HARVARD STUDIES IN URBAN HISTORY

Series Editors / Stephan Thernstrom / Charles Tilly

Town Into City

Springfield, Massachusetts, and the
Meaning of Community, 1840–1880

Michael H. Frisch

Harvard University Press
Cambridge, Massachusetts, 1972

To my Mother and in memory of my Father

Acknowledgments

This project would have been difficult to pursue without the assistance of many persons whom it is a pleasure to thank here. Miss Juliette Tomlinson, director of Springfield's Connecticut Valley Historical Museum, was most gracious and extremely helpful in guiding me through local material, as well as in discussing my work at great length and to my great advantage. At the Springfield City Library, Miss Dorothy Mozley's knowledge of the excellent local history collection smoothed the path of research considerably, and I am grateful to her and to Miss Margaret Rose of the library, who permitted me free run of the stacks. I am indebted also to Springfield City Clerk William Sullivan, who provided me with access to the City Hall vault and a comfortable place in which to work. Professor John F. Mitchell and Miss Gladys Midura kindly allowed me to use their helpful doctoral theses. I would also like to thank the Sterling Memorial Library of Yale University for permission to use and cite the Samuel Bowles Collection there.

I also wish to thank the Yale University Press for permission to reprint material previously published as "The Community Elite and the Emergence of Urban Politics: Springfield, Massachusetts 1840–1880" in *Nineteenth Century Cities*, edited by Stephan Thernstrom and Richard Sennett, 1969.

The illustrations on pages 73, 147, 148, and 150 are reproduced with the permission of the Connecticut Valley Historical Museum; those on pages 21, 75, 138, 141, 152, 153, and 189 with the permission of the Springfield City library.

I have appreciated the opportunity to talk with a number of
Springfield's people, who, through heritage and interest, combine a
deep respect and affection for their community with a profound
knowledge of its tradition. In particular, I profited greatly from discussions with former City Clerk Clifford Smith, Richard Garvey of
the *Daily News*, the late Mrs. Edward Broadhurst, and many of
those who participated in the Connecticut Valley Historical Museum's annual Institute on Local History in 1966 and 1967. On a
more personal level, I wish also to acknowledge my debt to a number of people who in a quite different sense taught me much about
Springfield and community dynamics in general. Oscar Bright, Ben
Swan, Henry and Bea Weissman, Celia Norrington, Muriel Moore,
Betty Fredericks, the Reverend Charles Cobb, Paul Dunn, Billy Van
Derzee, and many others I came to know and work with during
1966, my year in Springfield, were all trying to tell Springfield
something about the urgent need for racial justice and equality in a
twentieth-century American city. That they were so generally resisted and ignored only shows, I came to feel, how much an historically self-conscious community can misread the meaning of its past
and the needs of the present. In addition to these friends, my time
in Springfield owed much to the warmth of Herbert and Harriette
Michaels, who understand history and people. Finally, from a variety of vantage points since that year in Springfield, Carol Sipe has
been looking over my shoulder as this work progressed, and I hope
that when it reaches her in final form she will appreciate how important she has been to it.

In the academic world, my debts are even greater. I must mention
first my very substantial and sincere gratitude to the Samuel Fels
Fund of Philadelphia, for the dissertation fellowship in 1966-1967
that freed me to complete the doctoral thesis from which this book
originated. Since then, the task of revision has been assisted by institutional funds from Princeton University and from the State University of New York. Moving from financial to intellectual and
spiritual assistance, Kenneth Lockridge gave to several of the early
chapters the close reading and frank criticism one appreciates from
a good friend. Herbert Gutman offered valuable criticisms at several
points along the line, and I also profited from many discussions of
previous drafts with my colleagues first at Princeton, and now at the

State University of New York at Buffalo, including James Henretta, John Schrecker, Sheldon Hackney, Burton Bledstein, Peyton Mc-Crary, Marion Levy, Martin Duberman, John Gillis, David Hollinger, Lewis Perry, and Clifton Yearley. In addition, I have grown through contact and discussion with a number of the urban historians I met at the Yale Conference on Nineteenth Century Cities in 1968, especially Michael Katz, Stuart Blumin, and Theodore Hershberg. My greatest debt is to Professor Robert A. Lively, now chairman of the History Department at the State University of New York at Buffalo, who directed this project in its dissertation form at Princeton University. He allowed me the freedom to define my own questions and my own research and then, through close reading and pointed criticisms, helped me to strengthen my arguments and give the text whatever degree of readability it may have achieved. Stephan Ternstrom graciously read my dissertation and offered substantial advice and encouragement, from which this revised version has profited greatly. I must also mention my gratitude for the genuinely helpful criticism offered by Samuel Hays, who also read and commented thoroughly on the dissertation, although his reservations about my approach are so great that I hesitate to implicate him at all in the final results. And finally, I must make that absolution general, since responsibility for all errors of fact and interpretation, for all untaken advice in matters of thought, style, method, and content, rests of course solely with me.

Michael H. Frisch

State University of New York
Buffalo, New York
July 23, 1971

Contents

Illustrations

Maps

Town Into City

Introduction

The eleventh edition of the *Encyclopaedia Britannica*, published in 1910, is one of the world's great compilations of wisdom, an elegant, scholarly, authoritative, and monumental distillation of the best of nineteenth-century culture; it confessed to failure, however, when confronting the subject of the city. "The word 'city' is incapable of any clear and inclusive definition," it was finally decided, "and the attempt to show that historically it possesses a meaning that clearly differentiates it from 'town' or 'borough' has led to some controversy . . . The word implies no more than a somewhat vague idea of size and dignity, and is loosely applied to any large center of population . . . with little regard to its actual size and importance."[1]

Anyone who has ever worked with the historical statistics of cities has probably come to the same conclusion after much frustrating effort. Even in terms of the legal definition, from country to country, state to state, year to year, and often even among the categories of a single compilation, the population level distinguishing cities from towns has been set at anywhere from 1,500 to 15,000 and up. Part of the reason for this uncertainty, of course, is that the broader definition and meaning of the city has always been equally and unsurprisingly vague. In America, this was especially true in the last decades of the nineteenth century, when the swiftly accelerating growth of the nation's cities pushed such questions forward inexorably. Though nobody could say exactly what cities were, everyone recognized that something new was happening, that the emerging modern city differed generically from other communities preceding it, whatever their size. By 1900, most serious thinkers recognized that rapid urbanization was and would be among the era's most definitive characteristics, a leading edge, for better or worse, of a new civilization. Understanding the phenomenon of the city, its unique nature and implications for American society, became an intellectual priority of the first order.

In the present century, successive generations of scholars have taken up the burden, grappling enthusiastically and prolifically, if not always productively, with the nature of the city. Efforts to fashion general conceptions of the city as a unique form have until recently been made, for the most part, by sociologists approaching urbanization from a variety of perspectives, and several schools of thought have crystallized through the years, the study and classification of which has itself become an important topic of analysis. This has, of course, produced no general agreement on the meaning of the city and urbanization, nor even upon what should be the best framework for attempting such definition — ecological, demographic, economic, behavioral, or institutional. Each approach has had its champion, all seeking in some measure to provide the clarity the *Britannica* found lacking. In the past twenty years or so, American historians have added their energies to the study of urbanization, combining the traditional discipline of historical thinking with the insights of social science and the tools of modern methodology. That this contribution represents a needed perspective, rather than merely a desirable supplement, becomes apparent from even a brief consideration of recent approaches.

Most of the seminal work in American urban sociology shared at least one general weakness: for all the theoretical ambitions, this work tended to be descriptive of cities in a particular cultural and historical context, rather than definitive of urbanization in general terms. The "ecological" and "natural areas" theory of Park and Burgess, for example, has been criticized as accurate, ultimately, only for the modern American cities of the early twentieth century — particularly Chicago — which inspired these scholars. Similarly, Louis Wirth's influential behavioral definition of urbanism, and much work in this tradition, has been shown to explain, if anything, the traits of modern industrial society, urban or nonurban, more accurately than it does urbanization in various contexts. Thus, the criticism runs, most of such American sociological theory has been seriously time and culture bound, which is another way of saying that sociologists have often been careless about cause and effect. While observing and generalizing perceptively about social structures and traits, they have been less successful in examining how the city's characteristics developed, where they came from, and hence what they really represent. To raise such questions, to deal with the relation of development to context, of general to specific, of cause to process — to consider all these is to deal with questions in potentially historical terms, and to suggest the general value of the historical perspective.

There are, to be sure, any number of ways of studying the city historically, and American urban historians have accordingly produced to date a literature rich in detail but poor in focus and definition. The earliest works, and many since, were conceptually informal, usually narrative studies of particular cities or special topics that not only shed little light on the nature of urbanization, but also did little to give any coherence to the emerging interest in urban history. As this amorphousness became more and more pervasive, review articles began, at almost regular intervals, to call insistently and repeatedly for a more rigorous approach to conceptualization. Best represented by the complex yet rewarding writings of Eric Lampard, these arguments have tended, owing largely to the exciting possibilities of new social science approaches and methods, to suggest demography and cross-cultural structural analysis as the first priority for any overall history of urban development in a specific context, such as America.

When one considers how thoroughly this criticism has dominated the historiographical stage, the minimal impact of such suggestions seems all the more remarkable, leading Charles Tilly, for instance, to exclaim, "What a shame! Lampard has something important to say and nobody listens . . . Why don't other practioners heed this good advice?"[2] The question is important, and the answer perhaps more complicated for historians than might be indicated by the simple fear of rigorous methodology and conceptualization that characterizes much of their work. It is true, of course, that most urban historians have gracefully avoided the harder theoretical questions that must eventually be explored. But in a sense, they — including many who use the most advanced quantitative methods — have chosen to do so precisely because they are too interested in the very historical questions that generalists would have them defer. For many historians the limitations of such a theoretical and "macroanalytic" approach are the inverse of its virtues: to the extent that a more conceptual approach might be useful in abstracting the contours of urbanization as a general process, it can be limited in dealing with urban expressions in concrete cultural contexts, where the dynamics of change are never so precise. Its analytic power implies a certain descriptive weakness that becomes for historians a more definitive weakness as well, to the extent that they are committed to the fullest possible historical explanation of a given subject, to the goal of a *sufficient* explanation of change rather than to the discovery of a framework of general factors *necessary* to such an explanation in specific contexts. Insofar, then, as the interest of most American urban historians has continued to be the interrelationship of urbanization and American history in the broad sense of each, they have shown little enthusiasm for conceiving their subject to be the history of urbanization per se. And insofar as they have focused on urbanization, they have tended to understand it in terms that include a broader range of cultural and historical factors than a more analytic approach might include.

Perhaps it might be best to approach the writing of urban history in terms of this preference, rather than continuing to apply to it a standard that most American historians do not acknowledge. This hardly eliminates the deep problems that critics have found in the literature. Quite the contrary, the random scattering of subjects, the simplistic narratives, the fuzzy use of crucial terms, and the general lack of conceptual interest all stand in even sharper relief from this perspective, because they stem not only from an imprecise understanding of urbanization, but also from a more generally inadequate approach to those tasks and questions most appropriate to any historian. This approach does suggest, however, that the best solution to such problems may be found by aiming at a middle ground, by trying to ask the sort of historical questions about cities and urban growth that will draw from the detail of particular contexts the sort of theory and generalizations historians will find most useful.

The following study of one small city's growth over a period of time is an exploration of this general perspective. In order to learn something about the nature of the city, or at least the American city, this study of Springfield, Massachusetts, focuses on the process of community growth in broad historical and cultural terms: if urbanization has been as basic an American experience in the past century and a half as most historians believe, then something of this importance, and of the fundamental changes involved, should be reflected in the city-building processes of a given community. If there is general significance in a nation of cities arising from a nation of towns and villages, then some insights are to be gained from watching a single community grow from town to city. In almost any sense, this transition must include not only what happened to the community, in the objective dimensions of growth and the factors shaping it, but also how the people understood, reacted to, and contributed to the process of change. By presenting the details of urban biography with an eye to their conceptual implications, it is hoped that the transition from town to city can be understood as a human and cultural process, that it will be possible to explore how quantitative changes in condition and organization are related to qualitative changes in values and culture. In this way, perhaps, "the attempt to show that historically [the city] possesses a meaning that clearly differentiates it from 'town'" may prove more satisfactory than it seemed to the *Encyclopaedia Britannica* a half-century ago.

But why Springfield, Massachusetts? As must often be the case, the subject was bold enough to suggest itself long before any rigorous search for the perfect specimen could be launched, or even before the framework for investigation had been fully developed. Fortunately, as the study progressed to a more serious level, Springfield proved extremely well suited to the task at hand. It was and still is a small city, which made feasible the comprehensive study of an adequate span of years. Its roots are deep, providing a background of cultural and institutional identity against which nineteenth-century change could be seen in sharp relief. Because change was never sudden or substantial enough to completely overwhelm tradition, the more subtle and interesting interactions between old and new proved visible. No claim will be advanced here that Springfield is "representative," but at least it can be noted that there is nothing in the city's structure or experience to disqualify it as a guide to more general patterns. Unlike factory cities such as nearby

Holyoke, Springfield's economic base in the mid-nineteenth century was broad, as well balanced between trade, manufacture, and professional activity as that of most larger cities. Its population was heterogeneous, including a substantial but not disproportionate number of foreign born, and it had churches of every denomination. As the center of an important river valley, moreover, Springfield's growth had the regional dimension so important in understanding any modern city. And finally, its birth as a city came squarely in the middle of the period when America was first becoming conscious of the phenomenon of urbanization. This gives local experience an added dimension, for it opens the possibility of exploring how institutions, ideas, and developments so avidly discussed elsewhere were perceived and assimilated by an emerging city. More generally, it provides an excellent opportunity to observe the interaction between the experience of urbanization and the main currents of American history and culture, as seen in a specific context fully alive to each.

Part One
The Traditional Community, 1840-1860

1. The Shaping of the Town

Springfield, Massachusetts, is a community steeped in its own history, with a virtual surfeit of the colonial traditions that New Englanders have so worshipfully preserved and celebrated. People in Springfield today are properly proud and acutely aware of this rich heritage; in the mid-nineteenth century, however, their involvement in their own past was considerably more intense and immediate. People then stood closer to colonial forms, values, and events, still remembering many of the now-forgotten men for whom the streets are named. At the time, residents viewed Springfield not as the descendant of an early Puritan village, but as its lineal extension, and because of this historical consciousness, the two centuries of local life that preceded Springfield's municipal incorporation in 1852 represent something more than just a backdrop. Anyone wishing to understand the nineteenth-century town, restless in the bonds of its past and beginning the definition of a new form, an urban form of community, must accept Springfield on its own terms, and begin its story, however briefly, at the beginning.[1]

In the year 1636, William Pynchon, one of the original incorporators of Massachusetts Bay, led a group of emigrants from Roxbury, near Boston, to the banks of the Connecticut River, in the wilderness of the west. Pynchon's move followed by only a year or two the establishment of Wethersfield, Windsor, and Hartford, the first towns in that region, and his new village, further north along the Connecticut, was the first western settlement in the area that was to become Massachusetts. At the time, Pynchon had the limited objectives of tapping the fur trade and serving, with other Connecticut

Valley outposts, as a barrier to Dutch designs on the region. But within a few years, the settlers had established the framework of a more complete community, drawing up a formal covenant, securing official status as a town, and exchanging the original Indian name of Agawam for Springfield, after their founder's English home.

Because its unique geography was to shape Springfield's character and growth so profoundly, it will be useful here to see what the land looked like before it was peopled, built on, drained, graded, and hidden in the centuries that followed. Pynchon had originally selected a site at a broad bend of the river, on its west bank where the tributary Agawam River joined the Connecticut, about seventy miles up from Long Island Sound, twenty-five miles north of Hartford, and one hundred miles overland from Boston. It was a lovely location, with lush alluvial meadows stretching back from the river, but it was not to be the site of Springfield; the local Indians found it equally attractive and, driving an atypically hard bargain, they forced Pynchon to choose between land on the east bank or the abandonment of his entire venture. To call this site just across the river less promising is a considerable understatement. Instead of rich meadows, a sandy strip of humpbacked land ran along the water, less than half a mile wide between the river and a broad marsh to the east. Beyond the marsh rose a sharp wooded bluff, stepping further eastward and upward, almost like a natural terrace, to a broad and desolate plateau that reached back for miles towards distant mountains. Here and there, sudden ravines and valleys slashed the line of these north-south ridges, making the terrain rugged and unpredictable, and in fact hemming in on all sides the narrow riverside strip which was to be the heart of Springfield. To its north stood a high mound later called Round Hill, to the south another cluster of rolling hills dominated by a ridge called Long Hill, and behind each of these, curving around to the river in a great crescent, lay the "Hassocky Marsh," named for the large clumps of earth and grasses dotting it. Completing the picture and providing a further sort of symmetry, there was a modest stream to be known as Mill River joining the Connecticut below Long Hill, while a smaller one trickled out of the hills near the center of the strip, then turning north and meandering to the river above Round Hill.[2]

If nature seemed to be suggesting by this unpromising locale that

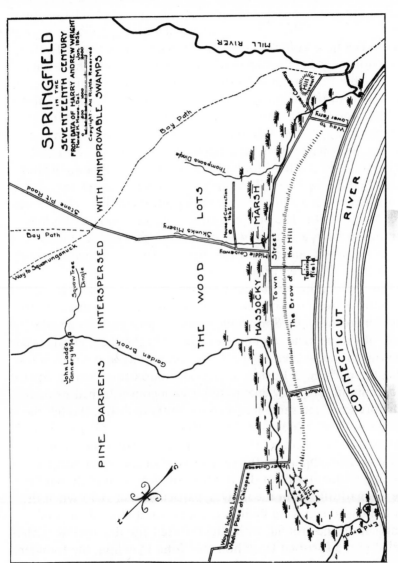

WITH UNIMPROVABLE SWAMPS

INTERSPERSED

PINE BARRENS

THE WOOD

LOTS

MARSH

HASSOCKY

MILL RIVER

Bay Path

Stone Pit Road

Bay Path

Way to Squawungonuck

Squaw Tree Dingle

John Ladd's Tannery 1674

Garden Brook

Thompsons Dingle

Skunks Misery

House of Correction 1662

Middle Causeway

Town Street

The Brow of the Hill

Road to Hadley and Northampton

Hill Meeting House

Way to Lower Ferry

CONNECTICUT RIVER

Training Field

Wharf Lane

Upper Causeway

Way to Indians Lower Wading Place at Chicopee

End Brook

Springfield in the seventeenth century

Springfield's future did not lie in agriculture, the settlers were slow
to learn this as the town struggled through its first century. They
parceled out town, wood, and farm lots on a lineal plan based on
Main Street, raised their crops, and traded with the friendly Agawam
Indians. The little colony soon had become more or less self-sufficient, with several craftsmen, a minister, a mill or two, and even a
jailhouse, the first building on the slope at the far side of the marsh.
At the time, Springfield had thirty or forty houses strung out along
the single north-south street that has remained the city's spine to
the present day, its east side then a border to the hassocky marsh.
Early on, the villagers had cut a ditch along this edge and turned
part of the little Garden Brook into it, so that the stream, dividing
about where Dwight and Worthington Streets now meet, ran
through town along Main, joining the Connecticut just below York
Street to the south. The one long street, one or two lanes leading
down to the river, a causeway across the marsh which would become State Street, and a few other paths — these outlined Springfield through the seventeenth century.[3]

In this setting, the town's early years were characterized by drama
and controversy. Pynchon feuded repeatedly with the towns to the
south, one reason why Springfield never became part of the new
colony of Connecticut, and he also figured in the theological battles
so central to the age, leaving both the community and America following the burning in Boston of an unorthodox tract he had written.
The community, equally energized by such concerns, had its own
witchcraft scare and sentenced two sorcerers to death, though the
penalties were set aside in Boston, a full two decades before Salem's
more successful assault on the Devil. More basically, the colonists
faced successive threats to the very survival of the town, threats
stemming frequently from the weather and less frequently but far
more dramatically from the natives, particularly in 1675 when the
local Indians joined King Philip's renegades and burned most of
Springfield to the ground, while the terrified and defenseless settlers
huddled in the fortified brick house of John Pynchon, the founder's
son.[4]

Springfield weathered these storms, and headed towards a more
secure and peaceful eighteenth century. In chronicling its life in this
period, faithful local historians continued to stress the exciting

events which helped to make their town unique or noteworthy, such as the ecclesiastical debates between a local minister and the formidable Jonathan Edwards of Northampton in 1735, or Springfield's role in the Revolution, or, most centrally, Shays's rebellion in 1785 and 1786, which had its political focus in Springfield's courts and its military denouement on the town's Armory Hill.[5] There is no shortage of such highlights, but tradition notwithstanding, surely the most important observation to be made about eighteenth-century Springfield is that with every year it was becoming more and more ordinary, more and more indistinguishable from the many villages that had filled the Connecticut Valley in its wake.

Western Massachusetts consisted of three towns when it was organized as Hampshire County in 1662, with the Court alternating between Northampton and Springfield, then still the official shire town. The Massachusetts town, one must remember, was what elsewhere might be called a township, a huge tract of land that was perhaps more a rural unit than anything else. As the villages within it grew, the towns regularly divided into smaller units. By 1800, such had been the region's growth that its first settlement was no longer its focal point, and hardly even noteworthy in any sense. Springfield's area had been reduced almost to the present-day limits as Westfield, Wilbraham, West Springfield, and Longmeadow split off one by one, themselves to be divided up in the same frequently acrimonious process. As new settlement had moved upriver and west into the Berkshires, Northampton had gained the ascendancy in the county, becoming the shire town and the permanent site of the County Court. Springfield did not have to look even that far to be reminded of its relative decline, however, for just across the river West Springfield, built on the meadows that had been Pynchon's first choice, had grown into a far larger and more prosperous community, finally splitting off from its parent in 1774. By the first federal census in 1790, its 2,367 people made it the largest town in western Massachusetts; Pittsfield and Northampton, also prospering, had about the same number. But the less well-endowed Springfield, notwithstanding its head start, had only 1,574 people to show for more than one hundred fifty years of continuous settlement.[6]

Physically, Springfield proper had hardly changed at all during these years. A new neighborhood appeared at the Mill River, and

farms had scattered more widely through the area. But aside from
the almost separate community at Cabotville, four miles to the
north where the powerful Chicopee River joined the Connecticut
from the east, "Pynchon's village" remained the center of the township, the location of almost all the homes and shops, boasting a few
more side streets and more substantial buildings, but otherwise still
the simple, small, and orderly village it had been for decades. A
famous traveler in 1794 described it as follows:

One mile below Springfield, we were presented with a very romantic prospect.
The river itself, for several miles both above and below, one fourth of a mile
wide, was in full view. Agawam, a considerable tributary on the west, joined the
Connecticut at a small distance above. The peak of Mt. Tom rose nobly in the
northwest, at a distance of twelve miles. A little eastward of the Connecticut,
the white spire of the Springfield church, embosomed in trees, animated the
scene in a manner remarkably picturesque . . . We arrived at sundown. The town
is built on a single street, lying parallel to the river nearly two miles. The houses
are chiefly on the western side. On the eastern a brook runs almost the whole
length, a fact which is, I believe, singular. From the street a marsh extends forty
or fifty rods to the brow of an elevated pine plain. The waters of this marsh are
a collection of living springs, too cold and too active to admit of putrefecation
on their surface, and for this reason, probably, the town is not unhealthy. Part
of the marsh has been converted into a meadow. The houses of Springfield are
more uniformly well built than those of any other inland town in the state except Worcester. An uncommon appearance of neatness prevails almost everywhere, refreshing the eye of the traveller.[7]

Thus Timothy Dwight. The Springfield he saw had its church, its
school, its town meeting, shops, merchants, artisans, farmers, and
paupers, and it was, in sum, nothing more and nothing less than a
typical New England town, moderately prosperous but hardly
promising, securely rooted in both its cultural typicality and in its
own century and a half of historical experience.

   With the nineteenth century, the period of "claiming the land" in
Massachusetts began to close. Few new towns were settled after
1800, and what had been a dispersal of population through the state
gradually became a trend toward concentration. In fact, notwithstanding the tremendous rise of the industrial cities after the Civil
War, the greatest rate of increased population concentration —

urbanization, in some senses — came in the prewar decades. Boston exerted the strongest pull, and the state's statistical center of population, which had been moving west through the eighteenth century, turned back to the east and by 1840 stood within thirty miles of the capital for the first time in nearly a century. Nevertheless, startling increases were shown in towns scattered throughout the state. Between 1820 and 1840, for example, Boston grew by 115 percent, Chelsea by 271 percent, Worcester by 153 percent, Fall River by 328 percent, and many small villages by equally imposing percentage increments. And the long-sluggish Springfield found itself prominent among the leaders of this surge. The 1,500 people of 1790 had grown to a healthy 11,000 by 1840 and almost 18,000 a decade later. This represented a rate of 180 percent between 1820 and 1840, and 400 percent for the 1820–1850 period, the third highest in the commonwealth. As a consequence of the whole area's initial expansion, the lower part of Hampshire County had been set off in 1812 as the new Hampden County, and Springfield, in anticipation of its rising fortunes, had been made a shire town once again. The faith in its potential proved well placed.[8]

There is no real mystery to the growth of Massachusetts, since the gods of trade, industry, and transportation worked openly, reforming America in their own image. But there is more interest in wondering why progress occurred in some places and not others, and at one time and not another. Why, to be specific, did Springfield suddenly become the most dynamic and exciting town in its area, regaining an ascendancy lost a century earlier? Why, to focus more narrowly, did West Springfield's population virtually level off at around 3,000 while its previously overshadowed neighbor soared so dramatically? At the root of this disparity was a complex of factors central not only to the early development of Springfield, but to the nature of the urban expansion that lay ahead.[9]

The establishment at Springfield of the United States Armory represents perhaps the most tangible of these factors, though the fortuitous nature of this act indicates how little there was to choose between Springfield and its neighbors at the close of the eighteenth century. An official arsenal had been located in Springfield during the Revolution, but when it came time to set up a full-scale manufacturing armory, in the 1790's, the government chose West Springfield for the site. Both towns were well located on land and water routes yet too far upriver to be reached by any enemy ships, but West Springfield's Agawam River seemed to offer a more dependable power source. To everyone's surprise, however, the farmers there would have none of it, for they felt no desire to see a factory and its workers disrupt their orderly rural prosperity. Thus it was that Springfield received virtually by default perhaps the single most important boost to future growth. The United States Armory was set up in 1794, with heavy work done at the Mill River and lighter manufacturing and assembly at the site of the original arsenal, on top of the large hill plateau overlooking the town. Even before the War of 1812 established its importance permanently, the new facility provided a core of sophisticated manufacturing, economically substantial in its own right, around which could crystallize a wide range of enterprise and a pool of skilled artisan labor.[10]

The Armory's establishment, however fortuitous, points to deeper structural differences between the two river towns that constitute a second major reason for Springfield's ascendancy. As the Armory soon illustrated, the very geographic disadvantages that had hobbled Springfield earlier now began to fit it snugly to the measured requirements of a new age. West Springfield's uniformly good farmland had been evenly settled throughout the town's area, including land near the proposed Armory site there. But across the river, the peculiar topography kept large tracts of land empty and unproductive, well removed from the center of settlement, thus rendering the Armory less disruptive to those who found it offensive, and making the later rise of diversified industry in general a much less complicated matter. Because of its geography, a modern student has concluded, "Springfield, unlike a number of other Valley towns, did not have to await the decay of agriculture before developing an industrial base."[11]

The inhospitality to agriculture also gave Springfield men more reason than others to turn toward the mercantile pursuits growing more substantial throughout the Connecticut Valley in the last decades of the eighteenth century, and since its regional location in terms of land and water routes was enviable, Springfield soon came to control a disproportionate share of the area's business, a third factor in its new-found growth. Though this activity was still relatively unsophisticated, involving little wholesaling and no direct foreign trade, Springfield's merchants conducted operations on a then imposing scale, as epitomized by the Dwight family, who from 1750 on built a small provision trade into a large mercantile operation with branch stores up and down the Connecticut Valley and a warehouse in Boston to keep them stocked. Such enterprises accumulated considerable capital, setting the stage for a local version of a more general story: the embargo and the War of 1812 thoroughly disrupted New England's trade just as new industrial techniques and credit facilities were opening exciting new possibilities for investment, and capital quickly began to flow from commerce to manufacture. In Springfield, additionally, the armory retrenchment following the end of the war left an oversupply of skilled labor, a further inducement to such investment. Much of this came from the east — Edmund Dwight of Springfield was one of the famous Boston Associates, and helped turn this group's attention to western Massachusetts, particularly to Springfield's village of Cabotville on the banks of the Chicopee River, where the Associates established major textile mills in 1825.[12] But a great deal of the investment came from local men and went into less spectacular enterprise in Springfield proper. In 1820, well before the Chicopee Mills or the later project at Holyoke, Springfield's many smaller mills and factories sufficed to have the town classified, by the census standards of the day, as a manufacturing rather than an agricultural town. Hardly coincidentally, this was the census in which Springfield overtook its rival across the river.[13]

The fourth element in Springfield's rapid nineteenth-century development was the commanding position in transportation and communication that the community won in the railroad era. Although superbly located before this time, with good highways east and west and a covered toll bridge across the river since 1816, Springfield lay in the shadow of towns like Hartford and Middletown because of the weakness of its river position. Frequent falls, rapids, and shallows cut it off from the substantial heavy trade to and from the sea, even with canals and locks smoothing the path; the steamboats that had such a deep economic impact elsewhere became, in Springfield, more picturesque than economically significant, as Charles Dickens found on his acerbic 1842 tour of America; describing the vessel that bore him from Springfield to Hartford, one typical of most serving the Massachusetts town, Dickens wrote, "It was certainly

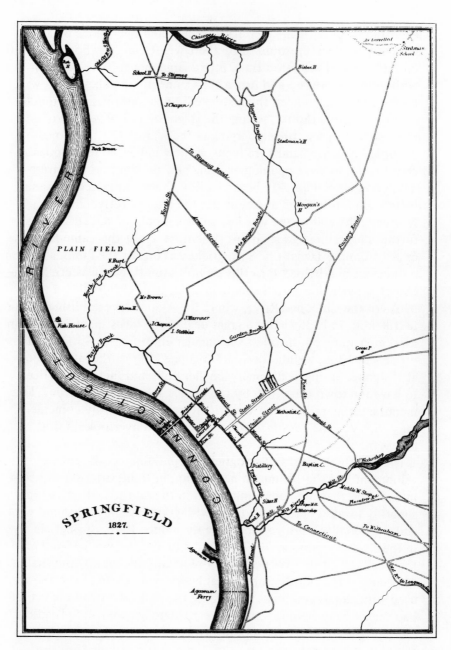

Springfield, 1827

not called a small steamboat without reason . . . I should think it must have been a half a pony power. I am afraid to tell how many feet short the vessel was, or how many feet narrow; to apply the words length and breadth to such measurement would be a contradiction in terms."[14]

With the railroad age, however, Springfield's facilities ceased to inspire sarcasm, and assured beyond any question the town's destiny as the leading city of western Massachusetts.[15] The start had, characteristically, been somewhat slow. When Boston capitalists completed the Boston and Worcester Railroad in 1835, they immediately began to plan the road's extension to Albany. But Springfield investors were initially quite skeptical and hesitant, and not until Hartford interests almost had the route plotted through that rival town did local businessmen support the plan actively. Their awakened interest soon secured the route, and the Western Railroad, as it was called, entered Springfield from Worcester in 1839, bridging the Connecticut and stretching on to Albany two years later. Once the ice had been broken, other projects followed swiftly — the Hartford and Springfield Railroad running south along the east bank of the river in 1844, and in 1847 a northern route through Northampton to connecting Vermont roads, which became the Connecticut River Railroad. Most significantly, Springfield played more than an investor's role in all this. Though both the Western and the Connecticut River projects had been financed mostly from Boston, operational control and direction soon settled in Springfield owing to the active entrepreneurial role of several local figures — men like George Bliss, Jr., from an old Springfield family, who supervised the building of the Western and became its first president; the remarkable Daniel L. Harris, a newly arrived engineer who ran the Connecticut River Railroad; and most important of all Chester W. Chapin, at this point president of the Western, but later the head of the consolidated Boston and Albany, Springfield's richest man, and one of the nation's foremost railroad entrepreneurs.*

*The town sustained only one defeat in all this, a failure to lure into Springfield the new route from New Haven to Northampton being built along the line of the old canal directly connecting those towns. When finally built after years of controversy, the Canal Road avoided Springfield and other river towns, intersecting the Western at Westfield, fifteen miles from Springfield. The loss, however, never proved as critical as the heated polemics of the route battle had threatened it would be.

At midcentury, then, Springfield enjoyed both good railroad facilities and significant influence in their operation. Its position, in
fact, was remarkably strong for so short a time, with major tracks
stretching north, south, east, and west, all meeting in the imposing
Union Depot built on the northern part of Main Street in 1851. In
helping to shape the growing town, geographic structure, the U.S.
Armory, mercantile development, and the railroads all overlapped,
each reinforcing and contributing to the others so that the total effect came to far more than the sum of the parts. By 1850 there
could be no mistaking the new character and promise remaking
Springfield, the town that at the century's start had been distinct
from its neighbors only in its relative lack of vigor and its decidedly
unexceptional prospects for the future.

In these years of rapid growth, the town had continued to follow
the pattern suggested by its topography, and by midcentury it had
developed a skeletal structure that it would retain even as the city
reached toward 100,000 people after 1900. There was, first of all
and still most basically, Main Street; in the 1840's it was lined with
stores, shops, frame houses, and even small farms, with the Town
Brook running alongside the unpaved roadway, providing water for
drinking and domestic purposes. About twenty small side streets
perpendicular to the river now bisected Main, some of them extending across the still soggy meadows that had been the hassocky
marsh. Main, however, was still the only business street of any note,
a dominance that would be permanent though it had by no means
been inevitable. For a while, in fact, it had seemed that State Street,
ascending the Hill and connecting the Armory to the town center,
might supersede Main. But in 1821, the developing rivalry came to a
head over the question of locating the projected county courthouse.
Aggressive downtown businessmen assembled a large parcel in the
very center of Main Street, where the steeple of the First Church
had attracted Timothy Dwight's attention. When they presented it
to the county as a public commons, they not only secured the location of the courthouse, but fixed as well the center of the town's
institutional life, for later the new city hall and the high school were
to join church and court around what became known as Court
Square. Other focal points along Main Street, particularly the
Depot, which brought new life to what was emerging at the North
End, heightened the Main Street orientation even more.

Court Square, 1820's

If Main was thus the major axis, State Street was not unimportant, for it led to the new Armory village growing atop the plateau, where by the 1840's many shops, homes, and churches were located. The street continued on past the Armory, dividing at the top of the Hill into roads to Wilbraham and Boston, and sending Factory Street — now St. James Avenue — off toward the mills on the Chicopee River. Farms and woodlands still covered this territory, but those familiar with modern Springfield will recognize the extent to which the lines of these early roads molded the course of later development. A third distinct neighborhood within Springfield proper had emerged strongly by this time, along the Mill River where the Armory's "watershops" were located. The newly opened Walnut Street linked this section to the hilltop plant, and Central and Maple Streets tied it to Main Street, with Maple, running along the edge of the bluff overlooking the town, soon becoming an exclusive and elegant residential street.

Thus Springfield was organized around the "Street," the "Hill," and the "Watershops," areas separated from each other by woods, fields, streams, and marshes, and linked by several rough roads. The scattered clusters made for considerable diversity within a small area, and, in fact, all this describes only central Springfield. The township still measured more than sixty square miles, and included several distinct villages far removed from the center's life. Cabotville had grown to be almost as complex and self-sufficient as the original village, raising problems to be considered presently. Further east on the Chicopee River was a newer textile center established by Springfield money and known as Indian Orchard, almost eight miles from the center of town. In addition, several tiny villages within the town lay at various points along the roads leading from Springfield — "Sixteen Acres" at the foot of the Wilbraham hills to the east; the isolated intersection near Longmeadow still known as the "X"; and "Five Mile Pond," on the hill plateau just that far from Court Square. People in these villages lived in rural detachment though they exerted a frequently disproportionate influence in town meeting; their communities would become more important as Springfield reached out to enclose them in a broad area of continuous settlement.[16]

And so Springfield in the 1840's and 1850's had quite suddenly become an exciting and bustling town, its prosperity not limited to a narrowly defined manufacturing or trade speciality, but diversified among a wide variety of mercantile, industrial, and professional activities. Moreover, it had won an image throughout New England as a dynamic place, where a career could be made in technology or theology, factory or finance. Accordingly, it attracted the educated and the well born along with the unskilled laborer seeking employment. One would hardly know it from present day Springfield, a struggling city fallen upon slack years in this century of the great metropolis, but the mid-nineteenth-century town was among New England's brightest beacons, a symbol of the progress and opportunity that men identified with America's future.

Between 1847 and 1852 Springfield pondered the wisdom of incorporation as a city. The story of the bitter and protracted demise of the Town rounded out the years of substantial and exciting growth, and forced the community into a sustained effort at self-consciousness, an attempt to decide what Springfield was and where it ought to be going. As such, the debates over incorporation offer both a summary of the town's development up to this point and an invaluable window into the workings of the community.

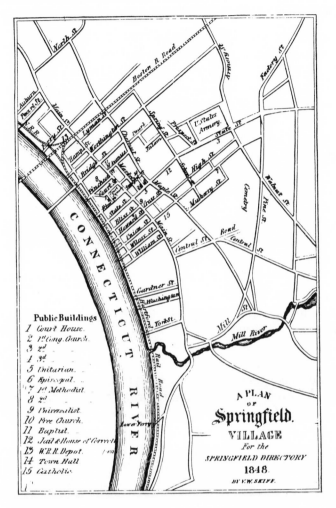

Springfield, 1848

In the 1840's, Massachusetts, the commonwealth of the independent small town, was beginning to give way rapidly to the commonwealth of cities and industrial centers. As late as 1820, the state had still not provided for municipal chartering, and even the 40,000 people of Boston were then still governed, after a fashion, by the ancient town meeting. But after Boston received a city charter in 1821, other towns began to follow — at first reluctantly and hesitantly, almost always amidst considerable controversy, but steadily and inexorably, since urgent needs spoke with a louder voice than tradition; the apotheosis of town-meeting government counted for less than its increasing obsolescence. Lowell and Salem incorporated in 1836 and 1840, and soon the state's larger towns tumbled over each other in the rush for the newly prestigious municipal status that was available to any community over 12,000 people. Roxbury, Cambridge, Charlestown, and New Bedford were chartered between March 1846 and March 1847, and at the 1855 census a full decade of such interest had produced a total of fourteen cities, holding about 35 percent of the commonwealth's population.[17]

Late in 1847, as this municipal snowball gathered momentum, many people in Springfield began to consider such a step. The town had more than the requisite number, and since there were then no cities west of the Boston area, it was urged that Springfield become the first, just as it had been the first inland town. More than local pride and ambition, however, was involved in this, for whatever the feelings about incorporation, almost everyone in town felt the urgent necessity for some structural reform: town-meeting government and administration by selectmen had manifestly reached its limit. In his study of Quincy, Charles Francis Adams, Jr., described the sort of breakdown many towns encountered: "That the town meeting should break down under the stress to which a city population must subject it is a matter of course . . . The indications that the system is breaking down are always the same; the meetings become numerous, noisy, and unable to dispose of business. Disputed questions cannot be decided; demagogues obtain control, and the more intelligent cease to attend." The last two points perhaps betray the perspective of an Adams, but many in Springfield anticipated his more general conclusion that there naturally comes a time when the meeting system "has to be laid aside as something the community has outgrown."[18]

In Springfield, it was not simply that population had outreached the capacity of the old form; more, the town meeting found itself increasingly hobbled by other conflicts intruding on the most innocent local issues. First there were the heated political questions related to the first stages of antebellum party disintegration. Second, pervasive antipathy to spending and taxes produced interminable squabbling about every proposal brought before the town. Finally, there was the traditional rivalry between the town's center and outskirts, particularly Cabotville. The Chicopee River village and the center area together claimed 14,000 of Springfield's 18,000 people, and town meeting government, as had happened so often elsewhere, could not really work to best advantage in what was emerging as a bipolar community.[19]

In December 1847, following considerable debate, the town meeting voted by a 4–1 ratio to apply to the General Court for a city charter. But geography, finance, and politics complicated the reception of this proposal just as they had helped bring Springfield to that juncture, and the opposition, largely from Cabotville, was vociferous. If Springfield had outgrown the meeting, people there argued, did it not make more sense to cut down the town rather than abandon a hallowed tradition of direct democracy? Reviving old petitions, they moved to have Cabotville set off as a separate town, and Springfield found itself facing a choice between division and incorporation.[20]

Friends of division pointed to the fact that Cabotville had become an almost self-sufficient community, and argued that other points within the township would soon become just as distinct. As "Citizen" predicted in an influential series of newspaper articles, Springfield would soon find its growing population "living principally in compact villages from one to seven miles apart; each having its own local preferences, prejudices, and jealousies, each urging its claim for a vigilant police, its fire department, the paving of its streets, with various other wants which real or imaginary will be put forth. I ask in all seriousness whether anybody supposes that *any* central goverment could make an approach towards administering the affairs of city over a territory so extensive and a people so circumstanced." And William Dwight spoke for many when he rose at town meet and was recorded as saying "he believed a city government wou sult in benefitting the center of town at the expense of the ou even if it worked at all, which he did not think it would."

This resentment of the center businessmen, among the charter's staunchest proponents, figured crucially in the debate. "It would not be right to take the last dollar of the widow and orphan to pay for paving and lighting the streets," asserted Elkanah Barton with appropriate hyperbole, while more to the point, "Citizen" argued: "Nobody expects that any considerable portion of the highways will be lighted, and it would be a gross injustice to oblige the large majority of the citizens to pay for what will accommodate only a small minority."[21]

In addition to sectional jealousies, traditionally endemic in New England towns, many opponents of incorporation feared the costs in general — some estimates saw incorporation inflating the budget by 50 percent. Many conservative businessmen from the center of town thus joined the opposition, led by Stephen C. Bemis, a Democrat later to be mayor of the city whose birth he fought to delay in 1848. And in a more general sense, a great many people in Springfield were wary of the very idea of a city. Demanding the division of Springfield into many little towns "already marked out by nature," the Democratic newspaper argued that only by fragmentation, could Springfield "postpone that era of extreme civilization in which the poor pay the taxes and the rich enjoy their fruits, and continue as long as possible the simple manners of a country town."[22]

All this resistance took charter proponents somewhat by surprise. They were prepared to offer statistics showing that the costs of municipality would be outweighed by rising property values, and to demonstrate that representative government would eliminate the advantages town meeting democracy imposed on citizens in the outskirts. But they had more difficulty answering arguments vision that could solve many of these problems more simply ating them. The best they could do was to assert that the inevitable in any event, would bind the vast township werful community capable of anticipating and en- growth; to hesitate would be to compromise every- . The town's leading newspaper, the *Springfield* ized this position concisely:

singularly adapted to the position in which we priate as we grow. Here is, and is to be, the

great center of an immensely driving and active population, devoted mainly to
those important manufacturing interests which are to give our country the ascendancy and lead among the nations. With such a prospect evidently before us,
is it not the part of wisdom to be binding ourselves together more indissol-
ubly?[23]

The majority of the town meeting agreed, rejecting division on
several occasions, but the decision was not theirs to make, and the
General Court in Boston, resolving the dispute in the way more traditional to the New England town, set off Cabotville, the adjacent
village of Chicopee Falls, and much of the surrounding territory as
the new town of Chicopee, Massachusetts, in March 1848. Chicopee
began with a population of 8,000 and Springfield was left with
11,000, two thirds of its former number and not enough to qualify
it as a city. Although the town's area had been reduced by half, its
reach was still extensive, for the new boundaries, running northeast
from the Connecticut to a point well upstream on the Chicopee
River, left Springfield a breadth to the east of seven miles, including
the factory village of Indian Orchard, still plenty of room for the
municipal glory the boosters had projected.[24]

As it happened, the issue remained a live one because the division
had not eliminated the faults of town-meeting government after all,
although politics and personal rivalry displaced sectional bitterness
as the major disruptive factor. In 1849, with Whig, Democratic, Free
Soil, and Independent tickets contending for even minor honorific
posts, the meeting could agree on only three selectmen, instead of
the usual five. This had happened before, but it was an ominous
sign, particularly with party framework and discipline fast melting
in the political furnace of the antebellum decade.[25] Everything came
to a head in 1851, when Springfield's town meeting collapsed so
agonizingly and so completely that none could doubt its day had
passed.

In that year, seven or eight overlapping tickets swamped the election process, and before it was all over there had been six consecu-
tive weekly meetings, loud and unruly affairs in which the boisterous
heckling came as a welcome relief from the interminable parlia-
mentary jockeying. In the tense and frustrating atmosphere little
could be done: one meeting finally produced three selectmen, but

the aroused opposition flooded the next one and declared the choice
void. Voting on all matters, such was the confusion, had to be done
by what was called "evacuation," which meant that the more than
thirteen hundred voters trooped outside and were counted as they
reentered the hall single file through one of several marked doors,
while party captains scurried about the street literally lining up the
faithful and cajoling the uncertain. At the somewhat incredible third
meeting, this nerve-fraying process was repeated six times in succession over questions of procedure and agenda, which makes it hardly
surprising that the exhausted citizenry could make little headway
with the more substantive matters reached many hours later.[26]

The voters finally accepted the three selectmen originally chosen,
but the real product of the two-month ordeal proved to be the end
of town government in Springfield. As Mason Green's standard local
history noted cautiously, "there may not have been any connection
between the convulsions of the village and its death, but it certainly
did die in a spasm." Whatever the direct or indirect impact of the
crisis, the arguments of 1848 took on a new cogency, and when the
requisite 12,000 population was certified early in 1852 Springfield
wasted no time in applying for a city charter. This time there was no
substantial opposition, and on April 21, 1852, in one of its last acts,
the town meeting ratified incorporation by a 969–454 vote.[27]

The new charter was similar to others recently adopted in Massachusetts. It provided for an annually elected mayor and city council,
consisting of an eight-man board of aldermen as the upper house,
with members elected at large, though one member stood nominally
from each ward, and an eighteen-member Common Council elected
on a ward basis. The two houses were not strictly separated, nor was
the executive branch, for the mayor sat as head of the aldermen and
served on several of the joint council committees that handled most
of the work of government. People in Springfield found the new
ward system the greatest novelty of the new plan, and the procedure
for drawing the lines became the subject of some uneasiness —
Massachusetts, after all, had invented the gerrymander. Nevertheless,
a blue-ribbon nonpartisan committee finally drafted a generally
satisfactory plan that provided for five wards in the populous sections and three in the outskirts. (See map.) Ward one represented
the North End; two and three lay along the heart of Main Street; the

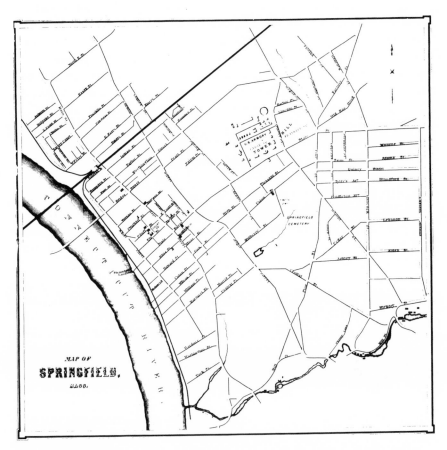

Springfield, 1852

prestigious slope of the hill up from Maple and Chestnut was ward
four; and five took in the hilltop plain and Armory area. These five
had three councilmen apiece, and their populations were moderately
balanced, ranging from 1,716 in ward four to 2,294 in ward two.
The other three divisions averaged around 700 people, and each had
one representative in the Common Council — ward six comprising
the South End, ward seven to the southeast, including the watershops, and ward eight taking in Indian Orchard, Sixteen Acres, and
the other far reaches to the east. It would not be long before the
strange new numbers and lines acquired a distinct character and
meaning in local life.[28]

Good feelings abounded as Springfield assumed its new form. Following a brief and notably genial campaign, the people chose insurance executive and county sheriff Caleb Rice as their first mayor by
a single vote over the prominent lawyer William B. Calhoun. As the
new city swore in its first government with great ceremony on May
25, 1852, its newly designed municipal seal offered silent comment
on Springfield's perspective: a central shield depicted boats on the
river and homes along the bank, the Armory, the railroad depot, and
the brick "fort" that had saved the early settlers from King Phillip's
wrath in 1675. But it did not depict farming; there was nothing at
all to indicate that agriculture had been central to local life for the
town's first two hundred years. Clearly, all eyes were on the future,
and amidst the speeches and celebrations that inaugural day, Joseph
Ingraham's florid script marked the transition on the final page of
the Town Records with a quaintly redundant self-consciousness:

Springfield, May 25, 1852. This day ends the town and commences the City
Government, having been a town just 216 years to a day, and now we go from
an old town to an infant city.

> Joseph Ingraham, last Town and first
> City Clerk of the old town and new
> City of Springfield.[29]

Springfield had arrived at the institutional shape and structure it
would retain for the remainder of the years covered by this study.
But Springfield, much like Joseph Ingraham, had only changed its

title, and the actual life that people there led could not be as swiftly altered by legislative decree. In many ways, in fact, the formal change obscures a deeper continuity in community life throughout the 1840's and 1850's, a continuity that gives the period unity and coherence sharply in contrast to the rapid change of the decades that followed.

2. The Meaning of Community

At a time when America's huge cities seem to be staggering toward institutional and spiritual collapse, it is difficult to remember the small towns of the past as other than models of uncomplicated simplicity. In terms of the paradoxes of urbanity, of course, this response is understandable, for the town possessed little of the complexity that makes the modern city so intractable. The problem, however, and the danger of romanticization, lies in the developmental fallacy of holding the town only against the later city, of seeing it only in comparable if contrasting terms. As historians have recently begun to discover, the earlier town represented a surprisingly distinct cultural context, and its institutional workings, formal and informal, need to be understood in somewhat distinctive ways, particularly when one deals with communities as deeply rooted and as self-conscious as those in New England.[1] In these terms, Springfield in the 1840's and 1850's contained many complexities and paradoxes, some of them inherent in its tradition, others a product of the newer currents already eroding that foundation with increasing force. Because this distinction soon would be virtually obliterated, it becomes particularly important to understand the nature of the older community, poised somewhat precariously on the edge of a rapid urban transformation.

At first glance, emerging social diversity would seem to be the most fundamental part of any description of town life and affairs in these years, for the Puritan homogeneity central to traditional Springfield had been steadily fading through the busy first half of the nineteenth century. The Hill and Watershops areas provided homes for many Armory workingmen, and early in the century Baptists and Methodists successfully established their first Springfield congregations there. Although the original Congregational Church still dominated the older center downtown, its hallowed authority had been weakened from within by the secession, also early in the century, of some of its richest, most established parishioners to form the Unitarian Society. The most portentous change, of course, beginning to be sensed at midcentury, was the influx of the Irish, who had arrived in Springfield with the railroad era. By the late 1840's, several hundred Irish Catholics lived clustered around the Depot in the North End; after some difficulty and resistance, they set up their first church in 1847, a visible reminder of their presence because of its central site on Union Street. In addition, some French Canadians had settled in the South End and at Indian Orchard, and there were about a hundred free Negroes, who had also established a small downtown church near Court Square, though most of them lived on the Hill.[2]

But whatever the later significance of this new social and religious complexity, it would be misleading and somewhat anachronistic to overemphasize its meaning at this point in time, for Springfield's traditional culture still retained great power, and people still lived among the institutions and ideas it had nurtured. To the extent that the tradition had been altered, moreover, its changes owed more to evolution from within than to the conflicts and challenges that a differentiating social structure often suggests. Therefore, one must look more squarely at aspects of this tradition itself, and deal with the so easily distorted and romanticized image of the cohesive, intimate New England town.

In the pre-Civil War decades Springfield still retained a genuine sense of community, despite its growth and size. The nature of social leadership and authority, the workings of informal institutions and the political process, and the conduct of community government all insured that community life and attitudes in Springfield suggested more the small town of fifty or even a hundred years earlier than the bustling urban center that would emerge in the next quarter century.

Central to the nature of this older culture, and to its tenacity, was the paradoxical nature of community leadership, at once strongly

elitist and deeply communitarian. In understanding this paradox,
the first point to consider is that in mid-nineteenth-century Springfield no fundamental distinction existed between a traditional, almost patrician social elite and the community's business leadership;
in fact, it is doubtful whether the patriciate was at all exclusive even
in the eighteenth century, when Springfield's imposing town elders
were known throughout New England as the "River Gods." William
Pynchon, after all, had been Springfield's first businessman even before he became its first citizen and founded its first family; through
the years, the ranks of these families always included great merchants and manufacturers, like the prestigious Dwights, along with
the expected complement of ministers, lawyers, and gentlemen
farmers. And in the nineteenth century, social prestige was even
more generally accessible. Wealth continued to bring influence, respectability, and after a decent interval a good measure of social
recognition. Since the opportunities for wealth and business success
were increasing so rapidly as the economy developed, the community leadership took on a somewhat broader and more open complex-
ion. Nevertheless, what separated the two centuries was more a
difference of pace and scale than a new process of elite recruitment,
and thus traditional concepts of social leadership seemingly remained viable.[3]

Basic to such continuity was the extraordinary degree of geographic mobility in New England at the time, an ironic relationship,
since this restless flowing of people was in other ways making the
older corporate exclusivity of the eighteenth-century town steadily
more obsolete. This mobility characterized not only the laborers
Stephan Thernstrom found drifting in and out of Newburyport, but
also — perhaps especially — ambitious young businessmen, clerks,
professionals, and craftsmen. Young fortune seekers might arrive in
a town, become successfully well known, involved in community
life, and in all senses established. Within a decade or so, they were
often indistinguishable from the finest of the "old citizens."[4]

By midcentury the local establishment was overwhelmingly composed of people like this. Although Springfield became a city in
1852, twenty years would elapse before voters chose a native son
for mayor, and this in a time when the office was still as much a
social honor as a political prize. More impressive is the evidence of

an 1893 volume of local biographies, a nostalgic tribute to the town's fast-fading nineteenth century aristocracy compiled by Charles Chapin, scion of a noble family that had been in Springfield since the beginning, two hundred and fifty years earlier. Predictably, his selection leaned toward the bluebloods and toward those community leaders who had flourished in the first half of the century. Nevertheless, of the almost three hundred respectables honored by full biographical sketches, only ninety, well under one third, had been born in Springfield, the city they had come to epitomize.* So much for the iron grip of the old families.[5]

Because of this fluidity, because the loosely defined establishment was not cut off from the dynamic forces of community growth, it retained considerable authority and continued, not seriously challenged, to embody the spirit and values of the traditionally homogeneous community. In other words, fading of this homogeneity in fact had not yet disturbed the dominance of older patterns of social leadership and socialization — the accepted articulation, rather than the imposition, of community standards, values, and practices by the social establishment.[6]

A number of informal institutions showed the vitality of this traditional process, defining a style of community life that touched almost everyone, with the possible exclusion of unskilled, itinerant laborers and many of the foreign born. There were frequent fairs, lyceums, and traditional celebrations in the calendar, and ongoing associations such as the colorful volunteer fire companies and the militia. Though the general level of formal culture was not particularly high, Springfield did boast a healthy press, including one already famous newspaper that was itself a major factor in providing a coherent sense of community, shaping public ideas and values as much as it reflected public opinion. The *Springfield Republican*, founded

---

*The full tally found 90 of the 294 born in Springfield, 30 born elsewhere in the Connecticut Valley, 80 elsewhere in Massachusetts, 77 in the rest of the nation, but mostly from Connecticut and New Hampshire, 2 in foreign countries, and 15 unknown. The figures are skewed somewhat by the fact that Chapin included separate sketches of each of the members of some prominent families, whereas all those in other equally important but not blue-blooded families are covered in the one sketch of the family leader. Thus, the 90 local-born citizens include 17 Chapins, 12 Blisses, 13 Dwights, and 7 Stebbins. Since this padding accounts for over half of the native leaders, it would appear that the actual position of the Springfield-born was even less substantial than the figures indicate.

in 1824 by Samuel Bowles, Jr., from the start pioneered a new sort of journalism that quickly drove out the party organs and bulletin-board newspapers previously prevailing. Especially after Samuel Bowles, III, took over in 1851, the *Republican* covered everything from local farming to international affairs with wit, intelligence, and judicious audacity, winning a national reputation for its editor and many of its correspondents. This latter Bowles was perhaps Springfield's most extraordinary man during these years, his influence as a man, an editor, and a political figure exceeding both the limits of Springfield and the limits of journalism.[7]

Religion, the original source of the communal orientation in New England, continued to bear most of the institutional responsibility for community values even after the denominational uniformity began to dissolve. All the churches, taken together, had a social function hardly separable from the purely religious, and few in town had more influence in general matters than the leading ministers, such as the First Church's Reverend Osgood, in the pulpit since 1809. The churches distributed Bibles to workingmen, and sponsored reading rooms, lecture series, and social events for nonmembers in an attempt to bring them more securely within the framework of community life and values. Revivals were frequent and enthusiastic, and an explicitly religious tone colored many of the period's efforts for secular and moral reform.[8] But it was the battle against rum, lasting through the century in varying degrees of clamorous engagement, that illustrates the meaning of community social control more precisely.

As Joseph Gusfield points out in his recent analysis of the temperance movement, the mid-nineteenth-century crusade must be distinguished from the more familiar rural-based campaign that pushed through Prohibition in the twentieth century, as well as from the highly aristocratic patrician tone of the earliest temperance efforts in the Federalist era. By the 1840's, he writes, the movement had been "converted into a popular movement to achieve self-perfection among the middle and lower classes of the nation." Temperance activity had become "a sign of middle-class respectability and a symbol of egalitarianism." Rather than being the desperate effort of a declining cultural group to retain prestige and influence, temperance in these years represented the bulk of the community and its well-entrenched values, and the temperance reformer, quite correctly, "assumed that his norms were dominant in society." Since those who were the object of his efforts did not yet represent a serious threat to the legitimacy of these norms, his crusade could be confident, benevolent, inclusive, and assimilative, at the same time as it sought, more deeply, to "consolidate middle-class respectability through a sharpened distinction between native, middle-class life styles and those of the immigrant and marginal laborer."[9]

This pattern describes Springfield's temperance involvement quite exactly, and explains its function in a community where status was both readily accessible and yet defined in quite stable, traditional terms. As the *Republican* commented, it was a battle between "New England Spirits and the Spirit of New England." The once-patrician movement in the town had become a broadly based community crusade in which all affirmed the virtues of temperance, in principle if not always in practice. The endless rallies, abstinence pledge campaigns, conventions, and meetings constituted an important focus of community life, and enlisted leaders from the Irish as well as the bluebloods. As Springfield attained the sophistication of municipality, the efforts were redoubled, for as Mayor William Calhoun said in 1859, the city lured the innocent young men most vulnerable to liquor's siren call. "Dollars and cents, all the accounts which have been audited since the flood," he intoned, " . . . sink into utter insignificance by the side of that record of desolation furnished by all our cities − the slaughtered young men. The root of all this evil is the Demon Rum, and here are scope and verge enough for a lynx-eyed and mail-clad police."[10]

Calhoun spoke of police because the old issue had recently acquired a dramatic new institutional form. In 1852, Massachusetts adopted a strict prohibitory statute banning all liquor sales, except for medicinal spirits available from a special state agency. This state experiment was never any more successful than would be the parallel federal policy of the next century, but it was years before this could be openly acknowledged, and in the meantime the policy generated a host of new questions around which temperance forces could focus their energies, pushing rum to the forefront of local life and, for the first time, local politics.[11] Questions of enforcing the ban, particularly in poorer neighborhoods, of cracking down on the

licenses of hotels and restaurants selling liquor under the table, of
the influence of rumsellers, especially the Irish, on the politicians,
especially the Democrats — all kept the pot at full boil for years,
and the fires of moral reform plus the heat of political battle could
produce a rather incandescent atmosphere, as a *Republican* editorial
illustrated:

Everything is swallowed up in the question of whether the IRISH GROG
SHOPS shall continue to have full sway or not, the most disgusting spectacle in
the history of local politics, . . . whether the intelligent, moral Americans and
decent citizens of any and all parties shall continue to govern the city for the
common good, or whether it shall be given up to men of low, sordid, and brutal
instincts, the party now ruled by KING ROTGUT.[12]

The political context of such vituperation — language like this usually appeared only around elections — suggests that it would be wise
not to overestimate the depth of ethnic and cultural conflict that it
represents. But to say this is only to beg larger questions: what was
the significance of political rhetoric and, indeed, political parties,
practices, and loyalties themselves in the mid-nineteenth century
community? The temperance reform tells much about the state of
social cohesion and the way in which community values were perceived, but a look at Springfield's political behavior will show a
somewhat more paradoxical and revealing picture.

In one sense, Springfield had traveled a great distance from the
eighteenth-century Massachusetts town in which, according to
Michael Zuckerman, overt political activity of almost any form was
considered a divisive threat to the consensual harmony of the self-
contained community, and was resisted institutionally and informally.[13] By the nineteenth century, such were the pressures of party
politics on state and national levels that towns like Springfield
found themselves awash in a flood of political consciousness. Party
organization and partisan rivalry pervaded the town meeting itself,
even extending at times down to the choosing of fence-viewers and
hogreeves. The election campaigns brought to each fall season a
burst of maneuvering, propaganda, gossip, energy, and excitement
quite in contrast to the community's summer diet of agricultural
fairs and quiet entertainments. The depth of this orientation and

the vigor of political combat were remarkable, and considering that the "Locofocos" stood strongest among the workingmen on the Hill while the Whigs rallied around the Court Square establishment, one is tempted to see in Springfield evidence of the era's supposedly incipient class politics and social conflict. A closer look, however, suggests quite a different reading of local politics.

In the first place, a preliminary investigation of local behavior tends to confirm the impression that little substantial economic and social differentiation can be made between the major parties. As Benson found in his study of New York, intracommunity neighborhood rivalries turn out to be the only moderately reliable guide to leadership and voting. Thus, a welter of old sectional gripes, personal jealousies, and other complex resentments of Main Street pushed many Hill people, from laborers to gentry and merchants, into the Democracy; the center of town, again from the top to the bottom of the social ladder, was traditionally more or less Whiggish. Both parties, in addition, found leaders among the same class of prominent merchants and civic figures. The Democrats, for instance, were never embarrassed by the fact that Chester W. Chapin, one of the party stalwarts, represented the ultimate anomaly for a Jacksonian, being the town's richest man, and boss of one of the state's most powerful and aggressive large corporations.[14]

And finally, though the rhetoric seems to show signs of social disorder in the community, the context of local political activity suggests that its function was as much to defuse and digest as to legitimize conflict. The banners, broadsides, loud caucuses, and torchlight parades offered everyone the opportunity of participating in local political life, and one cannot avoid the impression some social scientists have drawn in other contexts that the "play function" of political scrambling carried importance in its own right, particularly when it served as a means to integrate the citizenry through common activities and thereby reinforce the more traditional community orientation.[15]

This functional aspect of local political life comes into sharper focus when one looks more closely at the paradoxical structure of political leadership and office-holding. On the one hand, both parties were tightly controlled by a small circle of very similar men; the real political struggles and decisions took place only within this con-

text. Beyond the election-time ballyhoo, the involvement of the
general public was less noticeable. Although almost anybody could
vote — the only suffrage requirement then was a $1.50 poll tax —
the turnout was frequently slack, particularly in local elections and
particularly among less well-established citizens. Generally speaking,
the leadership of the propertied "best citizens" was rarely challenged, and a traditional sense of deference to them prevailed: political office still represented an honor, political leadership had not
yet become fully differentiated from social standing, and by and
large the traditional establishment, however divided amongst itself,
was seemingly permitted to embody the voice and identity of the
larger community.[16]

And yet this picture had another dimension, one which qualified
the deferential model and yet was equally rooted in the venerated
tradition of the New England town. This was the institution of
volunteer amateur service from almost all ranks of the community
and at almost all levels of authority, particularly in the community's
own government. A glance at the occupational backgrounds of those
serving in the most important elective offices illustrates clearly the
survival of this tradition. The new city's first mayors, of course,
tended to be prominent and important men — of the six who served
in Springfield's first municipal decade, two were lawyers, one an insurance executive and county sheriff, one a railroad president, and
two were merchant manufacturers. The general run of elected officials, however, represented a broader cross section, as shown by
Springfield's Board of Aldermen. This body was the source of virtually all power in the new city government; it consisted of eight men,
elected annually by the community at large, though one man nominally stood from each of the eight wards. In the 1850's, the slow
period before the city's dramatic change in the Civil War years,
Springfield's aldermen came, as one might expect, mostly from
three groups: 11 percent were lawyers, bankers, insurance execu-
tives, and leisured gentlemen; 28 percent were merchants and
businessmen; and 20 percent were manufacturers. Surprisingly
enough, 32 percent, almost a full third, were artisans and workingmen. Fragmentary evidence for leadership under the old town meeting indicates similar levels of participation extending back to the
early nineteenth century.[17]

The large workingman presence at a time when a traditional elite supposedly dominated a deferential community can be explained, in part, by the respect and visibility long enjoyed by Springfield's craftsmen, especially those at the U.S. Armory where the famous Springfield rifle was made. But nevertheless, this presence is impressive in its own right. In discussing the eighteenth-century Massachusetts town, Zuckerman showed that inclusion had always been a basic purpose of political as well as social institutions, and he found similar patterns of diversity in public office throughout the commonwealth. In Springfield, government and politics still expressed this older sense of inclusiveness and cohesion, however paradoxically. Just as elements of both elitism and fluidity existed in the social structure, political life in Springfield represented remarkable openness and participation as well as deferential, aristocratic, paternalism. In understanding this combination, and in appreciating its implications for understanding the meaning of community at this time, Zuckerman's reminder about an earlier era has great pertinence: "some forms of deference are innocuous," he observed, "others are quite incompatible with democracy. The issues are those of fixity and flux, of ascription and achievement, of authority and argument; which is to say, the issue is not deference but oligarchy." Zuckerman found little oligarchy as such in the older towns, and certainly Springfield had traveled even further away from it in the early nineteenth century.[18] But it had, in the same space, also departed from some of the earlier patterns. To fully understand these departures, and the way the Springfield of the nineteenth century had evolved a more distinctive notion of community, it is necessary to look beyond politics to the process of government itself, where the meaning of public and private life appear most clearly, and where the paradoxes in the notion of community can be understood more concretely and tentatively resolved.

The very pervasiveness of politics in community life makes the absence of organized conflict in the management of town affairs all the more striking. For all its excitement and turmoil, politics generally stopped after the nomination and election of officials, and did not extend to the actual conduct of government; local parties existed largely for the purpose of organizing county and state conventions, and for getting out the vote. Although there was thus a surfeit of politics in local life, local affairs themselves were not yet politicized to any significant degree.

It was not that local government bore no relation to matters of general concern. In fact, public involvement in trade and enterprise, not to mention charity and education, represented an ancient New England tradition. The general public had a duty for the good of the community to supervise, regulate, and stimulate the mercantile and productive systems as well as care for health and welfare. As they later developed on the state level, these responsibilities were only extrapolations of the earlier, direct experience of the towns; communities like Springfield had long been involved in regulating buildings, streets, health standards, conditions of markets, weights, and the like. This public involvement was hardly limited to regulation and supervision. The bulk of the government's business, in fact, concerned more positive involvement in hill grading, highways, bridges, sidewalks, and general property improvements. In all this, the aim was to further the public welfare, a concept that affirmed the symbolic priority of community over individual betterment. So expansive was the scope of this public role that even with the progressive weakening of the colonial era's rigid regulation, there were very few areas of business and private life in which the community did not maintain at least nominal purview.[19]

If this was so, then why was there so little political interest in government? Surely there can not have been perfect harmony on all these matters of concern, especially when involving property and money. Part of the reason is that the Massachusetts town had traditionally sought to avoid legitimizing conflict in any way, so important was the goal of consensus and harmony. Its institutions were deliberately designed to prevent divisions from becoming manifest. Conflict was minimal because "nothing in the norms sanctioned it, and no institutional arrangements accommodated it."[20] But these traditions would hardly themselves have kept politics out of government after the colonial era, particularly as the community grew more diverse and expansive. The answer lies in the fact that people were simply not very interested in local governmental policy, for reasons which say much about the prevailing meaning of community itself.

There was not a great deal that needed to be directly done by government, and its actual role in local life was quite limited. The categories of public expense in 1845 were identical to those of a half-century earlier — schools, highways, pauper relief, and miscellaneous expenses mostly involving property, all of which amounted to expenses of less than $25,000 per year. The sum rose to $70,000 in the next decade, but the distribution did not change much, and the quantitative jump itself meant nothing next to the meteoric rise of spending in the Civil War era to come.[21] These limited activities attracted the attention of a limited portion of the community, the taxpaying property owners, since most of the government's money and practically all of its time and energy went to matters related to property. In a real sense, the business of government was thus not public at all; the town and later the city government was simply the place where overlapping and conflicting private claims for public favor could be adjusted, a process usually bearing little relation to a search for general ends, and frequently followed closely only by the petitioners themselves. However broad the traditional concept of community interest may have been, it had grown correspondingly shallow with time. In fact, as Springfield grew, the tradition tended to become inverted: that is, if little in community life was purely private, then few functions could be considered purely public.[22] And as a corollary of this, people generally accepted the principle that policy was the concern of those most directly involved, and of limited interest to others. Poorer people in particular, for whom property taxes, the life-blood of city government, meant little, generally greeted its deliberations and decisions with virtual indifference. Certainly everyone "upheld the principle, once applied to all elections, that local government was a kind of public service corporation, in which only the taxpayers should share."[23]

These taxpayers had their own reasons for severely limiting the scope and importance of public activity. One of the most fundamental community axioms was that spending automatically meant distasteful rises in the tax-rate or in public debt, and this antipathy represented something more than parsimony: the "low-tax ideology," as it has more recently been called, was part of a broader business value structure that elevated thrift, minimal consumption, and avoidance of debt to the level of moral imperatives. This "psychology of scarcity" had already been abandoned in business by all but the most conservative entrepreneurs, but nevertheless it exercised an undiminished hold on public practice: proposals for spending invariably encountered constitutional aversion whatever their content.[24]

By definition, such a general characteristic cannot explain specific choices within the framework it supported; even the stingiest administration had to find some purposes worthy of support, and it is here, finally, that the heavily qualified notion of public activity most acted to limit the importance of government action. What was really limited, in other words, what was really remarkable about the functional expression of community before 1860 was not so much the reluctance to spend for public purposes, but rather how few were the purposes allowed to fall within this sphere of definition. For example, although with every year more of the business and social institutions of the city revolved around Main Street, people did not easily accept the legitimacy of improving the facilities there. When an appropriation for a proposed city library was suggested, Mayor Ansel Phelps, Jr., rejected the idea because: "Our citizens are scattered over a large territory and many who would be taxed for the support of a City Library could not, if they desired to, conveniently share the advantages to be derived from it." Similarly, there was stubborn resistance to the initiation and then the extension of public-sponsored gas lighting on the city's main business street.[25]

Local government in Springfield, then, was asked to do little, did little, and generally was reluctant to do very much more, concerned as it was with the interests and values of taxpaying property holders. Limited in theory and practice, therefore, governmental affairs rarely occasioned formal political conflict; it seemed neither appropriate nor necessary. But this apolitical, deferential community of taxpayers had another side to its character, and just as much as local government was a means for realizing the limited purposes of the propertied, it was also a means for expressing, through politics, officeholding, and its more general welfare functions, the larger sense of community cohesion and identity so central to traditional life. As a way of exploring this paradoxical character more deeply, as a way of sensing its reality for people in the 1840's and 1850's, it will be helpful to examine in greater detail an issue that brought out the tensions within such a notion of community. For this purpose nothing could be more suitable than the education question, since as one of the budget's major items, schools were a matter of great financial concern, and yet they symbolized more than anything else the common commitment to the development of the community's prime resource, its people.

There were, of course, few Massachusetts traditions more venerable than tax-supported public education. The famous 1647 law that began "It being one chief project of that old deluder Satan to keep men from knowledge of the Scriptures" was America's first law requiring public schools, and by the eighteenth century the Commonwealth had flourishing tax-supported primary and grammar schools in almost every town, under almost complete community control. Toward the end of the century, however, a rapidly dispersing population, widely diffused even within individual town limits, produced administrative and political problems that led to the evolution of the "district system," sanctioned in a comprehensive school law in 1789. Under this arrangement, the various villages and neighborhoods within a town managed their own school affairs, supported by a share of the town school fund. The districts — Springfield had twenty before its 1848 division, and twelve thereafter — were powerful and independent entities. They held their own little town meetings, could tax, sue, and be sued, owned the schools and equipment, and ran them with little effective supervision from the towns, even after an 1826 law mandated a five-man town school committee with expanded power.[26]

This state of affairs sounds quite attractice in twentieth-century America, where so many school systems suffer from an overcentralized, inefficient, and educationally stifling bureaucratization. In the mid-nineteenth century, however, the district system began to come under fierce attack by critics not unmindful of its attractions; as one later wrote, it represented "the high water mark of Modern Democracy, and the low water mark of the Massachusetts school system." Horace Mann called the 1789 law enacting it "the most unfortunate law on the subject of common schools ever enacted in the State." The trouble was, according to critics, that the extreme decentralization did allow local units to fit policy to their interests, but in so doing education always seemed to take a back seat to the desire for a low tax-rate, a situation that could entrench the narrowest and most provincial sort of particularism. Faced with the necessity of making costly decisions, the districts became notoriously stingy, a tendency that increased in inverse ratio to the size of the district, because the smaller the unit the larger bulked the proportional burden of basic expenses like buildings and teacher salaries. With towns fragmented into feuding districts, most of them too small to be viable, inefficiency, duplication, frustration, and, ultimately, apathy were left to rule, and critics held the district system primarily responsible for the generally acknowledged decline in the quality of public education in the early nineteenth century. The cycle was pernicious, since ambitious private academies took up the slack, luring away many concerned parents and increasing the burden on the districts. Consequently, a frontal attack on the district system became central to the crusade for the common schools launched by James G. Carter and carried forward so successfully by Horace Mann and his board of education.[27]

In Springfield, the town's districts were as parsimonious as those anywhere, their schools in as poor repair, as inadequately equipped, and as pedagogically provincial. From the early 1840's, school committee leaders had begun to plead for consolidation under town control, but found little response. The matter came to a head in the 1850's, as much because of the accelerating statewide campaign against the system as because of any developments in Springfield. By this time, the school committee's suggestions had become widespread demands, but so stubborn was resistance that consolidation of the districts could not be included in the new city charter for fear ratification might fail because of it. Despite a growing recognition that the districts were anomalous in an ambitious city, it still took three years of concentrated debate to push through a consolidation ordinance, and even then the districts sought to block the move in court, requiring several more years of litigation and ordinances before all the loopholes could be plugged.[28]

Such struggles often revealed deeper divisions within the community, with the forces of reform and centralization usually representing those middle- and upper-class interests concerned with promoting growth and maintaining social stability.[29] It is probably unwarranted, however, to read too much deeper significance into the district battle in Springfield. People differed over whether the reform, which few denied on principle or held inappropriate in a larger city, was necessary yet in a community like their own. Particularism, resentment of the center so common to Massachusetts towns, and skepticism about whether Springfield was growing fast or surely enough to warrant such modern arrangements — and their cost — seemed to fuel the opposition more than class or cultural divisions. Nevertheless, Springfield bears out the more general observation that educational reform can be correlated with a community's urbanization, particularly on the matter of the establishment of high schools. At the call of the commonwealth, Springfield had first established a high school in 1828. However, few felt it really necessary, and the costs soon eroded its initial support. By 1840, enervated by a bitter appropriation debate each year, the high school had disappeared. Nine years later, when a new law clarified the community's obligation, Springfield grumblingly resumed the burden of providing secondary education, agreeing with District Eight at Court Square to permit the high school there, established by and for that district, to serve the entire town. But the cautious town meeting carefully spelled out that the new law should be "so far complied with as to protect the town against a prosecution for the penalty, *but no further*," an eloquent comment on the community's interest in the project.[30]

These educational questions suggest how the limits inherent in traditional notions of community came to bear on matters of public policy, making it not very much more than the sum of the individual interests of the taxpayers. And these questions show Springfield still acting like a more traditional town, and thinking of itself in those terms. Its first years as a city were in this and almost every other sense a rounding out of an old era, rather than an inauguration of a new one. The Springfield described here had not yet gone through the changes that would make it an urban community.

Springfield before the Civil War embodied a number of paradoxes. In a functional and institutional sense, Springfield was a limited community. Identity with the town could easily break down into neighborhood squabbling and petty rivalries. People viewed government in the narrowest of terms, and held it accountable mainly to the interests of the taxpayers. On the other hand, the notion of community was rich and expansive, premised on a homogeneous culture and an immediate, informal community of association, at once structured and deferential and yet fluid, open, and inclusive. Instruments of social control were held to be agents of cohesion rather than differentiation, and politics functioned more as a mechanism for assuring broad cultural inclusion than as a means of expressing and managing conflict.

It is important to see how all these dimensions stemmed from a unitary outlook, a conceptual framework difficult to grasp in modern terms but comprehensible to people at the time, and basic to the way they understood their community. One approach suggested earlier is to recognize the absence of any actual or theoretical differentiation between public and private life in the mid-nineteenth-century town. The public interest could appear to be the sum of the community's many private concerns because there was not the degree of highly formalized, segmented, and fragmented contacts between individuals that characterizes modern life, and similarly the life of the community, and individuals within it, did not resolve down into various public and private roles. The curious blend of aristocracy and egalitarianism, "democracy without democrats," can also be more easily understood in these terms. A modern sociologist, in fact, has suggested that this is the basic distinction between urban and nonurban life, and that "the more clearly the polarity and the reciprocal relationship between public and private spheres are defined, the more 'city-like,' sociologically speaking, is the life of a settlement."[31]

This notion will be helpful in studying Springfield's transition to an urban community, but perhaps even more suggestive is a closely related framework that emerges from this overview of Springfield's background. All the aspects of community can be seen as complementary. People tended to think, act, and view their community in direct, personal, informal, and nonabstract terms. Community institutions, even formal ones, were strongest where they were rooted in this immediate sense of contact, in the traditional culture of cohesion — the volunteer fire companies, the temperance movement, the charities, even political campaigns and the concern with property improvements.[32] And the sense of community had the least meaning and reality where people were asked to think in indirect, formal, abstract, and projective terms about the nature of the general welfare or even about their own self-interest. Thus the meaning of education was discussed less than its cost, and the more or less abstract community advantage in street lighting for the business district was not generally appreciated, though in every other respect deference to business values and interests was substantial. The sense of community, in short, existed as a strong and meaningful personal reality linking individuals with the town's culture and history, but it was weak as a more abstracted conception, and as such inherently limited in its institutional expression and its capacity to adjust to drastically changing circumstances.

What was to happen to Springfield in the following decades can be described in its essential outline as the reversal of this conceptual situation: the divergence of public and private, the decline of community as a cultural reality and its emergence as an abstracted concept. The change really began with the Civil War boom, but no sharp line can or should be drawn at 1861. The crucial first step, of course, had already been taken with municipal incorporation in 1852, however slow its implications were to emerge. For what else was the meaning of the detailed charter, the representative democracy, and the implied bureaucracy, if not the substitution of formality for informality, of an abstract community for the personal association of the town meeting, of a vehicle permitting legitimate expression of community divisions for a concept of politics and government premised on harmony and intolerant of conflict, political or cultural?

To say that these implications were not fully grasped at the time is only to say that few in the 1850's could see how many ideas, attitudes, and institutions would soon go the way of the town meeting. As the nation shuddered on the brink of civil war, Springfield can perhaps be excused for not fully anticipating the dramatic changes imminent in its own life and culture. Meanwhile, the new city continued to live more or less in the manner of the old town.

Part Two
The Civil War Years, 1860-1865

3. Springfield and the Civil War

The Civil War years were for Springfield a period of growth and of a prosperity so sudden and concentrated that it dramatically transformed the city. The economic, social, and physical changes shaped the city's future, and the historical experience of the boom itself could not but work profoundly on institutions and traditional relationships. But apart from this wartime boom, the war itself had an enormous impact on Springfield. The conflict proved to be the most engrossing and traumatic event in American history; if it is always important to appreciate how local matters can be shaped by involvements that transcend the locality, it would seem, intuitively, to be particularly important in this instance. And in tangible fact, on several levels, the war and its demands dominated local life. When it was all over, Springfield emerged a much different place for having grappled with the exhausting challenge the war posed to its commitment, its resources, and its life as a community.

In one sense, the war and the issues that had produced it were exciting political phenomena, seen from afar through the eyes of the *Republican* — until 1864 Springfield's only newspaper — and reflected in turbulent partisan activity at home. The furious slavery debate had kept Massachusetts in political chaos through the 1850's, beginning with the famous "Coalition" between Democrats and Free Soilers that had routed the tottering Whigs, signaled the general disintegration of party lines, and sent Charles Sumner to the United States Senate in 1851. Passions ran high and when an unruly mob prevented George Thompson, the British abolitionist, from holding a planned rally in Springfield, the *Republican* placed the blame on

the provocatory appearance of "this vile slanderer of America and
her people, the fit associate of Garrison, Pillsbury, and other revilers
of religion and the Union." Most of "respectable Springfield"
seemed to join in condemning abolition in the early fifties, but there
was certainly no consensus; indeed, the Coalition battle and the
Thompson controversy proved to be major elements in the paralysis
of the town meeting discussed earlier. There were many outspoken
radicals, too, including the prominent Reverend Osgood, and the
Underground Railroad had stopped in Springfield for years, enjoy-
ing considerable support there. In fact, John Brown himself, though
hardly noticed at the time, had been a Springfield wool merchant
for several years prior to 1850, and returned in 1851 to help local
blacks organize assistance for runaways.[1]

As the decade progressed, Springfield began to listen to the anti-
slavery message more closely. The slow crystallization of opinion,
first against the expansion of slavery and then against the institution
itself and the South, mirrored closely the pattern familiar throughout the Northeast: as the nation began to fall apart, Springfield was
drawing itself together. Particularly after the Kansas-Nebraska Act
public opinion grew steadily, if reluctantly, more militant, and the
Sumner reviled in 1851 was a hero even before he fell under Preston
Brooks' cane. The process is dramatically visible in the columns of
the *Republican*, and there is no reason to doubt that the journal reflected the general drift of local opinion. Samuel Bowles himself
moved ahead of the people and his own paper, being one of the first
to call for the formation of a new Northern party. As a political
force, his influence was coming to be quite substantial, and he was
instrumental in the successful birth of the Republican Party. By
1860, in any event, Springfield was catching up with its editor and
the times. Fremont had not done well there in 1856, but four years
later Lincoln and the Republicans won a smashing two to one victory in Springfield, the county, and the commonwealth.[2]

When the outbreak of fighting ended the agonizing secession crisis,
the war enjoyed the general patriotic support one would expect it to
find in a New England town. But to say this is not to imply that
there was unanimity, or that the changing shape of the issues involved was uniformly perceived. On the contrary, there was a good
deal of movement and debate, even within the editorial columns of

the *Republican*, itself nearly an administration organ at the same time as it was a reasonably accurate barometer of public opinion.[3] It is fascinating to trace in the paper the long unresolved confusion over the aims and purposes of the war. At first, despite the call by local abolitionists for a holy war of emancipation, the *Republican* and most of the community insisted that restoration of the Union was the war's only valid goal. Gradually, it was acknowledged that emancipation might, after all, become a necessary means to this end. And thereafter, step by step and qualification by exception, people came to accept the legitimacy of emancipation per se, embracing Lincoln's famous proclamation "heartily if not with entire consistency."[4]

Beyond the intellectual or idealogical questions involved, exasperation with the war's progress, or lack of it, produced further divergence within the patriotic consensus. As usual, the moderate center could not hold; it corroded under pressure to the profit of the extremes on either side. Radicals in Springfield gained the most from this, as indicated by the appearance and immediate success of the brazen and uncompromising *Springfield Daily Union* in 1864. The conservative position gained more rhetorical bark than political bite — Springfield never had a significant Copperhead element, and there was little of the Irish antiwar sentiment often seen in other communities.[5]

General community support for the broad lines of the war policy was unmistakably apparent in local voting during the conflict. Governor Andrew, whose radicalism could occasionally displease the *Republican*, never lacked for public support. In each of his annual campaigns he carried the city by a wider margin, winning in the heavy 1864 turnout by a margin of more than three to one. And while Democratic voting strength was too traditionally rooted to drop precipitously in local contests, war conservatives supported by the party did not do well in Springfield. Thus in 1862, at a time when peace sentiment was gaining in the North, the largely Democratic-coalition "People's Party," saw its local meetings poorly attended and its best hope soundly defeated in a congressional race. The result is especially revealing because the loser was the locally imposing Chester Chapin, and the victor was Henry L. Dawes, an important Republican figure, but a man from elsewhere in the district who had not previously enjoyed any exceptional popularity in Springfield.[6]

The 1864 presidential race, of course, provides the best barometer. There had been considerable criticism of Lincoln from all sides in Springfield. The ambitious new *Union* delighted in attacking the administration from the left, and even the *Republican* was frequently impatient with the president. Bowles, who had never been an enthusiastic supporter, privately declared himself "sick of Lincoln's small village politics." But as election day approached, both papers closed ranks, there being no feasible alternative. And although the Democrats formed their McClellan Clubs, enthusiastically turning out for the torchlight parades, flag raisings, and street rallies that were the style of the day, there was never any doubt about the outcome. Many of the leading local Democrats, such as the former mayor Stephen C. Bemis, refused to support the dovish general, and Lincoln's landslide victory showed that the campaign noise had been hollow indeed. The president received 2,377 votes to only 790 for McClellan, which more than doubled the proportion of his 1860 victory, and exceeded the popular Andrew's three to one triumph. Even in ward one, reputed center of Irish and Democratic strength, Lincoln approached the same level of support.[7]

To know what people thought about the war is, however, to understand only a very limited dimension of the conflict's reality in local life. Beyond its importance as a political issue, the faraway war had a much more immediate impact in human terms. Never exclusively a newspaper abstraction, the military conflict was a human conflict that involved many local sons, a dimension particularly inescapable in the war's early years, when men were mustered into regiments recruited, organized, and trained locally, and often commanded by prominent local figures. Springfield, as one of the centers of western Massachusetts, saw an unusual amount of such military preparation. By the end of 1862, four regiments drawn from the area had been formed, all led by Springfield figures — City Clerk Horace C. Lee, Probate Judge William Shurtleff, and Oliver Edwards and Henry Briggs, both also prominent personages.[8] Three of these regiments mustered and trained in Springfield, amidst a swirl of excitement. The Tenth Regiment, Briggs in command, arrived for training in June 1861, setting up camp at the fairgrounds maintained by the local agricultural society in the North End, known then as Hampden and today as Pynchon Park. The city paraded and feted the new recruits with appropriate enthusiasm, and after a month of training characterized by equally unsurprising chaos and confusion, Springfield sent its first heroes off to war with a tumultuous celebration. The Twenty-seventh Massachusetts Volunteers, trained that fall on the Hill near what is now Winchester Square, enjoyed similar treatment, and there was only a slightly visible modulation in enthusiasm when Springfield welcomed the Thirty-seventh and Forty-sixth Massachusetts Regiments in 1862.[9]

This made the war more personal, immediate, and exciting for the home community, but the local identification with particular regiments also proved to be a two-edged sword, for when one of the Connecticut Valley regiments fought a bloody battle, the casualty lists would carry one familiar name after another. Such was the case when the Tenth was mauled in fighting near Washington, and when the Thirty-seventh fought at Fredericksburg, Chancellorsville, and Gettysburg. As the toll mounted, heroic romanticism numbered among the casualties. There were joyous celebrations when the regiments came marching home again, but relief was as apparent as exultation. The horror and reality of war were making their mark.[10]

And yet, such was the terrible magnitude of the Civil War that its impact would have been inescapable even without this local human investment. One sees this in the slowly changing tone of the *Republican*'s war stories, which were fed to the anxious crowds that waited outside its office for late dispatches or for the frequent extra editions run off during major campaigns. The first year shows the familiar romantic mode: each successful skirmish was a "glorious victory," and Massachusetts troops were always cited as being particularly "covered with glory" by their exploits. To judge from the rhetoric, setbacks and losses were as much dramatic as military defeats, partly because "Secessia" was perpetually pictured in rout and incipient collapse. Even with the impatience that quickly built up in 1861 ("On to Richmond?" grumbled the *Republican* on December 13, "On to somewhere, anywhere") optimism still ruled. As late as May 1862, a local leader wrote Henry L. Dawes that "We are all in high glee. We cannot doubt that the Rebellion is on its last legs." The other side of the next corner seemed always to promise vigor, progress, victory, and, of course, glory.[11]

It could never last. The shock of the summer and fall of 1862 still leaps from the pages of a century-old newspaper. The Confederate advances, the call for new troops, the threat of conscription — all had stunned the community, and yet nothing prepared it for the rebel invasion and the incredible destruction it brought into the North. After Antietam, glory was no longer the watchword; the *Republican* headlines now read "Slaughter, Horrible Slaughter." Appalled by the carnage, and fighting its own desperate battle to raise troops, Springfield still could generate excitement for the frequent rallies called, as one invitation had it, "to revive the popular interest and confidence, to declare and thus strengthen our fealty and devotion to the country and the cause." But grimness was never far from the surface.[12]

This was underscored by another form in which the war came to Springfield, the sick and maimed soldiers needing care, vivid evidence of the carnage. Springfield's location as a major rail crossroads imposed on it a special burden, for virtually all the wounded returning to eastern and northern New England passed through its depot, often waiting several days for connections. As the conflict became more bloody, the burden on local charity grew in proportion, with activity focusing on immediate care for these casualties rather than on the more common hometown activity of raising supplies for the distant front.[13] At first, this was taken up by a wide range of fundraisers, from church ladies to fire companies and armorers' groups. But the war demanded more intense and focused humanitarian effort, soon concentrated in the Young Men's Christian Commission, established for this purpose near the end of 1862. The group purchased a small house near the depot to care for the wounded, and aided by its ladies' auxiliary, it erected a larger and more adequate building there in the next year. Renamed the Soldier's Rest Association, the group channeled and coordinated Springfield's war relief effort for the duration.[14]

At the same time as it provided needed assistance to the wounded, this activity provided a needed outlet for war-generated tension and anxiety. And quite consciously, it was promoted as an important focus of community life, a way for all citizens to identify with and contribute to the war effort. The great Soldier's Rest 1864 Fair illustrates how local leaders sought not only to raise money and material, but to involve as many people as possible in the process. Saturation publicity and exhaustive planning occupied Springfield for weeks prior to the event, with virtually every person of note prominent among the organizers. Day after day, long lists of committees filled the papers, naming everyone involved in even the most trivial details of preparation. The fair itself lasted several days, featuring star speakers like Governor Andrew, and its success seemed as important a boost to the city's morale as to the soldiers who were to benefit from the $18,000 raised. It symbolized Springfield's impressive response to the need for war relief. The community raised over $80,000 during the conflict, and gave assistance to more than 17,000 transient soldiers. At the same time, the crisis had occasioned the most inclusive and extensive community activity in Springfield's history.[15]

To the extent that charity work functioned as an escape valve for wartime anxiety, it was only the most constructive of a variety of such outlets. For in addition to this positive involvement, there was also the need to escape, to mask the increasingly somber face of war. The same anxieties, fueled by the almost runaway prosperity, generated an often frantic rhythm in the city's social life. On the surface, all was gaiety and diversion. It was capped each year on the Fourth of July, when up to fifty trainloads of celebrants would arrive in Springfield for day-long festivities, but the celebration was hardly tied to patriotic themes, or limited to official holidays. People in the bustling city had plenty of money to spend on amusements that far surpassed the usual diet of parades, fairs, and entertainments high and low: the war spirit, it seemed at times, was turning Springfield into a perpetual carnival. "Amusements are more numerous than ever, and the crowds they draw are unparalleled," said the *Republican* in 1863. Again, the next year: "Still they come! The amusements season holds on as tenaciously as ever." Higher culture took several forms: the Library Lectures featured Emerson, Parker Pillsbury, Artemas Ward, and other familiar circuit speakers delivering their famous and familiar showpiece lectures; there were concerts by the Gottshalks, and many theatrical performances by touring troupes. John Wilkes Booth, an actor familiar to the city, played Hamlet in Springfield not long before assuming his role in real-life tragedy. Beyond this were the more popular circus-like amusements.

An endless line paraded through, competing for momentary favor: Springfield could choose among snake charmers, glass blowers, the marathon walking racers, a Jefferson Davis shooting gallery, public demonstrations of laughing gas, and so forth.[16] It is tempting to conclude, as some have, that all this shows how little the war touched distant communities like Springfield, how much the city was captivated by the abstract glory of war, and the more tangible gold it produced. But to say this would be to seriously misread the social atmosphere. The compulsive efforts at diversion were as superficial as they were frenetic, and it is significant that a similar "hectic gaiety" characterized Washington, D.C., a city hardly removed from war's reality by any measure. Springfield, its detachment only geographic, was hardly unique in this aspect of its response to the stress of a civil war, and the underlying tensions were far from hidden.[17]

The war touched Springfield in one final dimension — the difficult and deadly serious burden of raising troops and avoiding the draft. The complex business of meeting the quotas was the war's most direct manifestation, reaching deeply into almost every aspect of community life. It is here that one can observe the fullest interplay of interests, public and private, the most dramatic impact on politics and institutions, the most sustained personal involvement at all levels. Offering as it does the best insights into wartime Springfield, the community crisis of troop-raising will be examined here in some detail; the story is one of such richness that its neglect by Springfield's local historians, and in general by those of other communities, is as curious as it is unfortunate.[18]

Massachusetts found itself almost totally unprepared, institutionally and psychologically, to meet the extended military responsibilities imposed by the war. The ancient militia system was virtually defunct, and there was no machinery for raising large numbers of troops; nor was it expected, even late in 1861, that such might become necessary. In the first year of the war, at least, good intentions and patriotism sufficed. With forty thousand uniformed men soon filling thirty-two regiments, Governor Andrew could offer the secretary of war far more troops, in fact, than the government had requested or felt able to accept.[19]

The towns themselves did most of the work in this first mobilization, with little direction or instruction from the state. The approach resembled the old militia procedures where localities received enlistments and equipped their own volunteer units, all in an atmosphere that Springfield observers called "the true patriotic and working spirit of 76." Locally, the first steps had been taken in late April 1861, at a formal public gathering reminiscent of the old town meetings. With Mayor Bemis in the chair and the platform filled with all the city's former mayors, this assembly set up a blue-ribbon war committee to direct Springfield's recruiting, headed by Colonel James Thompson, George Townsley, Henry Alexander, and other prominent figures. Money quickly flowed in to fortify the spirit — this meeting raised $5,000, which more than matched the city government's initial emergency appropriation for equipment and recruiting. Given new taxing powers by the legislature in anticipation of state reimbursement, the city also presently acted to provide aid for the families of volunteers. Recruiting in this context proved easy, and over three hundred local men stepped forward during the war's first year.[20]

There is a fascinating if unsurprising parallel between the North's gradual appreciation of the severity of the war and the changing state and local approach to building the armies that would fight it. Not only did general attitudes grow progressively more serious and realistic, but the technical, financial, and administrative problems became as demanding, and as frustrating, as the military challenge facing the Union command. It was soon clear that the haphazard 1861 approach would have to be replaced by more comprehensive machinery. With the stunning call for 300,000 three-year troops in July 1862, the War Department began to take more general charge. For the first time, it assigned specific quotas to the states, which then in turn apportioned them among the cities and towns; in Massachusetts, the legislature authorized the local communities to tax or borrow to provide bounty inducements, and the mad scramble to meet the local quotas began. Hardly had the competition started, however, when Lincoln's August 6 call for another 300,000 men, these to see nine-months' service, visibly staggered the country. And this blow had frightening force behind it: should the quotas not be filled, Lincoln warned, the government would turn to conscription.

Responding quickly, the adjutant general of Massachusetts first ex-
perimented with old census and militia rolls, then ordered a comprehensive new enrollment of all men between eighteen and forty-five,
and a more accurate allocation of quotas by county, town, and even
subdistrict.[21]

Local communities felt almost immediately the pressure of these
two 1862 calls and the new quotas, and almost every town began
strenuous efforts to enlist recruits and raise money for the bounties
with which to attract them. Springfield now had an obligation of
250 men under each call, and during the bloody summer of 1862,
local affairs focused obsessively upon "that which pertains to the
war and filling up the quotas." Even before Governor Andrew suggested a similar procedure for all towns, the city clerk reported that
in Springfield "nearly all places of business were promptly closed at
3 PM, and mass meetings of the citizens, presided over by the
Mayor, were held daily, Sundays not always excepted, in front of
the City Hall, until the quotas were filled." The appeal was still the
patriotic one, although generally blunter in tone than earlier. "Men
of Springfield!" trumpeted the *Republican*, "What are *you* doing to
get young men enrolled? How much have *you* sacrificed? Throughout all this war we have enjoyed unprecedented prosperity and our
citizens have all made money. Let us, in the name of decency, do
something in response."[22]

While the speakers and bands raised money on the steps of City
Hall, inside, the council appropriated another $30,000 for more
bounties. By the end of the year local recruits could receive over
$300 for enlisting, a sum that then represented a good part of a
workingman's annual earnings and a great lure indeed. Springfield
could be proud of the results by the end of 1862 — more than 1,200
men had now entered service from the area, so far surpassing the
quotas that some of the surplus could be applied to the accounts of
towns less successful in recruiting. But it is illustrative of both the
growing competition and the price of success that bounties for
August's volunteers, who were to serve only nine months, consistently exceeded the sum adequate in July to attract recruits for a
long three years. The grim business gave signs of becoming less a
matter of mobilizing the yeoman and more one of purchasing near-
mercenaries.[23]

Throughout 1862, fear of America's first conscription case the longest shadow over local recruiting efforts. It would be difficult to exaggerate how deeply the North dreaded conscription, how alien and un-American it seemed, and with what real fear it was anticipated. New Englanders, constantly invoking their Revolutionary War tradition, viewed the prospect of forced enlistment with special horror. And even more than the threat of the call itself, communities like Springfield feared the shame and disgrace which they understood as attaching to a failure to meet the quota.[24]

For the time being, despite this new strain, the state-wide system still worked. Massachusetts raised 45,000 troops in 1862, exceeding its quotas on the two major calls. But new levies in 1863 proved overwhelming, and the dreaded draft could no longer be postponed. When it came to Springfield, it was regarded as a community crisis of the first order, with the tension especially great because the first drawings took place shortly after the appalling draft riots in New York City and a momentary eruption of violence in Boston. The city mobilized over one hundred special officers, virtually a roster of its most respected leaders, to supervise the procedures. Though there were no disturbances, this did not diminish the anxiety, which focused squarely on the draft itself. The events fully engaged the emotions and attention of the entire community, as indicated by the exhaustively detailed coverage and the page after page of names carried in the *Republican*. Considering the actual incidence of the draft, this fixation seems in some sense excessive — in this 1863 drawing, the only substantial one of the war in Massachusetts, only 3,068 men were taken into service, from the entire Commonwealth, and of these only 734 were actual conscripts, the rest being paid substitutes. But on the other hand, 32,000 names were called to produce these few recruits, which means that in Springfield several hundreds were touched by some phase of the conscription process; since nobody knew, in this first draft, exactly how many would be rejected or how many taken, it was with genuine fear that young men there formed "insurance clubs" to pay commutation or buy a substitute for any member unlucky enough to be tapped. And beyond this immediate fear, the symbolic meaning of conscription, its effect on the recruiting system, and the general administrative confusion that accompanied its operation all helped generate the enormous anxiety visible in Springfield and communities like it.[25]

The situation did not improve with the North's rising military fortunes after 1863. Though the unwieldy enrollment and exemption procedures were revised by state and congressional action, in Springfield this did not bring much greater efficiency or order to the task of feeding the war's appetite for troops. Some of the reforms, in fact, inadvertently increased the chaos at the local level — abolition of the patently inequitable commutation privilege, for example, forced communities to substitute increasingly scarce live recruits for the more accessible commutation dollars that had helped to meet the quotas. In this process, Springfield itself was relatively fortunate. It saw only minor supplemental drafting in 1864, and escaped later conscription entirely, despite ever larger quotas. But this had little effect on the level of tension, for even more than in the war's early years, the cost of escape was great. However odious, a comprehensive and efficient draft might have ultimately been easier to bear than what was taking place — a headlong rush into the arms of a bewildering, desperate, and thoroughly demoralizing bounty competition.[26]

The situation was genuinely frantic by 1864. With the call of patriotism growing fainter each week, recruits demanded and received more negotiable reasons for marching off to war. City leaders, in turn, began to use similarly more materialistic arguments in encouraging public support for recruiting, It was growing apparent that those interested in enlisting would sign up wherever inducements were most attractive, and more importantly, the larger pool of young men so crucial to the community's long range economic promise, would choose "safer" locations if unfilled local quotas loomed too large. Appeals late in the war were therefore routinely directed to self-interest as much as to patriotism. "Our city is not winning laurels and her interests are suffering for it," said the *Union*, urging more effort by the rich who were in no personal danger themselves. "If we don't act, bounty hunters will take over completely."[27]

This last point held increasing importance. Not only did the situation breed bitter, almost anarchic competition among various towns; it also led to swindlers, bounty jumpers, and the only slightly more legitimate bounty brokers. The entire system was clearly running out of control, and as with the draft, efforts to give it over-all efficiency often made the situation for individual towns and cities more difficult. This was particularly true of Massachusetts efforts to limit the bounty wars, mainly by assuming more of the burden on a state basis, distributing the costs evenly by taxation. The Commonwealth decided in 1862, for example, to reimburse the towns for bounties paid in that year, but this served only as an inducement to extravagance in those desperate towns most severely pressed already. Another law limiting local bounties to $1,000 was uniformly ignored, as were special efforts to prevent bounty raiding. Even when the state decided to take over the major share of the job itself, paying a direct bounty of $325, the local buying and selling of patriots went on apace. Bounties intended to replace each other merely piled up before prospective recruits.[28]

Many Springfield men at this time received the then astounding sum of $875 for their enlistment — $300 as a federal bounty, $325 from Massachusetts, and $250 from public and private subscriptions locally — the rough equivalent of offering $5,000 or more as a bonus to young men today. The average price of a draft substitute, when that was necessary was $600, and in all these figures Springfield was hardly unique in New England. Furthermore, the administrative confusion could be even worse than the expense. The cities borrowed and taxed for family aid reimbursed by the state; the state taxed and borrowed to pay for bounties and family aid; citizens subscribed money for direct bounties and for loans to the beleagured local governments. And when the mayor and aldermen headed subscription committees, as was standard practice in Springfield, the ambiguity was supreme; people could not really be sure whether they were making private gifts or advances to a public fund in anticipation of future government revenue and reimbursement. The poorly defined line between public and private concerns was never more in evidence.[29]

But somehow the creaky system worked, almost in spite of itself. Massachusetts surpassed all quotas, contributing 159,165 men to the Union armies, and Springfield itself furnished 2,265, including 96 officers, a respectable 206 above its quota. To provide them the city government had paid over $175,000 and individual subscribers in the community a great deal more. The sum may seem puny beside the state's $30 million outlay, or the $13 million spent by all the cities and towns taken together, but one must recognize that it represented a level of spending and debt, completely beyond Springfield's previous experience.[30] Given the attitudes toward government activity and public finance that prevailed at the war's start, such a drastic departure from tradition almost necessarily brought out special tensions and conflicts within the changing community. In shaping Springfield's growth, this was perhaps the most important dimension of the war's direct presence in city life; certainly it was the most complex.

The state government, trying to improve a faltering system, had realized that inefficiency was at least partially a product of inequity; the quotas benefited wealthier towns that could attract recruits and put unbearable pressure on those unable to meet obligations. The imbalance accounted for much of the momentum of the spiraling bounties. The principle of spreading the burden more equitably among all the towns and cities of the commonwealth therefore seemed both practically and philosophically attractive: by approaching the problem as a general public one, for which a general tax was appropriate, both ends could hopefully be served. Springfield encountered a parallel intellectual and administrative challenge. How much of the cost should be borne by the community, and how much by concerned individuals? To what extent was the draft a threat to the young men directly in its path, and to what extent was it a general community concern? And was government aid therefore a service to individuals or to Springfield collectively? In answering such questions, Massachusetts cities and towns did not have the option finally selected by the state, the direct assumption of the largest part of the bounty payments; this was financially and legally impossible. But the localities could, if they wished, adopt an earlier state solution, reimbursement, and it was this — the question of refunding individual contributions to bounty funds — that brought into focus for Springfield all of the ambiguity involved in its war role. Obscured during the fighting, the issue emerged into the light of bitter controversy shortly after the war ended. It revealed the confusion lying beneath actions taken in the press of emergency; in the process it also revealed, and shaped, public attitudes toward the community and its formal institutions.

In 1864 a new state law had first permitted localities to reimburse subscribers to the bounty funds of the previous fall, and Springfield promptly responded by returning $37,000 to local contributors.[31] But it was not made clear whether this was to be a general policy, and the frenzied recruiting of 1864 quickly swept the question from view. In 1865, when the guns had fallen silent and men could look to their wallets with less embarrassment, the advisability of refunding recent subscriptions arose again. The decision was more difficult this time, however, because a more recent state law specified that the localities could no longer borrow funds for reimbursement, but would have to raise the money for this from taxation. A wider range of interests in the community would thus be directly affected by any refunding move. Partly because of this, there was such intense public interest in the question that Springfield's City Council, ignoring a committee report supporting refund, let the issue ride pending a public expression in the December 1865 local election, so that the new government elected then could be guided through the controversial and acrimonious debate. By the fall of the year, local opinion was deeply divided, and the election loomed as a virtual referendum. Party organizations were abandoned in favor of pro- and antirefunding slates, their candidates solidly pledged to a clear position.[32]

The arguments used by each side in the debate are instructive. Refunders pointed to the previous state and municipal reimbursements, and reputed promises to continue them. Subscriptions were therefore held to be pledges that had to be redeemed by the community. Surely, the argument ran, the burden should not be borne solely by those whose age and station had made them most vulnerable to a draft, and most involved in forestalling it through contributions to the funds. Raising the army was a public responsibility, and the bounty donations had thus been public acts that now should be shared by all, including those unwilling to help earlier. The argument sometimes became more explicitly class-oriented by shifting the emphasis slightly: most contributors, it was claimed, were workingmen, who had saved themselves and Springfield from the draft "while the dividends of one class were accumulating in the factories." Taxes for reimbursement would hit the rich hardest, thus balancing the wartime donations of the poor. But such a view of the selective nature of the property tax was somewhat unusual at the time; generally, people still saw it as essentially a levy upon the whole community. In accepting this premise, the refund arguments thus usually came down to a plea that a tax on almost all replace the contribution by some.[33]

The antirefunders also employed a variety of arguments. They denied that the "poor" had given the bulk of the subscription, claiming instead that substantial property owners had contributed heavily to buy their way out of danger. Refunding, in any event, would only reward their reluctance to serve by reimbursing them for the cost of substitutes. Property, furthermore, had already borne a huge burden in the increased taxes for other war expenses; should the entire community be taxed again to pay this added cost? Veterans, naturally, were reported to be solidly against refunding: they felt they had paid their share in risking their lives, and resented the prospect of being taxed for the benefit of those who had not had to face the same dangers. And finally, to further complicate matters, it was widely charged that many of the poor, given the uncertainty of refunding, had already sold their claims on the subscription fund, at a fraction of their value, to speculators who would thus be the recipients of community revenue should refunding take place. In one sense then, antirefunders pictured bounty subscriptions as acts of individual self-defense; to the extent that they stemmed from other motives, or were made by those not directly threatened, it was offered that patriotism should be its own reward.[34]

Regardless of which side one feels made the stronger case, Springfield did not quite weigh its decision only in these terms. There was a good deal of money involved, and as Oscar Handlin observed in a wider context, in voting on such material issues "division arose from the immediate effects, rather than from the abstract nature of the question." As people expected, the antirefunders won the contest by a solid three to two ratio in the heaviest turnout for a local election in Springfield's history. Quite simply, most of the voters did not want any more taxes, and wished to put the war behind them. This was particularly so in the populous center districts that not incidentally, had carried proportionally lighter quotas and had subscribed proportionally less. Thus wards one through four had borne expenses averaging $130 for each recruit obtained, and though they had rarely voted together in the past, they each overwhelmingly rejected refunding, the total being 1,162 to 464. And in the outlying wards five through eight, where expenses had averaged $170, voters also crossed old dividing lines and consistently endorsed refunding, the tally here being 601 to 294. Considering the class appeal of some of the rhetoric, it is noteworthy that wards one and five, which had the largest and most vocal working class electorates, voted on opposite sides, and that ward one, where most Irish voters lived, showed the same pattern as the wealthiest Yankee areas.[35] *

Because records of subscription lists and amounts have not survived, it would not be wise to draw any further statistical conclusions from this vote. But clearly, even while citizens voted their pocketbooks, the argument had deeply challenged and confused Springfield. Part of the problem was that subscriptions were at once public and private acts, even before administrative ambiguity clouded their nature. Furthermore, the meaning of a pledge had varied not only from person to person, but with time through the long war. At the very start, most contributions were more clearly patriotic acts of witness, while toward the close, with men and towns running scared, pledges took on more particularistic meanings. Both sides in the debate, then, were correct to a degree, and perhaps this ambiguity remains the most important point — the war's agonizing realities eroded the patriotic meaning of volunteering, substitution, and bounties, and in the process transferred much of the ambiguity thus created to roles and obligations within the local community itself.

The bounty refund issue, then, helps to paint a more complete picture of the meaning the Civil War had for Springfield's people.

---

*Mayor Briggs was re-elected by 1,456 to 1,065, and although he was not directly involved in the bounty issue, there is reason to assume that the tally represents an expression on that issue, for it parallels all the various aldermanic totals in contests which were explicitly seen as a bounty referendum. The bounty cost figures are derived from the "Report of the Special Committee of the City Council," *SR*, June 13, 1865. Murdock, in *Patriotism Limited*, tries to answer, in appendix B, pp. 211–228, the question "Was it a Poor Man's Fight?" He concludes that "no clear correlation between economic status and commutation payments" can be determined. Methodological questions limit the value of this work, however. For example, Murdock arrives at his conclusions by comparing recruitment figures from different districts ranked by wealth. However, these rankings involve dividing total valuation by total population in a district, and cannot tell us who within the district, rich or poor, was actually commuting, substituting, or enlisting. His statistics are therefore only the broadest guide to the actual experience in a given locality, and the question must still be considered somewhat open.

Agreed on the general nature and policies of the war, they had initially responded with sincere enthusiasm to its demands. Rallying behind community leaders, volunteers stepped forward and citizens organized charity operations on a scale never before needed or attempted. But eventually, the war's horror evaporated the initial romanticism, generating intense pressure and making community obligations far more difficult to handle. The local sons in regional regiments, the troops training and the wounded returning, the recruiting and draft problems, the bounty tangle — all brought the war directly into the community's daily life. In all these dimensions, the experience was one of increasing tension and anxiety, a local crisis that illustrates how fully the tragedy of the Civil War reached a community so far from the battlefields.

But it is important to recognize that a good part of the difficulty was due to more internal considerations, for the war demanded of Springfield a community response on a new order, as well as on a new scale. The collective identification with the Union cause and the real desire to spare Springfield the shame of conscription combined with other more particularistic motives to enable the city to take public action — to spend, plan, and organize completely out of keeping with tradition. Only afterwards did it begin to be clear how confusing and unsettling were these steps. They called into question traditionally informal understandings of community responsibilities, and they put great pressure on the traditionally imprecise relation between collective and individual interests. Though Springfield had successfully met its obligations, it found that tradition offered no way of resolving the complex procedural and conceptual questions posed by the actions necessity forced it to take.

This break with the past had perhaps even wider influence on the community and its institutions, because the city was simultaneously facing a host of questions posed by the massive social and economic changes of the wartime boom, and the experience of vigorous public action on the war issues inevitably shaped the context in which these other questions were considered. But the pattern in more purely local matters was not to be identical. The imperatives of war and the quotas could not be ignored, misinterpreted, or contested: Springfield acted first and worried later. But in local decisions, tangled interests, contested concepts, and inadequate institutions in-

truded more easily, affecting both the ability to make public decisions and the forms that they took. War, as always, had the dubious
virtue of a certain clarity. In its direct impact on Springfield's public
life, the Civil War generated a crucially important momentum, but it
could not provide many answers for the local problems arising in its
wake.

4. The War Boom

The debate over the Civil War's impact on American economic
growth has filled library shelves and occupied delighted scholars for
years, without moving perceptibly closer to a resolution of the basic
disagreements. This academic battle, however, bears little relation to
Springfield, for whatever the war's diverse and ambiguous effects
elsewhere, it brought to the Connecticut Valley an enormous, sustained, and uncomplicated prosperity, which built on the region's
established foundations a solid framework for continued, long-term
economic growth. The reasons for this are not difficult to grasp, and
the substance and dimensions of the war boom could be meaningful-
ly sketched rather briefly. To do this, however, would be to risk
missing much of the larger meaning the war years held for Springfield, for prosperity meant not only production and dividends, but
also excitement, self-consciousness, conflict, ambition, and pride —
less tangible than profits and new factories, yet equally crucial to
the building of a city. In this sense, the separate details of expansion
and the actual processes of growth have a special reality of their
own, and a more intimate familiarity with these details is needed as
a context for exploring Springfield's development in any broader
historical terms.

The best place to begin any such survey is the United States
Armory, proudly overlooking the community from its hilltop site,
for it was the actual and symbolic trigger of the regional boom, and
its dramatic expansion under tremendous pressure illustrates the difficulties faced by other enterprises whose records have not been preserved as completely.

United States Armory, mid-nineteenth century

Initially, the Armory was quite unprepared for waging a long war.
Though James Ripley, its controversial superintendent from 1851 to
1854, had built an efficient factory in Springfield, subsequent years
had rusted his system badly. Production had been cut back sharply
through the 1850's, and at the outbreak of war a skeleton crew of
under two hundred men were pursuing leisurely experiments with
new mechanisms, turning out at a trickle the 1855 rifled musket
that would become the Union foot soldiers' basic weapon.[1]
Almost immediately after the outbreak of war, a flood of orders
from Washington engulfed the Armory, demanding the resumption
and expansion of production, instructions particularly detailed and
pointed because they came from James Ripley himself, now chief of
ordnance in the War Department. Steps were quickly taken to expand plant and machinery, to hire more men, and to operate at the
fullest possible capacity, but orders could accomplish only so much.
The Armory was a hybrid institution, controlled from Washington
yet dependent on local administration, labor, and a complex of relationships with area subcontractors and suppliers; expansion thus in-

evitably meant problems. The Armory had difficulty securing an adequate quantity or quality of iron, especially when British supplies were cut off, and it encountered constant delays in obtaining acceptable tools, machinery, and subcontracted parts, mostly from local firms. The burden of inspecting outside production and coordinating all the related efforts became correspondingly immense.

Equally imposing were the human problems. Skilled artisans were hard to come by, and a shortage of a certain critical specialty — barrel rollers, for instance — could and often did hold up production along the entire line. Even when skilled workers were found, so competitive was the valley's labor market that it often proved difficult to hold onto them. And all the new men, skilled and unskilled, created training, supervision, and discipline problems, which persistent financial difficulty only aggravated — payrolls from Washington were often as many as four months in arrears, lost in congressional haggling or Treasury Department delays.[2]

The Armory, however, seemed almost to thrive on these challenges. As one student observed, the pressure actually "awakened the Armory to something like a modern understanding of plant efficiency." Severe shortages of skilled labor and subcontracted parts led it to provide more exact specifications, and to give new meaning to the term "interchangeability." In 1860 the rifle had been made in 113 operations; by 1865 the same weapon's 49 parts were produced and assembled in 390 specialized steps. Progress was reflected in costs; Springfield Rifles made under full private contract cost the government $19 or $20, while all estimates of costs at the Armory suggest a figure of around $12.[3]

The dimensions of Armory expansion provide the most impressive evidence of its contribution to the war effort. The work force leaped in a few years from 200 to over 2,600 men, a figure especially imposing when seen against Springfield's population, then around 20,000. Allowing for workers who commuted from neighboring towns, it is still safe to estimate that almost one of every four men in Springfield worked at the Armory.[4] Even more dramatic was the meteoric increase in output. The Armory was producing 800 rifles a month in 1861; this jumped 400 percent in the war's first year, which led the most optimistic forecasters to hope that a peak of 5,000 per month might be reached, though this seemed extravagant

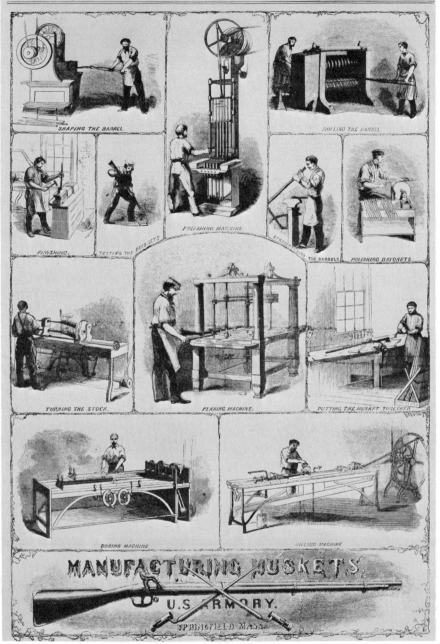

Manufacturing the Springfield Rifle, *Harper's Weekly*, September 21, 1861

to most experts. However, at the height of production in 1864, rifles were being sent out at the staggering rate of 26,000 per month, over 276,000 rifles yearly. The total Armory production for the war came to 805,538, far above the 650,000 produced by all of the private companies making the same weapon under contract.[5] This performance at Springfield dazzled the nation, as illustrated by an awestruck account in the *Atlantic Monthly* that described the many shops, the 2,600 workers, the miles of belting bringing steam power to hundreds of machines, all this "daily turning out enough to arm an entire regiment."[6] Springfield, of course, was equally impressed. But as its relationship to the Armory had always been intimate and complex, so its reaction to the phenomenon ran deeper.

In but not of the community, the Armory had always suffered from strained and often openly hostile relations with Springfield. A host of problems caused it to be resented by many townsmen — conflicts over land, arbitrary decisions made in Washington affecting employment and working conditions, and the like. All the tensions had traditionally focused in the debate over military versus civilian superintendency of the Armory. Military officers symbolized outside control, and it is not surprising that the community generally preferred civilian superintendents, usually chosen from the local area. Through the years, the Armory had swung back and forth between the two forms of administration. Periodically, after long hearings and heated debate, the War Department and Congress decided that now one and then the other was the more efficient system for the Armory. The old controversy had come to a head in the early 1850's, fueled at one end by complicated Washington politics and at the other by Springfield's exceedingly poor relations with Superintendent James Ripley, who epitomized the efficient but brusk, rude, and inflexible military expert.[7]

As a result of this controversy, the Armory was switched to civilian managers, but its relations with the community were still not good as the war began; among other things, Ripley's new position as chief of ordnance meant that the man so cordially hated by many in Springfield was once again in command, but from a position of greater power and distance. One would expect the situation to have worsened when he suddenly dismissed the popular and efficient newly appointed civilian head, George Dwight, a most respected

businessman and, as longtime mainstay of the volunteer fire department, an important civic leader. But the issue reveals instead how
wartime solidarity was breeding a new spirit of tolerance and cooperation; Springfield accepted without protest Ripley's decision to replace Dwight with a military man unknown to the community. The
old debate, it would seem, was relegated to a past era. Springfield
accepted the appointment of Alexander Dyer as a military necessity;
the question, as it happened, was resolved permanently by this
emergency switch.[8]

Further mollified when Dwight was kept on with supervisory
duties, Springfield embraced the Armory with new enthusiasm. The
people helped protect it from fires, and organized volunteer watches
to guard against rumored Confederate saboteurs. Armory workers
and officers participated fully in town recruiting efforts, and the
city responded with a paternalistic concern for the workers there,
establishing special recreational facilities for those whose late shifts
kept them from participating in community life.[9]

The war experience, then, "destroyed the ancient and traditional
antipathy . . . and broke down the last vestiges of restraint between
town and Armory."[10] Deeper, perhaps, than the pervasive economic
stimulus was Springfield's proud identification with the Armory and
its crucial national role. With Harper's Ferry part of the Confeder-
acy, Springfield was left as the only national armory, and the
famous rifle bearing the city's name was carried by almost every
Union soldier. Amidst the anxiety of war and the dislocating growth
of an undisciplined boom, this pride had almost tangible importance;
one should not underestimate the steadying sense of function and
status it conferred upon a rapidly changing city, or the special sense
of communal legitimacy attaching to the economic growth that the
Armory so directly stimulated.

That Springfield had a special relation not only to the war effort,
but also to the war boom, is highlighted by the fact that the young
city was, in Massachusetts, practically alone in its prosperity. The
commonwealth hardly provided a picture of bustling energy. Aside
from a negligible population growth, the growth rates of industrial
production were decreasing sharply. From 1855 to 1865, the dollar
value of production rose 72 percent, about half the previous decade's

rate. Whatever the value of this statistic, which is probably not very much, it is significant that Springfield's similarly calculated growth was 180 percent, from $2.5 to 7 million, a rate found only in the immediate Boston area and western Massachusetts. In fact, Springfield's Hampden County led all the other thirteen in the state, the only one to grow by more than 100 percent. State officials attributed the general fall-off to "the strain of a distressing war, with a large proportion of our industrial classes changed from producers to consumers." Springfield, plainly, shared neither the listless state performance nor this supposed transformation. Quite on the contrary, it had never seen so many producers making so many things.[11]

Ironically, few people in Springfield expected the war to bring such prosperity, nor did the first months of the conflict convert many to this view. In the winter and spring of 1861 Mayor Stephen C. Bemis held the unrelieved tension of the secession crisis responsible for the "present stagnation," which prevailed despite plentiful capital, labor, and production supplies. Continued uncertainty proved more important for business than the immediate outbreak of war — in August everything seemed to be "standing still," and the *Republican* reported that the question "How long?" was on the lips of merchants, manufacturers, and mechanics alike. Business saw only austerity ahead and everybody knew what to expect — the cotton mills would collapse; wholesalers would be ruined and merchants destroyed when the Southerners repudiated large debts; trade and consumption at home would fall off to nothing. Even in the autumn of 1861, as the first upsurge began to be felt, the *Republican* found it necessary to argue against the entrenched opinion that prosperity would return only with stable peace. But plentiful jobs, the clamor of orders, and the jingle of profits proved persuasive where the newspaper was not, and by 1862 Springfield happily submitted to the embrace of sustained prosperity, although not without a certain embarrassment — good fortune seemed at first inappropriate, almost dishonorable in the midst of national tragedy. Such reservations however, did not weigh heavily for very long.[12]

The Armory was at the heart of this, of course: the huge plant drew capital, skilled labor, and large contracts to the Connecticut Valley, particularly to the small arms industry already centered

there. Twenty companies had survived the lull of the 1850's, and by
the war's end they had been joined by nineteen new ones, so dominating the industry that in 1865 1,200 of the commonwealth's
1,500 gunsmiths and skilled armorers worked in Hampden County.
Of the 650,000 privately made Springfield Rifles mentioned earlier,
over half were produced in the area. But even more important than
these was the flood of subcontracts from the Armory, and the direct
government contracts for equipment not made there at all.[13]

The James T. Ames Company illustrates what the war could mean
for private industry. The plant's capacity plus Ames's many personal
contacts brought huge contracts, and his firm became one of the
major suppliers of large cannon to the government, which made
none of its own, while continuing as the nation's leading producer
of sabers, swords, and bayonets. In addition, with the work force
swelled from 200 to 1,000, Ames produced howitzers, caissons,
mortars, and ammunition, as well as vital heavy production machinery for the Armory and other large factories. The pace was frantic, contracts often coming on a "will take all you can make" basis,
and profits followed accordingly: despite heavy investment in plant
and equipment, the company paid dividends in 1863 alone totaling
44 percent.[14]

Others profited too, because one contract so often led to another.
Thus in 1861 railroad president and recent mayor Daniel L. Harris
was writing to Major Ripley:

I learn today that Mr. Ames of Chicopee has an order for a large number of
cannon for the government, and it occurs to me that you might like to have
carriages manufactured here to go with them. I take the liberty of suggesting
whether Wason's car shop here is not just the place to get that work well and
expeditiously done.

Ripley, familiar himself with Springfield's resources, probably did
not need Harris's prodding. Within months, double shifts at Wason's
were turning out the gun carriages alongside the railroad coaches for
which the company was already famous.[15] In similar fashion, contracts for hundreds of items found their way to Springfield. At Wil-
kinson and Cummings, where "ten hours a day is not the style,"
orders for military saddles, scabbards, belts, holsters, and other

leather work made eighteen hours more common. D. H. Brigham, Springfield's leading clothier, appealed throughout New England for seamstresses to help meet a four-month contract for 60,000 uniforms. All in all, statistics confirm that producers of such secondary items, including cartridges, accounted for as much economic activity as the armsmakers themselves.[16]

Nor were official government contracts the limit of war production activity. Because the Ordnance Department stubbornly refused to consider substituting the modern repeating breech-loaded rifle for the clumsy single shot muzzle-loaders — although many argued that the Armory could easily have made the transition — smaller private firms ended up handling this largely experimental work. In Springfield, for instance, Morris and Clement produced Remington carbines, while the Springfield Arms Company made its own design breech-loader; C. D. Leet's busy Market Street cartridge shop produced ammunition for the new carbines and for imported weapons, until its explosive growth was halted by a disastrously literal explosion in 1864.[17] The best illustration of growth independent of government contract was the now famous Smith and Wesson Company. Its .22 caliber pistol, though too small for real military use, was a popular present for the departing recruits, who carried it for personal protection. Smith and Wesson never managed to meet demand, despite double shifting in a large new factory and a production boost from 40 to 2,500 pistols a day; it often found itself a year behind wartime orders.[18]

Springfield quickly adjusted to the pace of war production. War matériel had to be produced somewhere, and Springfield was a logical focal point. But the community continued to be surprised by the more general prosperity it enjoyed in every branch of industry and trade. Official statistics show activity in over fifty categories and the diversity is impressive. Among the many items of major production were iron castings, buttons, clothing, boxes, dictionaries, and tools. Since the war was never far away, there was even a flourishing production of artificial limbs. Most impressive of all, however, was the rise of consumer and "luxury" production, faddishly reflecting the pace of local life. There were "rages" over the photo albums brought out by Samuel Bowles's Springfield Printing Company, and over the introduction of stiff, glossy paper shirt collars; both of these swept

New England and became major industries centered in Springfield. The list could go on and on — the Barney and Berry Skate Company; the Milton Bradley Company and its new "educational" parlor games; James Rumrill's gold chain factory — all were established in these years. Flush times brought new firms and ideas to Springfield, catering to people's fancies as well as stoking the fires of heavy industry.[19]

A broadly based new economy was the result of all this activity. In 1855, the twelve largest industries accounted for 70 percent of the city's total product value; in 1865, this had risen to 77 percent, not a great increment at all when one considers the tremendous weight of the sudden war contracts. War-related production, far from dominating the economy, represented under 30 percent of the total product. A listing of the major industrial groupings gives some sense of this balanced diversity.[20]

	Total product value
Cotton goods (Indian Orchard Mills)	$950,000
Arms	607,000
Military goods	600,000
Cartridges	589,000
Railroad cars	573,000
Building	399,200
Photo albums	237,000
Jewelry and chain	212,500
Candy	212,000
Iron castings	208,000
Woolen goods	140,000
Tools	132,754
Clothing	110,000
Buttons	104,750

Beneath all the success stories lay important structural growth. Consumer industries and broad markets evidenced a balance capable of generating continuing growth from within and attracting new investment from outside. Moreover, both cause and effect of the boom cycle, Springfield was coming to dominate the economy of its region as never before. Neighboring companies were relocating in the city, drawn by its capital, customers, workers, and communications. As a corollary, Springfield extended its mercantile reach over an ever larger area, developing wholesale facilities for consolidating this control. The Kibbe Candy Company, for example, which for years had sent its picturesque wagons through the adjacent country-side, grew into a large-scale producer and long-distance wholesaler during the war. More portentous was the emerging concentration of the writing paper and envelope wholesale trade in Springfield. Some claimed that half the nation's writing paper was produced within twenty-five miles, and one quarter within ten miles. Full control of production and marketing of these goods was still a distant dream, but Springfield businessmen had been stimulated to think in bolder, more expansive economic terms. As the city moved toward a new urban role in the complex economy developing all around it, such new ambitions represented a not insignificant step.[21]

All this vitality was mirrored in the swiftly changing face of Springfield's business district. The community watched proudly throughout the war years, and particularly in 1864 and 1865, as old wooden stores, vacant lots, and homes gave way to a succession of imposing business "blocks," taller, longer, stronger, and grander than the best products of the 1850's. These new structures, solid brick usually four or five stories, turned from Springfield's tradition-ally conservative architecture, and sported elaborate ornamental stonework in a more or less Victorian Gothic style, boldly if often crudely combined with the mansard roofs then considered "the sym-bol of modernity in the American commercial world."[22] These buildings reflected not only the fact of prosperity, but also some-thing of its character; their multiple uses, especially, revealed its di-versity and the way its energy could filter through the economy. Smith and Wesson rented space in one of its new buildings to a thimble manufacturer; Leet's Cartridge Company offered central steam power in its building to a variety of artisan-manufacturers. D. W. Barnes's 1863 block at Main and Vernon represented a more general diversity. This "ornament to the city" had four retail shops on its elaborate ground floor, business and professional offices on the second, a large public meeting hall on the third, and eight manu-facturing workshops on the fourth floor. Even grander was Tilly Haynes's famous "Exchange" on the north corner of Main and Pyn-chon, a unique brick hollow square covered by a glass dome which included stores, the post office and Western Union, offices, workshops, and an eighty-room hotel. Acknowledging as well the city's cultural pretensions, Haynes built the opulent new opera house and music hall across the street from the Exchange, when an 1864 fire destroyed the original.[23]

These individual projects had an important collective impact. They tended to reinforce, for example, the increasing concentration of life and business in the downtown center. There was substantial commercial and industrial building elsewhere — Allis's new block in the North End was, at six stories, Springfield's tallest structure — but the really important buildings were almost all on Main Street, between Court Square and the depot, and mostly on the west side of the street. The frequently coordinated styles and continuous frontage gave the street a more distinctly urban flavor while manufacturing buildings and warehouses also clustered nearby, though keeping to the side streets. No longer could anyone doubt where the focal point of Springfield's life would be; Haynes's Exchange and the other blocks around Main and Pynchon would, it was seen, "conclusively fix the business center of the city there," and there it has remained to the present day.[24]

More generally, because of the almost public character that popular fascination conferred on the development of Main Street and the imposing new business blocks, physical change worked with other aspects of the boom to reinforce the community's growing sense of identification with its economic growth and business leadership, something that proved to be a crucial dividend of prosperity.

The picture of exciting and sudden development receives vivid confirmation from a look at the people who composed the community. This is dramatically illustrated in the dry figures of state and national censuses. Just as business did not flourish statewide, so too population growth in Massachusetts was "very trifling" during the war, an almost negligible increase of 2.92 percent that census compilers attributed to the slack period of "war and business interruption." And not only did the commonwealth as a whole cease to grow, but the earlier shift of population to the cities slowed considerably as well. Though the state's fifteen cities gained modestly between 1855 and 1865, only ten of them grew at all during the war years, and only four by over 20 percent.[25]

To the statisticians, Springfield must have seemed to be in another

world, or at least another state. It had grown by a respectable 30
percent for 1850–1860, and a sluggish 10 percent in the last half of
the decade. But in contrast, its growth for 1855–1865 was a remarkable 65 percent with the rate between the 1860 federal census
and the state tally in 1865 amounting to 45 percent, more than
twice that of the closest Massachusetts competitors. From tenth in
1850 and twelfth in 1860, Springfield became the state's seventh
largest city by the war's end, trailing only Worcester, Lowell, and
the several cities of the Boston area. Similarly, only eight of the
fourteen counties had gained any population, and at 12.73 percent
Springfield's Hampden County headed the list, surpassing even Suf-
folk County's 8 percent rise.[26]

This singular performance, of course, was a corollary of the economic spurt. The demand for workers and the bustling city's
promise of long-range opportunity acted as powerful magnets, and it
is not surprising to discover that Springfield grew at the expense of
its neighbors, even within the county. For the first time, the number
of towns losing population in Hampden exceeded the number gaining. Furthermore, the area's other commercial and industrial centers
– Holyoke, Westfield and Ludlow – which previously had kept pace
with Springfield, now fell rapidly behind. As a result, Springfield
was really responsible for almost all of Hampden County's impressive gains: without it, the 12.74 percent county growth tumbles to
.87 percent. Clearly, the area's only city absorbed the region's natural population growth and captured the new population entering
it.[27]

Other census figures buttress the relationship between population
growth and economic opportunity, particularly employment.
Throughout the state, say the figures, there was not only a percentage drop, but also an absolute fall in the number of men between
twenty and sixty, the "producing ages"; a number of factors, chiefly
the absorption of so many into the army, accounted for this. But
Springfield, though giving more than its quota to the war, actually
gained 2,000 men in this category, most of them young, single, and
unattached, or arriving for work in advance of their families.[28] The
city's increment not only offset the rest of the county's decline in
this respect; it even enabled Hampden to rank first in the state. In
fact, the city's increase, at 60 percent, exceeded its own over-all

population rise. And where the state averaged 19.7 percent of its people in this twenty to sixty male grouping, Springfield had 26.7 percent, a remarkable comment on the city's dynamic economy and its pull on human resources elsewhere.[29]

Springfield's unusual population growth was not created by a flood of immigrant labor. The city had never seen an unusual number of foreign born, its long-standing 20 percent proportion similar to county and state averages, and this continued to be true in the war years. While the percentage of immigrants in Massachusetts held virtually steady, falling from 21.16 percent to 20.95 percent during the war, Springfield's portion rose, but by a similarly slight degree, from 20.51 percent to 21.62 percent. The total number of immigrants in the city grew from 2,829 to 4,765, an increase only marginally greater than that of the total population of the community.[30]

Taken together, these figures present a picture of dramatic and solidly based growth. Springfield was attracting a wide variety of new citizens, Yankees and immigrants, some from far away but more from the surrounding region, most of them young, ambitious, and hopeful, attracted by the great opportunity the city seemed to offer. While the rest of Massachusetts stood still, Springfield grew strong as never before in the one crucial resource that nature had once been so capricious in providing.

These were, however, people flooding into the young city, not statistics, and as such they had very human needs which played an important part in the wartime reshaping of Springfield. If employment was not a pressing problem, housing certainly was. First near the Armory, but soon everywhere, newly arrived workingmen encountered an acute shortage of houses, tenement apartments, and even boarding places. As early as August 1861 the *Republican* reported: "Every tenement [on the Hill] is occupied and every boarding house is full to overflowing. Good tenements would rent readily by the scores at first rate prices anywhere near the Armory grounds, could they be had." Throughout the next few years, demand continued to outrun supply, even as new building accelerated, and not until 1865 did the pressure slacken perceptibly. "Extreme scarcity" remained the consistent state of the market, which suffered in addition from "a general rise in rents owing to the anxious bidding of would-be tenants against each other." Modest apartments that had rented at $50 a year before the war soon brought over $100, and that was moderate, with many far more expensive. Boarding houses frequently demanded the then outrageous price of $5 per week, while many men who could find no room at all helped fill the coaches and trains that daily carried commuting workmen from Agawam, Longmeadow, and even as far away as Northampton.[31]

This housing shortage gradually became a matter of some concern, particularly when people realized that without adequate housing it would prove difficult to hold many of the new arrivals once the boom inevitably slackened. But action was slow to follow; there were so many more attractive investment opportunities than building that few would risk the large-scale projects needed, for fear of being stranded after the war with undeveloped lots, unsold houses, and unrented tenements. From the first, others joined the *Republican* in trying to dispel such fears, arguing that there were substantial and certain profits in tenement building. "Will our capitalists and builders take the hint?" asked the paper in 1861, only to acknowledge sorrowfully two years later that the rhetorical question was receiving a negative answer: "We have grown so rapidly nobody realizes it," with the result that little had been done toward "making our increase of the past two years lasting and secure."[32]

The hint was, however, finally taken, and by 1864 such reluctance had evaporated, opening the way to a building boom of striking proportions. Contractors suddenly could not find enough masons and carpenters to work on the hundreds of houses springing up everywhere, often fully rented before building began. Real estate changed hands at "an unheard of rate" — at times over one hundred deeds were being filed in a week — and the city's largest dealers astounded other businessmen with the volume of their trade — over $100,000 in April 1864 alone. Yet in contrast to soaring rents, prices on this brisk market remained fairly reasonable. There was too much real demand, it would seem, to permit much extensive speculation buying; tracts were developed and houses built for immediate occupancy. By the war's end, this activity had somewhat compensated for the long delay. Springfield then had 3,556 dwellings, up from the 2,801 in 1860, with most of the increase consisting of small frame tenements and modest homes suitable for an armorer or skilled craftsman. Though this was far below the rate of population growth, the 27 percent jump in dwellings more than tripled the building rate of the previous five years. During 1863 and 1864 alone, it was claimed, more houses were built than during the entire previous decade, and although the boom shifted to business buildings in 1865, it still had represented a substantial response to Springfield's most pressing need as well as a substantial contribution to its over-all economy.[33]

The new population and homebuilding gradually began to alter the shape and appearance of the city in the same way as had the business blocks rising on Main Street. Even in 1865, of course, Springfield still "retained many features of an overgrown country town," with cattle grazing within mooing distance of City Hall and many prominent families living on downtown estates that stretched from Main Street to the river, "as in the first distribution of the land over two hundred years before."[34] But all this was changing. Given the previously diffuse settlement throughout the city, the boom period's pattern of integration and concentration meant that new growth took an inward direction — a filling up of the old centers, not a spreading outward. The bounds of the most populous sections remained about what they had been before the war, and though urban growth was hardly planned, this situation insured a certain orderliness. Small builders put up their frame houses on older, half-filled streets, while larger developments followed the traditional "estate carving" procedure — old tracts purchased, streets laid out, and lots opened for sale.

The filling in was noticeable all over Springfield. Charles Winchester bought six acres of a South End estate, opening up the new Loring and Lombard streets through it; on the Hill, houses and tenements for armorers consumed vacant lots on old streets like Florence, Bay, Hancock, Florida, Oak, and Stebbins. The heaviest activity, however, seemed to be on the slope of the hill behind the Armory, down toward the railroad. Here, Pearl Street, which had been extended from downtown in 1859, suddenly filled with modest frame houses, many still standing today. Later in the war, Summer Street was opened to the hill, and developers made the first inroads into several estates in what is now the Matoon-Elliot area, behind the Museum Quadrangle.[35]

Within this filling pattern, to be sure, significant shifting of population and neighborhoods occurred. To the extent that the settled area expanded, it was gradually spreading north past Round Hill, where substantial projects opened the Bancroft, Osgood, and Morgan Street section. Projections of future development all agreed that North Main Street, from the Depot to the Chicopee line, would be thickly settled in the next decade, a result of the dual northward pull of Main Street business and the railroad depot.[36]

Considering the extraordinary strength of the Armory on the Hill to the east, this northward stance and Main Street focus become all the more significant. Twenty years earlier, observed the obituary of Elisha Gunn, a noted Hill merchant, "the Hill, more than it is now, was dividing trade with the Street, and having the first chance at countrymen as they came into the city."[37] The railroad eliminated much of that advantage, and the Hill's gradual decline as a semi-independent community had been long noticed. Paradoxically enough, it was the war period which seemed to seal the fate of Gunn's neighborhood. That commercial and even residential attention could focus elsewhere during the time of the Armory's great expansion is eloquent testimony to Springfield's balanced development. The smooth expansion, moreover, shows how much more integrated Springfield was becoming, physically, commercially, and psychologically, through these years. The same Armory expansion, in earlier years, might have been identified more with that area alone, and enormously aggravated fragmentation and neighborhood jealousies. Now, though these were certainly still present, the growth was identified with the entire city. It was an agent of integration, generating among Hill people, for example, demands for better transportation to the Depot and to the Main Street business area, which they no longer attempted to rival.[38]

As a result of all this growth, Springfield was now firmly oriented around a right triangle having the Depot, Court Square, and the Armory as its points, and Main Street as its base. On the downtown flats, for the first time, more people lived north than south of City Hall, and the North End's ward one ranked second in population to ward three, at the city's center; next, significantly, came ward five, the Armory Hill area. Other differences among the wards had emerged clearly by 1865. Ward two, the major business and residential district between State Street and the depot, together with ward

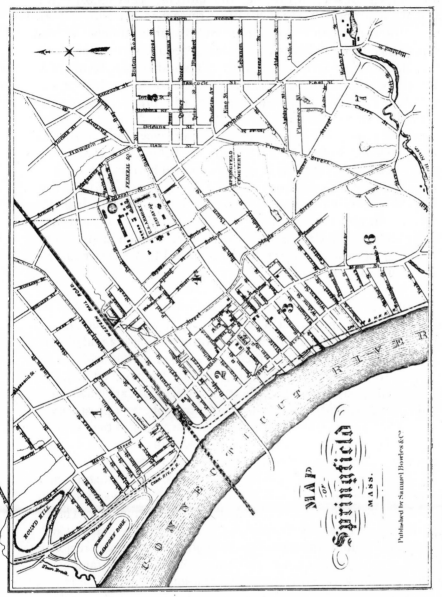

Springfield, 1865

four, which housed many of the "first citizens," paid almost twice
as much in property taxes as the other three central wards, and ward
two, although fourth in population, had the largest number of legal
voters. Significant patterns also characterized the settlement of the
foreign born, who were mostly Irish and working class. Ward break-
downs are not available for the years before 1865, but there was no
mistaking the North End as the center of Irish life. Ferry Street and
Railroad Row were as notorious in 1865 for the deplorable conditions that respectable society linked with the new immigrants as had
been Mechanic Street and the "Irish Huts" behind City Hall in
earlier years. Ward one was 25 percent foreign born in 1865, and
home to a much higher proportion of the city's Irish. This was concentration, but by no means was it a ghetto. Over half the Irish distributed themselves through the other wards, except for ward five,
where the Armory attracted primarily skilled workers, and most of
its foreign born were English; the Irish tended to live closer to employment available to them.[39]

In all these dimensions and in all these ways did the energy of the
Civil War touch Springfield. The boom may have been loud and sudden, but for the community and its future it was also a remarkably
deep phenomenon. Its major theme, in a sense, cannot really be abstracted from the details of growth, for it lay in these very details,
in the tremendous vitality, confusion, anxiety and excitement of
rapid change, all suffused by the heady atmosphere of prosperity
and patriotism. Its major significance, however, lies in the over-all
impact. The boom transformed Springfield profoundly. Its momentum and its structure definitively shaped, for years to come, the
city's emerging economy, physical framework, and population pattern. Moreover, the particular nature of Springfield's war boom enabled growth to have a special meaning for the community. The
patriotic basis of prosperity, the degree to which it was shared and
general throughout the economy, Springfield's developing regional
power, the focus of business and community life on the rapidly
built-up Main Street area, the impact and implications of rapid
population increase — all of these led people to take a more collective pride in the city's prosperity, and to view the excitement gener-

ated as a community phenomenon. The boom was thus helping to produce, and was somewhat sustained by, a developing self-consciousness, a view of Springfield as a unique, bold, and ascendant city whose leaders charted a promising course for the future.

5. Institutional Responses to City Growth

On the surface, Springfield was a remarkably harmonious community during the war years, showing few of the signs of social dislocation and confusion one might expect to find during a period of rapid change. The war and the boom seemingly diverted such tensions into channels more external to the local community, while also neutralizing mechanisms that traditionally had expressed the deeper anxieties of social change. The highly visible patriotism of Springfield's Irish and their leaders, for example, may have been part of the reason overt criticism of Catholic morals was far less frequent than in earlier years; more significant was the dramatic eclipse of the perennial temperance crusade, which found attention and interest, much less support or opposition, exceedingly hard to come by.[1]

This is not to say that the traditional concern with community morality had diminished, or that symptoms of social stress were absent. People continued to regard with the same combination of indignation and morbid fascination what was commonly viewed as the declining state of social morality and standards. But, significantly, the focus of this concern was shifting. Community spokesmen began to see the supposed deterioration not as ethnic or individual inadequacy, but rather at least partially as a function of specific institutional weaknesses in the community, themselves a product of extraordinary circumstances. Again and again, they called crime and vice a "natural result" of the influx of so many single workingmen, who lacked the stabilizing restraints of home, family, and familiar surroundings; increasingly, they stressed the importance of developing ways to provide direction and orientation.[2]

To the extent that this concern found a specific focus, attention centered on the matter of a public library. Faith in the socializing power of reading matter was, of course, deeply rooted; Springfield's first reading rooms and libraries had been opened long ago by benevolent groups for the uplifting of workingmen. Springfield's rapid growth during the war helped strengthen the belief that the community much needed a genuine public library to serve businessmen as well as workingmen, old residents as well as newcomers.* This became explicit when in 1863 George Bliss offered a large, valuable plot at State and Chestnut towards the erection of such a building, crystallizing sentiment, discussion, and activity. Springfield should have a real library, said the *Republican*, to "give tone and direction to the popular taste and feeling" at a time of hectic business activity where one sought "in vain for circles in which general culture is maintained." The mayor called for action "individually and as a municipality," stressing the "influence of the Library on the taste and character of the people." Responding promptly, private sources raised an imposing $77,000 and the government initiated appropriations for the library. Construction and completion were years away, but people felt enthusiastically committed to the community project.[3]

Reliance on such solutions does not speak impressively of the depth with which Springfield's leaders understood the problem of social cohesion, but it is perhaps more important to emphasize here their perception that the web of local life wanted strengthening. Traditional concern with the quality of the community and its people was shifting to more tangible concern with community institutions conditioning that quality. This, in turn, was part of something broader: Springfield's increasingly collective and institutional in-

---

*Failing the establishment of a municipal public library in 1857, a group of local leaders had established the City Library Association, setting up its small collection in two rooms of the City Hall, donated as a token of public sanction. Between 1860 and 1865, however, the library grew from 2,000 to 18,000 volumes, from 400 to 500 subscribers paying the one dollar borrowing fee, and from a 40,000 to 80,000 circulation. Similar to the library campaign was the effort to have the proposed Massachusetts Agricultural College located in Springfield. The prospects were good, until the passage of the Land Grant College Act stimulated interest in other communities, and after some controversy the school was established in Amherst. As this became the huge University of Massachusetts, it is interesting to speculate about what would have happened to Springfield had its efforts been successful.

volvement in the process of city-building. In these years, most public interest in the community centered on the many questions that
growth pushed forward, especially matters of public services and
property development, the community meaning of which had never
been precisely defined. It is here, not in older, more informal social
concerns, that one can best see Springfield responding to change,
here where old concepts and institutions confronted suddenly
altered needs and pressures. The resulting dynamics of perception,
conflict, and response proved crucial to many important public decisions, and lay close to the heart of less tangible changes in the
nature of the community.

To explore this dimension, three areas of concern — schools, water
supply, and property improvements — will be examined in some detail. But first, a brief look at Springfield's local political situation
during these years is in order. People at the time were quite conscious of the broader political relevance and the general financial
implications of any position on a given issue, and so the framework
in which matters were defined and discussed becomes important if
one is not to have a distorted view of the specific questions involved.

Daniel L. Harris, the successful Republican candidate for mayor in
1860, was the most prominent citizen to have held that office in
years. President of the Connecticut River Railroad, a nationally
known engineer, mainstay of the Library Association, the temperance crusade, and other civic concerns, Harris was an ambitious executive who, on taking office, embarked on a vigorous building and
improvement program. Despite his prestige, however, his projects,
especially an elaborate waterworks plan, were unpopular and invariably controversial; Harris himself, whatever his virtues, was a blunt,
stern, and tactless man who made enemies effortlessly. His subsequent defeat for reelection at the hands of conservative Democrat
Stephen C. Bemis illustrates the extent of public dissatisfaction, for
it followed by only a month the stunning local triumph of Lincoln
and the entire Republican slate.[4] Bemis was also an active and aggressive businessman, with coal interests in Springfield and a paper
company in Holyoke. On public issues, however, he had long worn
the mantle of frugality. Looking back on Springfield's days preceding incorporation, which he had strongly opposed, Bemis pledged to
alter the paths by which "we are fast departing from the simple and

economical habits of our fathers." The sentiments seemed to fit the mood of the uncertain winter of 1860–1861, and he maintained this posture throughout his two terms.[5]

Bemis was followed in 1863 by Henry Alexander, Jr., brother-in-law to Samuel Bowles but a politician and banker prominent in his own right and, according to his enemies, Springfield's closest approximation of a big-city "boss." Alexander roundly attacked the conservatism of his predecessor, urging throughout his two terms a more active and positive approach to the city's problems.[6] This policy was generally approved by the voters, who supported Alexander's slate and chose as his successor a close political ally, Albert D. Briggs, later to be one of Charles F. Adams's railroad commissioners. Briggs led three highly popular and similarly aggressive administrations, leaving the weakened Democratic opposition to criticize in vain "an extravagance doubly culpable because of the growing burdens of war."[7]

It would be unwise to draw from this progression from Harris to Bemis to Alexander and Briggs any very conclusive picture of changing public values on local issues, since each election was shaped by many factors, both peculiar and external to Springfield's situation. But the general trend toward more substantial public activity is a valid generalization, one confirmed by the standard then most respected, the statistics of municipal finance. Expenses leaped from $72,000 in 1860 to over $238,000 five years later, a great change even allowing for the war spending and increased population: non-war-related costs more than tripled, and per capita expenses rose from $4.77 to $10.82. Some of this was absorbed by a city debt that from $120,000 had reached $344,000 in 1865, but the biggest bite came in taxes. A property valuation rising by 45 percent from $8.9 to $12.8 million slowed the tax rate only slightly, as it jumped from 1860's $2.20 to $16.50 in 1865, touching $18 at the end of Briggs' third term in 1866, a figure not topped until the 1920's.[8]

Whatever their impact now, these figures and the change they represented seemed frighteningly imposing in the 1860's, even to those enthusiastically championing expanded public activity. It is interesting to note, in this connection, that the rhetoric they employed did not reject the traditional identification of virtue with frugality, but rather sought to work within this old "low-tax ideology" by proposing a variation that in a more slogan-minded age might have been labeled the "True Economy." Extensive spending, ran the argument, would be cheaper in the long run because needed work could be done comprehensively and efficiently, substituting planned permanence for patchwork and stop-gaps. "True economy consists in doing things at the time they should be done, and in doing them thoroughly," said Mayor Alexander. Mayor Briggs argued that "procrastination is not economy. This has been the besetting sin of the city. There is no greater wastefulness than to leave undone that which ought to be done, or in half doing that which is undertaken." The *Republican*, as usual, put it the most succinctly: "It is better to pay full price for something than half price for nothing."[9] Such arguments, of course, immediately beg the question of just what it is that "ought to be done," which is precisely the point: so often discussed in terms of spenders vs. savers, budget, debt, and taxes, local issues involved, more deeply, differences over how Springfield was and should be changing. And because they were so easily expressed in terms of traditional economy, these differences were not always explicitly articulated or confronted. Within this older framework, then, Springfield debated profound questions of local policy, measuring new demands and interests against tradition.

As 1861 began, Springfield's School Committee reported proudly: "Since the abolition of the district system when the city assumed this responsibility, nearly all sections of the city . . . are now provided with substantial and convenient buildings . . . [The system] is in a thriving and promising condition."[10] If so, it was a promise almost immediately betrayed by Springfield's explosive growth. It took two years for the change to be noticed, but the war boom was steadily filling the schoolhouses past capacity. The school-age census, rising almost as fast as the general population, increased by 50 percent from 2,500 to 3,700, and the situation became pressing, especially downtown where only one schoolhouse had been built in the preceding fifteen years. In the State Street building, the four teachers suddenly found themselves responsible for over four hundred pupils, ranging in age from five to sixteen.[11]

By the end of 1862, an anxious School Committee warned that it

might soon become "utterly impossible to receive all the children
seeking an education." The mayor, joining in the next year, shocked
many in the city by terming the schools "wholly inadequate," the
buildings "inferior, uncomfortable, and unhealthy." And the 1864
school report, titled "Urgent Call," struck a more strident, almost
desperate note, declaring that the very viability of the public school
concept was at stake.[12] Despite all these pleas, however, by the
war's end not one new schoolhouse had been built, and only makeshift emergency accommodations had been arranged. Why, with
such seemingly critical problems, had so little been done in Springfield?

The poor response was certainly not due to lack of trying. The
School Committee was at its most dynamic and capable point in
years during this period, led by the august and imposing Josiah
Hooker, whose entire public life had been devoted to education in
Springfield.[13] The first and most basic need, of course, was money,
and the School Committee, the mayor, and the press repeatedly,
often eloquently, demanded larger appropriations for expansion, all
in the language of the "true economy." At every step, they labored
to convince the public and the City Council that their requests were
but minimal responses to a general crisis. Hooker was more pointed,
charging that cynical stinginess, not frugality, was denying the
schools necessary support, and he liked to refer to the war profits
for justification: "Our city was never more prosperous in business,
and it will not be wise in us, from any narrow view of economy
while everything about is thriving, to suffer these seminaries of the
people to languish."[14]

As would so often prove to be the case, facing one problem almost
automatically revealed others, or more exactly altered the light in
which they were seen. Confronting the physical overcrowding inevitably brought local officials to critical reconsideration of the
structure of the system itself. "System" is probably a misnomer, for
a "school" at that time was limited to what we might call a class-
room, with several housed in a building, each largely independent of
the others and under the charge of individual teachers who suffered
little supervisory control beyond the general overview of the School
Committee. In Springfield's less populous areas, the "mixed school"
still prevailed, the old one-room schoolhouse with all ages mixed,

while in the more thickly settled sections a rough gradation of primary, intermediate, and grammar schools had emerged. In any event, it was far from the full graded and thoroughly supervised school system that had become a major goal of school reformers throughout the nation, but especially in Massachusetts. Prodded by the wartime overcrowding, Springfield's school guardians plunged into the mainstream of this reform movement.[15]

Whatever the familiarity with this campaign elsewhere, it still seemed a great local novelty when Josiah Hooker proposed that Springfield adopt the new approach when and if it got around to raising new schoolhouses. In the city, with its thirty-nine "schools" loosely grouped in sixteen buildings, this implied that the new structures would have to be quite large, consolidating and absorbing several of the old neighborhood schoolhouses. When proposing in 1863 the construction of several three-story, six-hundred-student buildings on these lines, Hooker argued that concentration of educational facilities was only a corollary of the city's own accelerating concentration and growth. Again and again, he urged Springfield to accept the new concepts if it wanted schools that could keep up with the community, and offer an education equal to the needs of an urban industrial society. The point was well put in his summary 1866 report:

In times past, the opinion has widely prevailed that every neighborhood must have a schoolhouse, with the children of the neighborhood duly gathered into it, constituting a school independent in character, with hardly any relation to or connection with other schools. [This is suited to rural conditions, but] in cities there is no such necessity, but on the contrary, the varying circumstances in this respect justify and require a very different system. And the City of Springfield, it is believed, has now arrived at that point when the introduction of the new system is urgently called for.[16]

Calling for a new system was about all the hamstrung School Committee proved able to do for years, though there may have been some consolation in the fact that a parsimonious approach to school spending was a problem for committees all over Massachusetts. Many towns at the time were reported as "inclined to retrench," and in 1863 total school appropriations throughout the commonwealth dropped, only the third time this had happened since collection of statistics began in 1837. Despite energetic support from Mayors Alexander and Briggs, and extraordinary public appeals by Hooker, Springfield also shared in this trend.[17] Appropriations hovered around $20,000, reaching to $30,000 in 1865, with more borrowed for the as yet unbuilt new schools. But this hardly kept up with population. Yearly expenditure per school-age child dropped from $7.53 in 1861 to $5.67 in 1863, and had barely climbed back to prewar levels by 1865. Considering Springfield's singular growth and prosperity in the Massachusetts context, its decline from thirty-first in the state to thirty-ninth by this measure of expenditure gives some support to Hooker's contention that economy was ill-serving the community.[18]

But just as the School Committee sought more fundamental changes than an altered level of expenditure, so too there was more to the opposition than a narrow economy. The new and strange-sounding ideas for the school system generated widespread hesitancy in the community. Mayor Bemis, for example, saw the large graded houses as impersonal, mechanical, anti-individual, and unhealthy: innovations, he said, that could only lead to excessive homework and inferior teaching, leaving "many children ruined in their health and means of usefulness." More fundamentally, smaller neighborhoods and the outskirts of town opposed the idea as just one more step in the dominance of the center, a banner raised by the *Union* in 1864 when it charged that Hooker's plan for "grand edifices" would "break up existing educational arrangements and centralize matters to the inconvenience of children and the damage of taxpayers."[19]

However tempting, it would be wrong to overemphasize the role of this quasi-ideological dispute in preventing Springfield from reaching a decision about how to proceed on the school question. For whatever the specific differences, the fact remains that the community did generally support the public schools, and seemed agreed that some positive action had to be taken to enable them to stand up under the pressure of rapid growth. And yet it found deciding what to do almost impossible. Perhaps the greatest obstacle of all proved to be the inability of the government to make a decision even when committed to doing so by inescapable necessity, and this was due as much to cumbersome political machinery as to conflicting interests or ideas per se.

The School Committee itself was fully at the mercy of the City Council, unable even to spend its appropriation without the specific approval of major items by the council's watchdog Committee on Education. The council, however, was hardly in a position to provide much leadership. On proposed school construction, for example, its Standing Committee on Education made reports that had to be approved by both branches of the council. Then, special site-choosing, building, or investigating committees were appointed, whose reports had to win similar joint acceptance, often resulting in special conference committees to resolve differences. Debate might begin anew over appropriations, with the entire matter often recommitted for further study. In addition to being frustrating, duplicatory, and wasteful, this complex procedure offered anyone opposed to any phase of the planned action almost infinite opportunity for creative obstruction. Furthermore, unrelated but deeply rooted rivalries between the Common Council and the Board of Aldermen were particularly manifest on school questions, regularly producing a sort of legislative ping-pong, with spitefully rejected reports shuttling back and forth from one branch to the other. And to make matters worse, the one-year tenure of each administration frequently meant that months of patient negotiation, bringing a complex question near to resolution, would be wasted when it was left over in December for the new government, which often would prefer to start at the beginning. It was a system with few advantages for the general will of the majority, yet it granted great power to even the smallest minority, whatever the basis of its opposition.

Intractably complex school issues, particularly site location, seemed designed to bring out all the weaknesses of this hobbled procedure. Thus the search for school land in the desperately pressed center of Springfield began in the fall of 1863; after debating several alternatives for most of that year and 1864 as well, the council finally purchased a lot at Main and Willow Streets. But the action stirred up a storm of opposition to the low and reputedly swampy site, and the 1865 government reopened the matter, seeming to prefer a lot on the higher ground of swanky Maple Street. But this, in turn, enraged the rich and powerful residents there who vowed to outbid any city effort to buy property in the section. Finally, the harried councilmen sold the Willow lot and bought another site at Elm Street on Court Square — land which had been initially considered and passed by almost three years earlier.[20] Springfield was discovering, through experiences like this, what so many other communities, then and now, have learned — how difficult it can be to turn a generally acknowledged imperative to do *something* into generally acceptable public policy, how difficult it is to weave public decisions out of the tangled skein of community interests, attitudes, traditions, and opinions. The only substantial result of five years of crisis and debate were the purchase of lots in wards one, three, and four, and initial appropriations for the first of the new model houses, soon to rise on North Main Street, in the first ward.[21]

That ideological resistance to reform was not the most basic element involved is further illustrated by the fact that the School Committee's ideas, when not touching directly the complex and confusing web of pressures, could be acted on far more easily. For years, Hooker had been demanding the appointment of a superintendent, a full-time professional official who would bring system, efficiency, perspective, and responsibility to school administration. This too was a widely discussed reform at the time, part of the general movement in Massachusetts; in fact Springfield had been the first town to appoint such an official back in 1840, though the experiment had then been dropped almost immediately. The step was an obvious corollary of the educational assumptions in the graded-school proposal, and a long stride toward the substitution of bureaucratic professionalism for the traditional service of dedicated town elders. But though it was conceptually no less a departure than the new-model schoolhouses, this reform was easily passed and popularly accepted in 1864, while the building program was still hopelessly stalled in committee.[22] This suggests that while the major problems of Springfield's schools may have been fundamentally institutional, requiring new concepts and mechanisms for realizing a general mandate, the obstacles to change consisted of more traditional political, social, and economic interests. That is, it was not so much differences in perceiving new needs and evaluating new ideas that inhibited consensus at this stage, but rather the community's traditional and almost institutionalized particularism, which bred a resistance to seeing public needs in larger, more comprehensive terms, and which made collective decisions exceedingly difficult to formulate.

A recent scholar has taken a critical view of the educational reform movement of these years, and of men like Hooker, viewing their efforts as merely "imposition of the values of communal leaders upon the rest of society. There was little of the humanitarian in educational reform; it was principally indoctrination, an attempt by promoters to remake the rest of mankind in their own image." An earlier student, on the other hand, took an equally unkind view of those who resisted reform: "Nowhere is the conservative influence more apparent than in the history of the New England schools. Every important innovation has run afoul of those whose only interest in civil affairs has been to reduce taxation. To this open hostility of the niggardly has been added the inertia of the ignorant." Unaware of this later debate, Josiah Hooker offered his own opinion on the meaning of the school issue in wartime Springfield: "Our citizens were not fully prepared at once to assume and discharge their new responsibilities . . . The public sentiment did not keep pace in this respect with the rapid strides in our growth, and time, discussion, and reflection were necessary to accomplish the desired result."[23]

All three of these views are complementary, in a sense, but normative assumptions aside, it may be that Hooker is the most accurate. For looking past the quaint self-righteousness of his words, written just as his program had begun to be accepted and implemented at last, one sees the process described here, in which new ideas from a more general context, strong local leadership, and the self-evident demands of internal growth all combined to wear down obstacles to educational innovation, for better or worse, and to alter community attitudes at the same time.

The water-supply question presented Springfield with somewhat different problems. The town had always depended on private wells and springs for its water, although the town brook running along Main Street had long been unsuitable for drinking. Then, late in the 1840's, stimulated perhaps by much discussion of water supply in Boston, a private Aqueduct Company to bring water to the downtown section was organized by Charles Stearns, the contentious figure who had been Major Ripley's nemesis in that period's battle over the Armory's superintendent. This new pursuit proved no less controversial. Stearns's project, like aqueduct companies elsewhere, soon became embroiled in a series of bitter disputes concerning the rights and privileges that could be granted it by the town, especially in the matter of crossing private land for pipe lines. Several years of acrimony ensued, sustained by deep personal animosity between Stearns and several powerful community figures, all of which did little to resolve any of the outstanding questions, or to clarify what was the community's relation to the general matter of water supply. By the late 1850's, the Aqueduct Company was providing modest service from springs in the ravines north of the railroad tracks through wooden pipes to the downtown section. A number of houses and buildings along Main Street enjoyed domestic service, and some fire protection was afforded by "reservoir" tanks set up at strategic locations.[24]

It was in this last respect that the water question came into focus around 1860. The Fire Department, of course, depended on water, and as the city began to grow faster, there was increasing concern about whether Springfield could be protected from a major fire disaster. As with the school situation, some significant steps in response were easy to take, others surprisingly difficult. Perhaps the parallel to the innovation of a school superintendent was the 1862 purchase of Springfield's first steam-pumping fire engine. This had considerable symbolic importance, for it was understood generally as spelling the eventual doom of the colorful volunteer system, presaging the emergence of a professional fire-fighting force. Nevertheless, transition to the new steam companies, and the connected reorganization of the Fire Department aroused few objections; the first limited steps came easily, a direct and uncomplicated response to an obvious need.[25]

But this was hardly the case with the Fire Department's real problem, assuring enough water for the steam engines to pump. This challenge forced Springfield to face the question of urban water supply, and unlike the school issue, it was not one that could be handled by merely extending traditional public responsibilities to cover enlarged demands. After years of intermittent agitation, the matter first attracted serious attention in 1860. A group of promi-

nent citizens, including Mayor Daniel L. Harris, P. B. Tyler, and
Judge Reuben A. Chapman, later chief justice of the Massachusetts
Supreme Court, proposed an imaginative plan based on their belief
that the Armory Hill itself was a vast natural reservoir, consisting of
a concave clay base like an ice-cream dish, filled with porous sand,
that held the water deposited by underground springs and rainfall,
and needed only to be tapped. The City Council found the idea
interesting, and though wary of proceeding itself, it contracted with
an ad-hoc corporation formed by the promoters to have the system
begun experimentally. If the city were pleased, they agreed, it could
buy the company and its work.[26] There was considerable interest in
Springfield about the so-called "Harris Plan." Heretofore, most people had thought of city action only in terms of fire needs, but the
new plan promised such a vast supply that the gravity flow pipes
from the Hill might provide "an abundance of the purest and best
water, for all domestic, mechanical, industrial, and sanitary purposes." And if this were undertaken, the City Council committee
speculated, Springfield might eventually have to shoulder the
burden itself: "Should the city, in its corporate capacity, elect not
to adopt the project of procuring water from the Hill, a private
company will be glad to undertake it . . . But we are of the opinion
that the supply of large towns and cities with pure water is one of
those matters that ought not to be placed under the control of individuals."[27]

Such reflection was considerably premature, for there was much
opposition to even the tentative step taken on the Harris Plan. Many
resented the prospective cost, especially Hill people whose private
wells were more than adequate for their own needs, and whose an-
noyance turned to rage when it appeared that the deep wells Harris
sunk into the Hill were drawing off many nearby springs and private
wells. The lopsided margin by which voters there rejected Harris in
his try for reelection, providing the margin of his defeat in a very
close contest, indicates how deep was this resentment. Mayor
Bemis's succeeding administration took the hint. Although it did
buy the experimental works just before the contract expired, in
hopes of possible future development, it pulled back from the lofty
goals of the Harris Plan, deciding to aim only at a level of supply
that would "serve well for fire purposes without injury to property."
And since in any event the new system dried up in the summer of

1861, the city was back where it had started — seeking adequate fire protection, with only a batch of reports, much wearisome debate, and $3,000 worth of wells and piping to show for two years' effort.[28]

Tired by the controversy, the city did little for two years. But in 1863, Mayor Alexander ordered a new investigation to discover ways to bring "pure and wholesome water for the westerly portion of the city." The committee assigned to this broad task looked elsewhere for help, hiring as consultant William Worthen, a noted engineer who had recently designed Hartford's water system. Worthen's scholarly report, submitted at the end of 1863, came as the rudest sort of shock. Where the Harris Plan, which had been too radical for Springfield to accept, estimated needs at a maximum of 300 million gallons per year, Worthen showed that the city's current requirements were more than three times that amount, and that any system aspiring to permanence would have to provide nearly two billion gallons annually, or five million or more *per day*. And where Harris's proposal for a $50,000 investment had been viewed as rashly extravagant, Worthen's lowest estimate was a staggering $250,000. His report also demanded a new sophistication regarding sources: any plan depending on the fickle local springs or the supposed underground reservoir he dismissed as nonsense. Though he made no specific recommendation, Worthen declared that water would have to come from the Connecticut, Chicopee or Agawam Rivers, or perhaps from springs and watersheds far away, conducted to the city via large aqueducts, similar to the system Pittsfield had recently built.[29]

With its own most ambitious plans dismissed as hopelessly provincial, Springfield retreated quickly from this sophisticated vision of a modern urban response. The sum of $250,000 was quite beyond the reach of even the most daring "true economy." But nevertheless, the situation continued to grow worse, aggravated by a very dry summer. Particularly symbolic was the July 1864 fire in which Haynes's Music Hall — the "pride of the city" — burned to the ground partly because the water supply suddenly failed in the midst of the battle to save it. As the chief engineer later reported, the loss showed Springfield to be virtually defenseless against major fires in its most settled areas.[30]

Confusion and hesitation seemed Springfield's only response, when suddenly a new development suggested a way out. The old Springfield Aqueduct Company, still piping water to a few hundred homes, shops, and offices near Main Street, found itself near the brink of collapse, its old wooden pipes rotted and leaking, and the limit of its capitalization long ago reached. The company boldly decided on a major rebuilding and reorganization, and applied to the legislature for power to double its capital, the money to be used for new cement and iron pipes and a huge reservoir in the Van Horn area north of the railroad. Encouragement came from many members of the city government, who proposed that the city contract with the rejuvenated company for its needs, in effect creating a subsidized franchise.[31]

With the municipal construction of an extensive water works rejected by almost everyone, this seemed a feasible solution, despite loud objections to giving so much responsibility to an inept concern that owned only "five fountains and fifteen miles of rotted logs." After all, the only alternative was a very limited city-built project, and after a year of swirling, nasty debate, proponents of this solution acknowledged that however desirable it might be in theory, agreement on a specific construction plan seemed virtually impossible. The *Republican* spoke for many in expressing its frustration with all available options, declaring that "now, in the miserable puddle which remains to us, we wash our hands of the entire matter."[32]

It was well into 1865 before the contract with the Aqueduct Company was finally drawn up and signed. The firm was to build a forty-million gallon reservoir at Van Horn and lay new pipes downtown. It agreed to supply the city for ten years, at $2,500 annually, with all the water necessary for fire safety and public buildings. The careful contract included guarantees by the company to extend its facilities when necessary, and, reaffirming the public's stake in the enterprise, it reserved to the city the right to purchase the company and its property at any time, for cost plus 10 percent. Springfield had, for the next few years, finally provided for at least some of the public need for water.[33]

Despite the meager results, there was considerable importance in Springfield's long wrestling with the matter of better fire protection. Although in several ways the city was not yet ready for the scale suggested by the Harris Plan and the Worthen Report, discussion of such comprehensive approaches introduced Springfield to the eventual necessity of a general water system for the community, and to the problems and questions such a commitment would involve. The pressures for action on the water question resembled those at work in the school issues: a combination of manifestly increasing needs, the leadership and perspective of those close to the situation, and the general context of responses being made by other, larger cities, a context which Springfield was becoming increasingly familiar with as it grew. The factors that restrained these pressures were also similar: the web of conflicting particularistic interests, the rejection of the new proposals on grounds of economy and principle, and the plain difficulty of cumbersome machinery in making public decisions. But there is a significant difference between the two areas, which is that the government and the public were asked to make a far broader intellectual adjustment concerning community responsibility for water than concerning schools. A totally different scale of involvement had been proposed, methods undreamed of a few years earlier, and, most important, it was suggested that the public assume responsibility for a basic need that had never been seen in collective, or community terms. Because this difference made for greater conceptual, political, and social complications, the result was a far less ambitious and ultimately less successful response.

However intractable the water and school questions proved to be, Springfield's rapid growth generated even more vexing problems in the area of property improvements. Always ambiguous in the past, the public stake in private development was made more manifest by sudden wartime prosperity, which bred a considerable sense of collective identification with the city's economic progress. At the same time, however, this increased correspondingly the pressure on government from energetic business and property interests, and so the problem of deciding public policy became that much more complex. Though specific administrative determinations were demanded, tradition provided only informal and vague distinctions between public and private interest, and this contributed substantially to the controversy that these new questions repeatedly raised. It is in this area that Springfield faced the confusion of change most self-consciously and explicitly.

These points are vividly illustrated by the debate that took place over a proposed street railway for the city. After years of talk, local capitalists led by Mayor Alexander and Chester Chapin, the railroad president, launched and chartered the Springfield Horse Railway Company in 1863. Their plan was to run cars up and down Main Street, and up to the Armory and perhaps the Watershops as well. It was a popular idea with almost everyone — it would benefit business, it would be "the poor man's carriage," it would tie the city together and symbolize its new stature; the community felt ready for what its larger rivals, Providence, Worcester, Albany, and Hartford, already had.[34]

But while the idea found general acceptance, it encountered much specific opposition. There was the usual run of particularistic objections — residents of some sections feared disruption of quiet streets by clattering horsecars, for instance; cab and hack interests resisted the threat of formidable competition. But more of the opposition stemmed from the general fear of granting a subsidized monopoly to a private corporation. This was similar to the suspicion of the Aqueduct Company contract at about the same time, but became more substantial.[35] As was so often the case, the general matter of defining public and private rights took the form of a relatively trivial point: for how much of the roadway was the company to be responsible? How much would it have to keep in repair, and on what territory would it be liable for injuries and damages? The dimension of privilege and responsibility, not their granting by the city, was the issue, and it proved substantial enough to doom the project. For two years, the city and the new company haggled over feet and inches without reaching agreement. Finally, the city passed a license ordinance providing for a strip one rod, sixteen and one-half feet, in width; the company rejected this final offer, and the project collapsed entirely. Everyone, it would seem, had been overly cautious, especially the city government, which demanded more than most other cities involved in similar relationships. Even in the exciting wartime context, Springfield was suspicious and hesitant in dealing with such a new form of public service, the collective value of which, however apparent, seemed indirect and abstract next to the tangible open-ended opportunity for profit that the company sought.[36]

The problem of the streetcars was only in part a conflict over corporate rights and service. That it was equally a question of the community relationship to a new improvement neither wholly public nor private is shown by the approach to related property improvements. The public role in the general process of property growth had long been established, of course: new streets had to meet rigid specifications, sidewalks on private land would be built under the direction of the city engineer, with the cost assessed on the abutters, and so forth. In fact, the bulk of routine City Council work consisted of petitions for such street and sidewalk work.[37] But here too, Springfield found great difficulty in extending old procedures to cover drastically altered circumstances. In the first place, it learned that greater order and discipline would have to be imposed over the many individual steps being taken. Work was often sloppily done in the rush of building and expansion, with lot and street lines inaccurately drawn. If, as Mayor Briggs remarked, "some of the abutters know as little of the boundaries of their land as the sources of the Nile," this could become a serious public problem when the city attempted to act on petitions for improvements, producing obstructive bickering and lawsuits. In response, therefore, the city began a comprehensive resurvey of all streets, grades, sidewalks, and boundaries, as well as private sewers and drains. Public supervision of private activity was also advanced by Springfield's first modern building code: in response to general authorization by the 1861 legislature, the government declared the land on both sides of Main and State Street in the center area to be a fire district, in which no new wooden buildings could be raised.[38]

More important than supervision and regulation, however, was a new positive involvement in improvements: beyond responding to random private petitions, city administrators became more active in pursuing their own improvement plans. Grading and repair of streets proceeded at a moderate pace, despite frequent obstruction by litigation, the favorite resort of disgruntled abutters.[39] The most symbolic and important step was a greater departure from tradition: Springfield began paving its major streets with macadam. This, like the lighting of the business district, had once been staunchly opposed by those not directly benefited. But now neighborhood jealousy seemed to give way to the generally recognized ascendance of the downtown area, and to the pride that permitted more of the population to identify with Main Street. The "True Economy," meanwhile, could here be argued with telling effect; it was obviously pointless to regularly pour loose gravel into Main Street's mud, when macadam could produce a "smooth street, hard and solid in all weather, needing little attention." When Mayor Alexander initiated paving in 1864, there was little opposition. Macadam, of course, was far from new or untried — it had been widely used for decades and most larger cities had graduated to more sophisticated materials. But for Springfield, it seemed to open a new era. Main Street was soon paved from Union Street to the Depot, and State Street up as far as Maple.[40]

Similar comprehensive patterns of regulation and more positive action characterized the approach to sewer needs in these years. Drains and culverts were then regarded as property improvements, not in terms of public welfare, and certainly not sanitation. The primary purpose of the small sewers built before 1860, mostly downtown, was to drain surface water from the low and soggy flats. But for several years prior to the war, some citizens and officials had urged that the small drains be linked in a system designed to serve the entire area. In particular, it was proposed that a large culvert be built from the division of the old brook in Worthington Street directly to the Connecticut River, constituting a trunk to which branch drains could connect. Legal and financial questions disuaded successive administrations from taking the proposal seriously until the ambitious Mayor Alexander revived the idea in 1863, faced with a glaring need for better drainage in the increasingly dense center district. He obtained sanction from the General Court to build up to three such large drains "for the purpose of protecting private property and the streets of the city from damage during seasons of freshet." One third of the expense, at least, was to be borne by the community, and the rest could be assessed not only on abuttors, but on all those in the area judged "bettered" by the improvement.[41]

By the end of 1865, the Worthington Street sewer was finished and another one through Cypress Street well under way. But innovations were not to be won so easily, as the government soon discovered. Once again, the question was to express tangibly a general principle, the public and private sharing of costs. No guidelines existed for deciding the extent of improvement in such cases, and the concept of a betterment area proved vague and difficult to work with, especially in contrast to the traditional assessment of direct abuttors only. It was even hard to devise a method for apportioning costs once this area had been determined — should gradations of benefit be recognized within it, as the basis for assessment, or should the whole zone be taxed according to property valuations? In light of the bitter argument that surrounded the final allocation of costs, the *Republican* predicted that "there will undoubtedly be trouble, if not litigation." In fact, there was both, and it took several years and three separate court cases to sustain the city's action under the 1863 act.[42]

While the city was thus getting a taste of complexities that were to cause much difficulty in later years, it was learning more constructive lessons too. The first efforts to apply the "true economy" to drain work convinced those close to the problem that a far more comprehensive approach was imperative. As the city engineer concluded in 1865, Springfield had to look beyond the start represented by the large new drains:

What this city needs . . . is a general system of sewerage. Hitherto, with the narrowest limit of expenditure running the gauntlet of petition and remonstrance from the abuttors . . . a solitary sewer has here or there been constructed, without regard to any general plan. Such a plan should provide that every house-lot, particularly on the flat or lowlands, have its drain into the street sewer.

He went on to sketch a network of major drains, parallel and perpendicular to the river, which would serve this end.[43] It was all as sweepingly premature as the other grand visions discussed above — the comprehensive school system, the water works, even the horse railway — but this is somewhat beside the point: what matters here is that those in closest administrative contact with these concerns were drawing similar lessons from their experience.

In each of the areas surveyed, it is true, these men responded to different problems and encountered different obstacles in securing public support for their plans. In education, the pressing needs soon became generally apparent, and controversy arose over how a traditional community responsibility should be extended and restructured to meet them. In the case of a new water supply, the very need itself was unclear, making the major issue a drastic redefinition of the public obligation, together with the intellectual and financial costs of this step. And in the various improvements, problems arose not so much because of disagreement over either means or ends, but rather because old procedures and understandings were being stretched too thin to cover new situations; assumptions based on individual private improvements with some public meaning were beginning to break down when relied on for carrying out comprehensive public works projects.

All these matters did have much in common, however, and Springfield's experience with them can be seen in terms of a set of more or less general forces at work throughout. Although it was only beginning to be recognized in these terms, at issue was an increasingly structured, comprehensive, rationalized, and professional approach to local problems, and beyond this a more collective and abstract notion of the nature of public authority itself. The emergence and implementation of this approach depended on the play of what one can almost think of as two opposing triangles of forces, triangles because in each case the various points were closely tied and mutually reinforcing. One triangle includes the impact of wartime change on both attitudes and environment; the role of strong leaders whose perceptions, interests, and energy led them to champion new ideas; and the influential context of thought and experience from outside Springfield, especially from other cities toward whose stature and modernity Springfield aspired. But a parallel triangle of forces acted to restrain these impulses. In the first place, there was opposition to many of the new ideas per se, opposition fueled in part by deeply rooted traditions of proper public activity and finance. Second, the tangle of particularistic pressures surrounding every question made all sides suspect, contributing substantially to confusion and division. And finally, the government's own more purely institutional inadequacies crucially hobbled the process of formulating policy and making decisions.

In many ways, the positive and active approach championed by aggressive community leaders represented the governmental equivalent of wartime energy and activism, intoxicating prosperity, and collective self-consciousness. The tremendous increase in public spending and government activity was fully a part of that mood. And it is in the same sense that the very limited success of these leaders becomes particularly instructive, for it illustrates vividly how much more demanding were the complex processes of change in those public institutions where the people of Springfield sought collectively to shape their growth. Simply perceiving the dimension and implications of change, much less agreeing on a proper response, proved job enough for the community in the hectic war period.

Part Three
The Postwar Period, 1865-1873

6. Continuing Prosperity and Growth

Springfield in 1865 was a city grown fat on the profits of war, and not without a real sense of guilt it expected peace to bring swift and crushing retribution. Everyone knew that with the Armory stilled and private manufacturers deprived of lucrative government contracts, the bubble would have to break: Springfield would rapidly lose the false prosperity, the transient population, and the grim vitality born of war. The community braced itself, waiting for the crash.

Nothing happened. In May 1865, the *Republican* ventured hopefully, "We don't see it yet." And in October: "We have waited long enough, but it hasn't come. Merchants and trades of all classes discover no falling off in their business, but all have plenty to do. Tenements are snapped at as eagerly as ever." In mid-1866 and again in 1867, the *Union* declared Springfield to be "never more prosperous," notwithstanding the "croakers predicting dullness," and the "sages" who had warned of disaster.[1]

To be sure, there had been ample grounds for apprehension. The most dramatic blow came at the Armory, where a payroll of 2,300 employees was reduced to 300. But the Armory retained a core of its best skilled workers, and it was not long before the pace of work increased again: the government finally adopted the breech-loading rifle, keeping the Armory quite busy with 500 men producing 20,000 weapons a year and working on development of what would be the famous 1873 model Springfield Rifle, the Army's basic weapon through the Spanish-American War. Though the Armory's role was less central, it was still one of the community's largest em-

ployers, and its postwar contraction did not, it turned out, shake
the city more than momentarily. The *Republican* proved correct in
its 1865 prediction that "it will take more than the discharge of
2,000 Armory workers to bring down the city."[2]

Peacetime readjustment was a more complicated matter for private war manufacturers. The bigger more diversified firms had relatively little trouble – the Wason Car Company, for instance, soon
had an enlarged work force busy on a huge backlog of railroad
coach orders. But many were left hopelessly stranded by the re-
ceding tide of government contracts, and had either to convert to
new production or sell out to new enterprises. C. D. Leet, the cartridge manufacturer, was soon producing Hooker's Cough Syrup; the
Massachusetts Arms Company sold its plant to a Springfield knit-
ting-machine maker; and the American Machine Works was given
over to the Hampden Watch Company, a young but substantial firm
lured from New York City by an attractive offer from Springfield
capitalists. In all, though the outbreak of peace ruined some individuals and companies, the community's economy as a whole
proved able to absorb the shock without serious disruption.[3]

This confirms the point made earlier that even during the war
Springfield was developing a remarkably diverse and broadly based
economy. With the mushrooming, almost frantic growth of the war
years behind, the city settled down to sharing a less spectacular but
sustained prosperity with the rest of New England. There were the
usual ups and downs, the jitters and intermittent complaints of
"dullness," but the momentum did not really diminish until the
great depression beginning in 1873. In the immediate postwar
period, Springfield's economy grew stronger and deeper in quantitative terms; more important, its structure matured and the city took
on an increasingly powerful and more sophisticated economic role
in its region.

Accurate estimates of over-all economic growth are almost impossible to make because of structural weaknesses in available statistics,
particularly in the state's industrial censuses of 1865 and 1875. But
these surveys do show that, comparatively, Springfield was still one
of the fastest growing cities in the commonwealth; its total product
dollar value increased 90 percent between 1865 and 1875, a rate exceeded only by Lynn and several cities in the Boston orbit, and a

figure particularly impressive because Springfield began the period already at peak production, while virtually all the others had been unnaturally restrained by the wartime slowdown.[4] Moreover, the figures suggest that Springfield's tendency toward small, highly diversified enterprise became more pronounced than ever. By 1875 the city had 250 manufacturing establishments and 444 "occupation" concerns — carpenters, blacksmiths, machinists, truckers, and other service business not actually creating wealth or products. In the state perspective, this was an unusually high number, and the average product of local businesses was correspondingly low. Factory cities like Holyoke averaged over $200,000 per manufactory, for example, while in Springfield the figure was only $40,000; the average for all local businesses was $18,000, one of the lowest among the cities of Massachusetts. And the size in terms of employees was similarly limited: the industries averaged twenty employees, the occupations under five. When it is remembered that hidden in these averages are several very large operations employing hundreds, one can appreciate how very small was the median size of businesses in Springfield.[5]

These shops poured forth an ever more varied flow of goods and services. Freed from war demands, the leading industries included cotton goods, arms, railroad coaches, paper collars, cuffs, and boxes, water pipes, gold chain and jewelry, soap, candy, clothing, buttons, and iron castings. A random page from the classified city directory in 1873 perhaps better illustrates the range of local activity. Here were headings for "beds, bells, billiard balls, blank books, boilers, boots, bricks, bridges, and buttons." Another page listed "dress makers, dyers, dentist's materials, elastics, electrotypers, engravers, envelope makers, fertilizer, foundries, gas-fitters, gold chain and leaf, grist mills, and gunsmiths."[6]

Many of these were new, newly relocated in Springfield, or first solidly established during the postwar period, and the community watched the parade with pride. Frequent newspaper summaries of business growth and the expanded city directory displayed the success stories in great detail, an answer to the "plenty of croakers who could not see who was to occupy all the new buildings." Perhaps the best illustration of opportunity well seized, one constantly cited at the time, was offered by the Morgan Envelope Company. Started in

1864 in one room by a railroad freight agent, it set up a large factory after the war, incorporated in 1870, and was soon one of the city's largest producers, landing a huge prize in the federal government's first contract for its new postal cards. By the 1880's, its ultramodern Harrison Street factory, six floors high and 230 feet long, was one of Springfield's showcases.[7]

It was not only the presence of opportunity and prosperity that made such success stories possible. There were many conscious efforts to create opportunity, which often took the form of large workshop buildings providing power, heat, and lighting for individual workingmen and small companies. Emerson Wight, a builder who had been putting up such structures since early in the war, filled Main Street from Worthington to Tyler with interconnected buildings fed from a single power source. In 1872 his newest block was occupied by a gas-fitter and plumber, a marble-slate mantle company, a job printer, a spicemaker, a box manufacturer, and several metal workers. This type of investment was widely hailed and encouraged in Springfield, for many businessmen felt that the city depended on the continued growth of such small scale enterprise, and that prosperity might be indefinite if "capital should [continue to] hold out such a generous hand to ingenuity and skill."[8]

While the Wight workshops aided artisans, large sources of capital were crucial in attracting established firms to Springfield, and in permitting local companies to expand. The seven business and three savings banks were particularly strong, as evidenced by the imposing new buildings five of them erected, but they were not enough; the Chapin Bank was organized in 1872, specifically to handle the diverse investments of railroad magnate Chester W. Chapin and his associates, but more generally in response to "rapidly increasing business and the accumulation of capital here, as well as enlarged demands for its use by our manufacturers and merchants." As the other banks "passed more under the direction of enterprising businessmen," few could complain of over-cautious capital hindering progress. The increased activity of finance, as well as a new sophistication, found expression in the 1872 formation of a clearing house among the banks of the city and the region.[9]

Beyond such organized sources of capital, the greatest support for new investment came, as it always had, from the profits of trade. Within the city, prosperous merchants competed eagerly for impos-

ing stores in the business blocks rising everywhere along Main Street.
Where there had been seven major clothiers in 1868, there were
twelve in 1872. D. H. Brigham and Theodore Haynes in ready-made
clothes, or the McKnight brothers and Forbes and Smith (today
Forbes and Wallace) in dry goods, or Pynchon and Lee in groceries
– all expanded their stock and, significantly, their markets. Continued prosperity could only broaden Springfield's reach into the
towns around it. Throughout the valley, customers who usually
ordered goods from Boston began to find Springfield's stores far
more adequate than before. The "large and steady increase of the
country trade" became the most widely noted characteristic of the
postwar period.[10]

Whatever the extent of this tendency in retail trade, even more exciting and dramatic was the growth of wholesaling, which embodied
most fully the powerful regional role devolving upon Springfield as
it matured. The incipient centralization of the paper trade, it will be
recalled, had first been observed in Springfield toward the end of the
war, and within several years the trend became clearer: Springfield
was to be the mercantile center of western Massachusetts not only
in paper, but in many items of trade. By 1869 the awed community
discovered the quiet growth of wholesaling to be little short of phe-
nomenal. Where there had been virtually no economic reach forty
years ago, and only a small orbit up until "the electric touch of
war," in recent years the principle of "trade draws trade" and the
concentration of capital facilities had revolutionized the valley's
business, or so it seemed. Springfield merchants claimed control
over a region stretching hundreds of miles in every direction except
south, where Hartford provided stiffer competition. In 1869 sixty-
seven firms reported a wholesale trade that totalled $18 million; in
addition to paper, this came from volume transactions in flour and
provisions, wool, cotton waste, hardware, coal, iron, lumber, oil and
paints, boots and shoes, dry goods, clothing, leather products,
candy, and notions, to say nothing of the liquor traffic whose agents
were "too modest," amidst the prohibition controversy, to permit
publicity. An 1870 survey concluded proudly that "Springfield is
the natural business center of a wide extent of territory. There is no
reason why our dealers should not command almost their entire
business."[11]

Such imperial claims represent considerable exaggeration, but in a sense it is not that important to gauge the exact proportion of hyperbole and fact in Springfield's assessment of its mercantile reach; what is significant in any event is that local businessmen were setting their sights higher and wider, defining their ambitions in a broadened and more cosmopolitan framework. And the development of wholesale power was only the most dramatic and visible of the ways in which sustained prosperity was working important qualitative changes in the city's economic and business outlook. In several other senses, Springfield was becoming more important in the region, and more genuinely urban in and of itself.

In addition to a central trade and financial position, the city assumed a more specialized role in regional manufacturing as well. In the paper industry, primary milling and manufacture came to be concentrated in the mills at Holyoke and elsewhere, while secondary manufacture of a wide range of consumer products gravitated to Springfield. While it still had some mills, most of Springfield's paper production lay in boxes, envelopes, cardboard, blank books, and the like, especially paper collars.[12] Another more sophisticated development was the increasingly high proportion of consumer-serving enterprises throughout the city's business life. Whatever the faults of the industrial census, its voice on this point is louder than any reservations. Springfield's 444 "occupation" businesses, which could range from an individual blacksmith to a large trucking firm, were more than the number in any other city, and the almost two to one ratio between these and the manufacturing shops ranked highest in the state. At the very least, this suggests that, perhaps because Springfield was farther from competitors than were the clustered cities of the east, a far wider area was coming to depend on it, as were its own citizens, for the goods and services that in an urbanizing community people found they could not, or did not wish to, provide for themselves.[13]

In all these ways, then, eight years of postwar prosperity did a good bit more than make many individual businessmen more wealthy. As the boom lengthened into a steady hum of trade and production, with a continued influx of new energies, progress created a more organized and complex regional economy, a structure within which Springfield found itself coming to play a central and increasingly urban role. However surprising the continued prosperity had first seemed, Springfield adjusted smoothly to this new position, viewing itself and its prospects in ever broader, more sophisticated economic terms. But perhaps because the scope of so many individual businesses remained comfortably small, this proved to be a process not nearly as disruptive as it was exciting.

A similar blend of continuity and qualitative change appears in Springfield's population growth and in the rhythm of community life in the postwar period. Here too, Springfield's sustained growth was less than unique in the context of an awakening Massachusetts, although in losing uniqueness the community gained a perhaps more valuable and exciting sense of sharing in the profound urbanization of New England, a phenomenon just then becoming the source of much general interest and comment.

Sometime after 1870 and probably before the 1873 depression, Massachusetts crossed an important divide. For the first time, the 1875 census revealed, a majority of the people, 50.6 percent, lived in the state's incorporated cities, which then numbered nineteen. These cities had accounted for fully two thirds of the state's growth in the preceding ten years; generally speaking, this had taken place in the larger or more heavily industrial of the cities, while older shipping ports like Newburyport and New Bedford sank into a gradual and permanent decline. What earlier had been a trend was now an imposing reality that became more inescapable as the shape of a society dominated by city needs and problems began to emerge in many aspects of state affairs.[14]

Not only was Springfield not unique in this statewide development, it no longer led even its own area. Hampden County's growth, at 46 percent, ranked third among the fourteen counties, and within it Holyoke tripled its population, while smaller centers — Westfield, Palmer, and Chicopee — began to respond to the pulse of urbanization. These three towns contributed a third of the county's growth, Holyoke accounting for slightly more than a third, and Springfield, which previously had been responsible for virtually all the growth in the county, now only registered slightly under a third of the increment. This does not necessarily mean a weakened position, of course; the other centers were hardly rivals to Springfield, and their growth is best seen as part of the growth and maturation of the entire region, a process Springfield continued to spark and one that was certainly more a benefit to it than a threat.[15] Within these regional and statewide patterns, Springfield's growth was steady and strong. The 22,000 people of 1865 grew to 26,704 by 1870, and had just passed 31,000 at the 1875 census. This represented a healthy increment of 41 percent for the decade, considerably below the 68 percent growth of the state's cities not counting Boston, but close to the 44 percent average of all nineteen municipalities, and far ahead of the entire state's 30 percent population growth.[16]

A closer look at the effects of this growth on the Springfield community yields some surprises. Just as there had been remarkable stability amidst the hectic Civil War explosion, so in the years that followed there still was little of the manifest dislocation so often associated with urban growth, despite the depth and rapidity of the change taking place. Some of the reasons for this can be seen by looking at the place of the foreign born in community growth and life. Springfield remained close to the state average, here as in other categories. While factory towns like Holyoke and Fall River were already half foreign-born in 1875, Springfield fell much below this figure, as did Worcester and many more medium-sized commercial cities. The immigrant population in Massachusetts rose from 21 percent to 25 percent, paralleled in Springfield by a rise from 21.6 percent in 1865 to 24.8 percent, from 4,765 foreign born in 1865 to 7,713 in 1875.[17] With every year, of course, the immigrant presence must have been greater than these bare statistics indicate. For one thing, because all new children born to immigrants counted as census "natives," the foreign-born share of the population contained proportionally many more adults than the native tally, and thus the immigrants represented a good bit more than 25 percent of Springfield's adult population. And the higher birth rate of immigrant parents swelled the portion of the "native" community in direct contact with the immigrant experience. By this time, not only the rate but the actual number of babies born in immigrant families exceeded those born in native families; new children with two native American parents represented less than 39 percent of all those born in the state in 1874, for example. Further statistics in this direction are imperfect, but one can estimate that as few as 8,000 of Springfield's 27,000 people in 1870 were natives with two native American parents.[18]

However suggestive these figures may be, statistical reality is not necessarily social history, and these striking percentages in particular represent an imperfect guide to the impact of the rising immigrant presence. For several reasons, Springfield remained largely undisturbed by this massive and progressive dilution of the native stock and did not seem to sense any increased threat to its structure and tradition. A good part of this equanimity stemmed from the fact that so many of the immigrants were the skilled and easily assimilated English and Scotch, 10 percent of Springfield's foreigners in 1875 and the source of a higher proportion of the first native born generation. Furthermore, fragmentation and isolation among other nationality groups softened the community impact of the over-all increase. This was particularly true in this period, for the influx of the relatively aggressive Irish had slackened considerably; 70 percent of the immigrants present in 1865, they were only 59 percent in 1875. They were replaced as the ascendant group by the French Canadians, who tripled their numbers from 600 to 1,700 in the same decade, accounting in 1875 for 22 percent of the immigrant population, and who were, significantly, among the most passive of the new nationality groups. Poorest and the most unskilled, hampered by a language barrier, the French Canadians huddled closely together without much institutional strength or identity, hardly visible, much less assertive, in community life. Equally invisible to "respectable" Springfield were the scatterings of Germans, Italians, and other nationalities. The small Negro community — it had been one or two percent of the city for many years — was more prominent and better organized, supporting several strong churches, but if blacks were an accepted fragment of the larger community it was only because there were hardly enough of them to pose any problems or generate much tension within it.[19]

The large Irish community, of course, must be the test for any generalizations about immigrants in Springfield, and here too no discontinuity developed in the postwar period. On the formal and explicit level, the Irish were increasingly recognized as a legitimate part of the community. All Springfield joined in celebrating the consecration of the new St. Michael's Cathedral in 1866, or the more important selection of Springfield as the seat of the new Diocese of Western Massachusetts in 1870.[20] The Irish, in turn, contributed leadership and energy to community activities such as charity drives and, especially, the temperance crusade — in the early 1870's one of the most influential and in membership one of the largest temperance groups was the Catholic "Father Matthew Total Abstinence Society," named after the Irish anti-rum crusader who had visited Springfield decades before.[21]

But harmony, whatever its occasional institutional expressions, did not, in any event, mean equality, brotherhood, or lack of prejudice. Discrimination was more informal but undoubtedly substantial, as the frequent complaints about jobs and housing attest, including the interesting variation on modern "blockbusting" that occurred when a real estate broker at a large auction used dummy Irish bidders to scare the Yankees into paying higher prices, so that they might thereby "protect the reputation of the street." Beyond this was the even more casual prejudice of press and pulpit, the ritual denunciations of "Irish" crime, "Irish" drunkenness and rowdyism. And yet, if Springfield was hardly a tolerant community in any enlightened sense, it still tolerated the Irish in the more literal meaning of the word. In a period of confident growth and expansion, Springfield seemingly felt relatively undisturbed and unthreatened by the Irish presence.[22]

A large part of this attitude stemmed from the fact that the Irish themselves generally accepted their role and had as yet felt little need to challenge it; apparently Springfield's prosperity continued to offer them more than its prejudice withheld. In local politics, so typically a mode of Irish expression, they were still noticeably unassertive, accepting the traditional rewards and advantages doled out by those playing the game. At a time when naturalization laws and poll taxes offered few real obstructions to those who wished to vote, and with more than a quarter of the city's adult males foreign born, only 9 percent of the voters were naturalized citizens. Arranged differently, these figures explain that half of the native adult men, and only 20 percent of the foreign born held the franchise. Similarly, in party leadership, ward committee, and in the issues of local politics, the immigrants in general and the Irish in particular were still quite inconspicuous. It seems clear that traditional patterns of community life, in this and other respects, had not yet been seriously affected by the rising number of immigrants in Springfield.[23]

If ethnic tensions had not much disturbed local institutions and relationships, one might still expect to find class consciousness, arising from sustained industrial growth, posing a threat to tradition. Certainly the atmosphere in the nation was becoming conducive to such awareness; the late 1860's saw constant skirmishing on questions real and theoretical concerning unions, strikes, hours and wages, class relations, and industrial regulation, all a prelude to the more general labor crisis of the 1870's. In Massachusetts, the new Bureau of the Statistics of Labor set up in 1869 reflected a new sensitivity to this question. One might logically expect to find in Springfield a similar focus on labor matters, given the rise of industry, the huge profits being reaped by business amidst rising prices, and the disproportionate share of this wealth trickling down to the workers, so many of whom were new to the community. The local press reflected the predictable view of respectable society; though disagreeing on almost everything else, the *Republican* and the *Union* joined in rejecting the premises of the rising labor movement. Legislation of wages and hours was termed foolish, unions themselves "a form of tyranny by which the ignorant are enabled to share wages with the higher class of workingmen." The true answer to the problems of labor, advised the *Union*, lay "not in the antagonism of labor and capital but in their cooperation . . . not by keeping up an 'irrepressible conflict' between the two classes, but in securing their harmonious efforts for the same end."[24]

One expects such words in the mouths of the masters, but in Springfield the workingmen also seem to have held to the same affirmation of traditional relationships, rejecting the idea that divergent interests seriously divided elements of the community. The labor movement had made only a tiny and tentative foothold in Springfield at the time; there were a few craft unions and occasional shop walkouts, but very few real craftwide strikes, and these collapsed or were quickly crushed. When a bricklayers union struck in 1868, nine leading contractors banded together and easily defeated it, destroying the union and blacklisting those involved. Similarly, a young stonecutters union disintegrated at the first show of opposition to its 1872 wage strike.[25] There is more positive evidence that these sporadic efforts far from characterized the position of Springfield workingmen, for what successful labor activity there was pointed in quite another direction. Springfield saw in these years the formation of a powerful Workingmen's Association, explicitly dedicated to the older concept of the community of all producers, from laborer to contractor and even, in Springfield, including merchants. This effort grew out of a local labor dispute that, significantly, had the peculiar ability to unite the entire community. It concerned the efforts of Armory workers to receive the benefits of the 1868 federal eight-hour law, without any reduction in wages. The complicated issue took years to work out, involving many hearings, presidential decrees, and congressional action, but Springfield supported the armorers throughout, sustained by its pride in the great factory, traditional antipathy to Washington interference, and the logical if not legally obvious validity of the armorer's case. This warm public support spilled over into efforts to keep alive the old labor-reform spirit through the new Workingmen's Association. It soon had over five hundred members, mostly artisans and middle-rank clerks, who busied themselves with rallies, speeches by visitors like Wendell Phillips or Henry Wilson, and that most traditional response of an earlier age to wage-price imbalance, a co-op grocery that enjoyed, as in previous incarnations, a shortlived success.[26]

Thus, whatever the turmoil and conflict elsewhere, nothing in Springfield yet seriously threatened deeply rooted views of the relationship between workers and the general community. The unskilled poor were too unorganized and isolated to complain; the more articulate workers simply did not feel complaint was appropriate or necessary. Faith in mobility could be sustained by the new businesses and industries prospering on all sides, and meanwhile wages in Springfield were demonstrably higher and more secure than elsewhere in Massachusetts. A good artisan could make from $15 to $25 a week, and mill conditions were good, with workers there averaging $12 a week. At the 1875 census, before wages began the really precipitate depression tumble, Springfield's average annual wage income was estimated variously at from $555 to $603, one of the highest among Massachusetts cities and towns, and far above anything available elsewhere in Hampden County.[27] Workingmen enjoying this relative prosperity were still far from challenging the assumption that their well being and the progress of local business, industry, and community growth were one of a piece. If the workingmen, then, and the foreign born, did not challenge such assumptions it is hardly surprising that the solidly entrenched middle classes and their leaders still accepted traditional social attitudes and relationships. The differences were there, and the material for conflict increasingly abundant, but prosperity and the momentum of exciting, generally shared growth continued to mask these profound social changes.

If it was too soon for the social structure visibly to reflect the impact of years of sustained change, community life in other ways had been deeply affected, and showed through a new pace and tone important adjustments to the altered environment. In the same way that the frenetic social life of the Civil War years reflected the tensions of that period, the rhythm of community life and the patterns of association can be seen as a response to continued change during the postwar years, as if Springfield was trying to digest the confusion that inevitably attended rapid expansion.

Two trends can be seen in the clutter of local social life, both hardly new but with a sharp new focus nonetheless. First, Springfield spawned a host of clubs and organized groups for purposes cultural, charitable, political, and purely social. This grouping tendency, as Tocqueville had noted decades earlier, was so pervasive throughout the society as to represent almost a characteristic American instinct. But the sudden proliferation of such voluntary associations in postwar Springfield does still suggest, within this general context, that many in the community must have felt at this time a need for closer institutionalized contacts in a community, flooded with new faces and concerns, where informal social relationships had become more difficult and less satisfying.

Every level of society demonstrated this. The already noted coherence of the Irish community, focused in the church, found expression also in a host of special groups organized around regular gala events, such as the annual Catholic Fair, or the St. Patrick's Day parade. And the labor movement, such as it was, clearly satisfied the need for fellowship and association more than it furthered class aims. Higher up in society, among those who could not claim to have shared less than fully in the traditional life of the community, the same impulse was even more prominent, particularly with

younger people. There was the active new G.A.R. veterans' organization, new chapters of the Knights of Pythias, and a number of sporting clubs; there were new groups like the Women's Suffrage
Association, the Springfield Scientific Association, and any number
of smaller, usually ephemeral, literary or musical clubs.[28]

Some of these assumed more significance than their nature would
seem to indicate; the fact of contact and association per se, whatever
the official purpose of the group, often proved to be its most important activity. Thus the Springfield Club, formed as a sporting
club to promote horse races and regattas, was composed of many of
the more dynamic young businessmen of the city, and not surprisingly, it soon became less concerned with horses and rowing than
with business, civic affairs, and, eventually, active politics. Even at
the very top of local society, the need for more formalized association was striking, as well illustrated by the emergence of "The
Club." This group had existed informally off and on since the
1850's, but first assumed formal structure and prominence after the
war. As the name indicates, the members felt they needed no further
identification to themselves or outsiders: they were fifteen or twenty
of the most powerful business and social leaders in the city, most of
them closely tied to the *Republican* establishment, including men
like former Mayors Daniel Harris and Albert Briggs, Reverend Buckingham, and Samuel Bowles. "The Club" at this time functioned of-
ficially as a discussion group, with vacancies filled only by vote of
the members; unofficially, of course, it was a center of enormous
power and influence, not to be confused with a similarly named but
less exclusive literary club of later years. While a great many influential and prestigious men were not members, and had no particular
desire to join this large clique, its control of community power is
not the point; what is significant is that the powerful leaders involved apparently felt the need for such an institutionalized, not to
say stylized, vehicle for communication and identification among
themselves, and for representing their stature to the community
looking on.[29]

Another trend reflects the emergence of a more complex social
community. While the entertainment season contained just as many
lectures, clowns, games, races, and fads as ever before — now chess,
now baseball, now velocipede rinks — the number of large scale,

highly organized activities requiring weeks of preparation and dominating local life for days, increased rather dramatically. Fairs and
sporting events in particular came on an order and frequency new to
Springfield. The National Horse Show was revived, exceeding by far
the already substantial success of prewar exhibitions, but it was the
new fascination throughout the East with boating and crew races
that best illustrates changes taking place. Beginning in 1867 the
Springfield Club organized and hosted a series of regatta on the Connecticut River attracting prominent college and club crews from all
over the East. Thousands of spectators would flood into the city for
the matches and side events, which could last for several days, creating great excitement for weeks before and after. Springfield seemed
as proud of the wide attention these regatta received as it was
pleased with the business they generated, and even the disadvantages
had some appeal: press and pulpit condemned the gamblers, confidence men, and prostitutes attracted by the carnival atmosphere,
seeing Springfield endangered by such importations from the big
cities, "those hotbeds of occidental depravity and prosperous in-
iquity." But like the teenage boy complaining of the inconvenience
of shaving, these preachings also carried a certain pride, an excited
resignation to the fact that Springfield shared the problems as well
as the energies of other, grander, cities.[30]

This redirection of community social life altered Springfield, in
one instance, quite symbolically. While everything about it pros-
pered, the venerable Hampden County Agricultural Society had fallen upon hard times; people no longer took much interest in its old
style agricultural fair, with the jams, pumpkins, and blue-ribbon
sheep. All the interest had been absorbed by the horseraces, originally a side attraction, and many felt the group should not continue if
that were its only purpose. "If our agricultural societies are not a
failure now," wrote the *Republican*, "their decadence is plainly visible and their final collapse prospective." After struggling through
several poor seasons with the expense of maintaining Hampden
Park, the local society gave up, leasing the property to an ad hoc
citizens group that was to conduct the race season. And just as the
farm fair disappeared, Springfield hosted its first Mechanics Fair.
For weeks, two hundred exhibits of machinery and industrial products from all over New England filled the City Hall, attracting large

and enthusiastic crowds. The symbolic juxtaposition was not lost upon the community.[31]

All in all, postwar Springfield seemed a curious blend, changing rapidly yet demonstrating considerable continuity. In both economic and human terms, the surprising persistence of a high-powered prosperity brought substantial growth, without disrupting the basic social fabric of local life. The community was still relatively cohesive, with lines of social status, power, and influence remaining clear. But if it was not disrupted, the old community had continued to evolve into something else. The prosperous shops, offices, and factories were fashioning a more sophisticated economic environment, expanded functionally and geographically, within which Springfield's businessmen learned to think and plan in more comprehensive terms. In social life and structure, activities and contacts expanded in a similar fashion, while growth produced a felt need for more formalized expressions of personal association within the larger community.

In all of this, there is more than a suggestion of an intimate and reciprocal relationship between the people and the city's economic and social environment. As the latter changed, so too did the community, slowly and subtly. Its outlook, its framework of thought was becoming correspondingly more broad and abstract, and less informal and personal.

7. Physical Change and the Community

In the decade following the Civil War, and particularly between 1869 and 1873, Springfield as a physical entity changed far more drastically than its economic and population growth would seem to have justified. Rapid development transformed not only the city's face, but its basic physical form and structure as well, a process accompanied in the community by a remarkable new physical self-consciousness. The community was discovering the implications of more than a decade's expansion at the same time that it was discovering and experimenting with the power to alter its environment according to its needs. In a variety of suggestive ways, these discoveries had much to do with each other.

In understanding the historical relationship between city people and the streets, land, and buildings that surround them, considerable assistance is given by one of the most important recent books on modern cities, Kevin Lynch's *The Image of the City*. Here, Lynch explores the ways in which people perceive and comprehend the totality of the physical city around them, how they orient themselves within an environment they cannot visually grasp in its full scope. By a city's "image," he means the public's conceptual organization of this environment, and the bulk of his book is devoted to examining what it is in various cities that determines the strength, or "legibility" of the image. Why are some cities said to have interest, character, and vitality for their residents, while others are faceless and numbingly oppressive? Lynch finds the answers in the physical components of the over-all image — in the streets, neighborhoods, landmarks, and special interest areas, or "nodes," which by their variety, placement, and conceptual graspability produce a city landscape high in definition. This matters, he argues, because of the important role of the city's image. Men have a basic need to structure their world, to locate themselves within their environment, and much of the coherence of the community depends on whether its people understand and share the physical city they inhabit. Particularly in the modern metropolis, a strong and meaningful image can be crucial in helping the individual to overcome the isolation and fragmentation of his urban life, just as it helps him see beyond the confines of the street and tall buildings which block his view.[1]

Although Lynch does not deal with the interesting question of how a city image changes and develops over time, his approach has exciting historical implications, particularly when considering a period in which local people were making some very basic decisions about the physical future of their city. By dealing with the perceived environment as well as physical reality, the concept of the city image helps to clarify the symbolic nature of individual steps in the city-building process, and the cumulative effect they can have on the way subsequent or more general questions are perceived and dealt with. A changing city image, therefore, indicates not only a response to change, but the basis for even more dramatic departures. In many ways, this was precisely what was happening in Springfield just before the Panic of 1873. As a result of rapid growth, the image of the city — the scope and scale of perception — broadened in almost every dimension. Larger buildings, new neighborhoods, more imposing architecture, greater unity: inextricably bound up in the type of city being built, was the changing image of physical Springfield. As people began to conceptualize its form and growth in ever more abstract ways, the city-building process itself changed profoundly. This will be apparent in an examination of several aspects of the physical transformation that so occupied the community in the postwar decade.

Where growth during the Civil War had not really altered the pattern of settlement but consisted more of a filling-in of older patterns, the story after 1865 was quite different. Population flowed swiftly, now to one area, now to another. New neighborhoods were created out of pastures, and others dramatically changed in character, while the central district took on an altered appearance and a somewhat altered role. The bare statistics of population shifts provide perhaps the best overview of these developments.[2]

Ward	1865	Increment	1870	Increment	1875	Approx. percentage growth
1	3,775	2,514	6,289	1,564	7,853	100
2	3,417	765	4,182	–505	3,677	5
3	4,051	507	4,558	–131	4,427	10
4	2,880	194	3,074	316	3,390	20
5	3,470	130	3,600	1,660	5,260	50
6	1,405	271	1,676	618	2,294	60
7	1,494	–61	1,433	184	1,617	10
8	1,546	345	1,891	644	2,535	60
Total	22,035	4,668	26,703	4,350	31,053	40%

Springfield's North End, ward one, received the bulk of the city's total increment after the war, and by 1870 it had become the most populous ward, outdistancing ward three, the traditional center, and more than twice as large as ward four, home of the wealthiest citizens. In the next five years, however, the pattern changed. While ward one's expansion remained substantial, the momentum was stolen by the Hill areas, especially ward five. Even as Springfield's over-all population growth slackened in these years, the Armory wards grew even faster than they had during the Civil War.

The statistics show dramatic changes as well within the center of the city, for while the outside was gaining, the inside was losing. As the center became more commercial and industrial, it relaxed its hold on the majority of the city's population. What, in wards two and three, had been a steady 34 percent of the total, dropped by 1875 to 26 percent; even more surprising in a growing city was the numerical decrease of these wards after 1870. Seen another way, the figures show that in the first six wards, the "city wards," which together held a constant 85 percent of the people, the balance shifted away from wards two, three, and four, the central three wards, and by 1875 for the first time a majority of the "city ward" population lived in wards one, five, and six, outside the center core.

A whirlwind of new construction put these changes in sharp relief;

the annual survey of building, the *Republican* warned its readers in
1869, "will seem to border on the fabulous." From 3,556 in 1865,
the number of dwellings in Springfield rose by 41 percent to 4,997 a
decade later, an increase proportional to the rising population and
hardly diminished from the wartime pace. Real estate was still responding to the unsatisfied demand for housing, and plentiful capital encouraged many large-scale projects. "In all parts of Springfield," summarized the proud city directory in 1872, "wide awake
folks are studying where are to be the new centers of population.
The excitement in real estate is thus far a legitimate result of the
large and active demand for lots for immediate building purposes.
There is little speculation, buyers reap the advantage as land is
brought into the market, and at the same time the public welfare is
best promoted."[3]

Not only did construction change several areas, but development
took many different forms as well. The North End, first to feel to
postwar energy, grew at first along traditional lines, through the sub-
dividing of older lots and the opening of a few new streets through
old estates, with the pace of construction often furious — a reported
fifty homes, for example, being built in one small area in the first
months of 1867.[4] After 1869, new trends in the area became visible. Projects began to free themselves from Main Street, clustering
along other promising arteries such as North Chestnut, parallel to
Main and to the east, where many finer homes were built, stimulating further building on all sides. And land began to be developed in
larger parcels than had been customary, often with public assistance.
Thus the city opened Jefferson Avenue, a malled street 125 feet
wide, through what had been the old poor farm, creating sixty-four
building parcels. With four parallel north-south streets in close prox-
imity and strong east-west ties like Jefferson Avenue, the North End
had a new and solid framework for continued growth through "filling in." Its lots were being covered, furthermore, by a variety of
houses, from small frame two or three family workingmen homes to
more substantial $10,000 residences for prosperous businessmen,
and the entire area was emerging as a coherent neighborhood, with
settlement spilling steadily north from Round Hill. This became explicit when Memorial Church, a small evangelical congregation founded almost as a mission to the North End in 1865, raised a magnifi-

cent new building near this hill, at the intersection of Main and Plainfield. What had once been the northern boundary to settlement was becoming the center of a unified new district.[5]

Even more dramatic departures changed other parts of the North End in these years, developments unlike anything Springfield had ever seen, though quite in the context of things being done in other, larger cities. The prosperous Wason Car Company, cramped in its Lyman Street shops near the Depot downtown, had come to learn that the heart of a city was no place for heavy industry. Fortunately for Springfield, there was room for it elsewhere in the city, and turning down an offer of free land from West Springfield, Wason began in 1871 to move to a seventy acre tract of pasture and grassland in the northwest corner of the city, an area known then and now as Brightwood and today one of Springfield's most depressed areas. Within two years the Wason Company had doubled its facilities, occupying sixteen acres with factory, workshops, paint sheds, warehouses and spur tracks to the railroad; ancillary firms such as Talcott Forge had also begun to follow Wason to Brightwood. But the most unique feature was the development of a planned, balanced residential area. Wason had little interest in creating a factory village, and deliberately sought to attract businessmen and artisans of middling means. The company therefore prepared twelve streets, centering on Plainfield Road and the new Fisk Avenue, installing drains, aqueduct pipes, and fire hydrants. To insure the "quality" of the neighborhood, it strictly controlled the sale of lots to builders, requiring that all houses erected cost no less to build than $3500. The project demonstrated vividly to Springfield the power of large-scale capital investment and the northward flow of growth, confirming the eventual continuity of settlement with Chicopee. The planning steps, furthermore, were seen as an exciting advance in shaping Springfield's growth as a balanced, which is to say essentially middle-class, community.[6]

As the North End grew, ambitious businessmen began to look to the inviting plateau in the city's west, and to the rolling hills in the south. This was land of quite obviously ascendant value — close to the center yet removed in height and character from the downtown flats, and still relatively cheap. Attention centered primarily on the area around the intersection of the Boston and Wilbraham Roads,

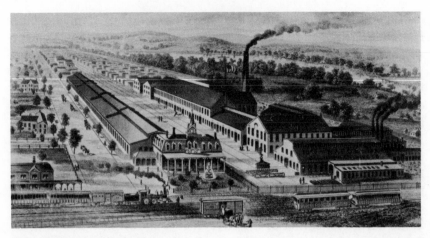

Wason Car Company, 1872

soon to be called Winchester Park. On the Hill, back two thirds of a
mile from the Armory and bordering on a small pond locally known,
through a substantial flight of imagination, as Lake Como, this was
an area of large farms, estates, and private woodlands, with a few
clusters of settlement in which most of Springfield's few Negro citizens lived.[7]

Development here, as in the North End, came on a scale unprecedented in Springfield, but the form was somewhat different, and
more portentous. North of State Street, men like George Tapley,
James Thompson, Tilly Haynes and especially the two McKnight
brothers began between 1869 and 1873 what was to be almost
twenty years of comprehensive neighborhood development. Starting
with the land they already owned in the area and buying up adjoining plots, these men were soon opening streets such as Westminster,
Buckingham, and Sherman at a steady clip. As Wason had done,
they usually sold the lots with stipulations as to what kind of houses
could be built, but they did more: led by the McKnights, they began
building homes themselves, often in advance of sale, foreshadowing
the more extensive speculation building in the area during the
1880's. Styles were coordinated, trees planted, sidewalks and drains
built, and other steps taken towards establishing ordered and unified
neighborhoods. By 1873, filled with many fine homes and a larger
number of modest middle-class dwellings, which still characterize

the area today, the Winchester or McKnight section was a recognized district boasting several community-wide institutions — the new Children's Home, the City Hospital, and the Oak Street School, one of the large new-model houses. Before the depression interrupted Springfield's growth, the process and pattern of its eastward expansion had been firmly established.[8]

The hills and bluffs to the South, which had long been attracting many wealthier people, saw yet another variation on the theme of expansive development. If less extensive, growth here was far more elaborate, best illustrated by the deluxe project from Pine to Locust along the Mill River. The developers retained Frederick Law Olmsted's firm for landscape planning, and the streets and lots were laid out with an eye to vistas, curves, and trees. The whole project was hailed as confirming the harmony between private development and public progress; as the *Republican* said, Springfield was fortunate that the land had "fallen into the hands of men with the taste to plan, and the wealth to execute, such an extensive scheme of public improvements."[9]

This relationship was acknowledged more explicitly by the city's official assistance in opening the virtually unsettled areas below Mill River to private development. In 1871, after a good bit of hesitation, the city agreed to convert the old road to Longmeadow, an extension to the south of its own Main Street, into a wide, well-graded avenue that swept grandly along the river past Long Hill. The project's success led to others: Fort Pleasant Avenue, an elaborate boulevard one hundred feet wide, was opened due south from Mill River, and the city straightened and relaid the old east-west road to the intersection called the "X," a street soon to be renamed Sumner Avenue. All of these improvements underscored important new directions in public policy: Springfield recognized the need for better links to neighboring towns, and for integrating into the city proper the suburban villages within its limits, such as the "X." More important was the indication that the community was trying to give some sort of shape and direction to future expansion, planning, after a fashion, far in advance. The area that these new roads blocked out would in the next decades become the Forest Park section, Springfield's fastest growing district, and the first buildings there were well under way by 1873.[10] In another light this public assistance illustrates the power of real estate pressures within and

upon the City Council, but perhaps nowhere was the absence of a
perceived incompatibility between public and private purposes more
apparent. Handling each request on its merits within this traditional
value structure, the city was little bothered by the broader implications such actions might come to have.

There was an interesting and somewhat curious relationship between this turning outward and the initiation, at last, of horse
streetcars in Springfield. A new effort at establishing the long-de-
layed service was mounted by new sponsors in 1868, and this time
the problem of roadway obligations offered no obstacle, for the city
was guided by the prescriptions of the state's 1864 general street
railway act. Service began by 1870, with the horsecars running every
fifteen minutes from Carew Street in the North End down Main to
State, and then up the Hill as far as Oak Street at the Armory. The
fare was eight cents, or six and a half cents with a book of tickets.[11]

The operation generated controversy and dissatisfaction almost
from the outset. Hill people demanded extension of the route to
Lake Como, on top of the Hill plateau, and those in the South End,
not even partially served, pressed for streetcars down to Mill River.
The company, however, steadfastly refused all these requests. In addition to having sectional prejudices — most of the directors and
stockholders were North End or Main Street businessmen — the
management was financially quite conservative, plowing most
profits back into servicing the construction debt. Not until those in
the outskirts actually acted to organize competing lines did the
company respond with route extensions.[12]

The reluctance seems remarkable, considering that elsewhere in
New England street railways were pushing their tracks into virtually
empty suburban tracts, realizing that homebuilders and profits
would follow their lead. But in Springfield the company still tended
to view its service in the older terms of center business communication, along the old right triangle, rather than as a conduit of suburban commuters. The very terms under debate tell something of
the conceptual limits of the issue — Winchester Park was only a mile
and a half from Court Square, and the extensions demanded were
only half a mile in that instance, and a full mile to Mill River at
Locust Street in the other. But lessons were being learned slowly
through this petty dispute, and the 1873 stockholders' meeting that

Horse streetcar on the Hill, 1870's

approved the extensions also authorized study of possible lines to
Longmeadow and Chicopee, prompting the *Republican* to comment
that "the company seems to have suddenly comprehended the object of its existence." Still, it was symbolic of the confusing dimensions of change and the qualified nature of Springfield's urbanity
that this enterprise, already a major stimulus of growth, took so
long to recognize the direction in which lay Springfield's future and
tremendous profits for itself.[13]

In a similarly hesitant way, Springfield was moving toward a more
sophisticated and modern understanding of city needs concerning
its central business district. Here prosperity received direct expression in the elegant business blocks rising in rapid succession. The
1866 city directory listed forty-seven of these blocks, the 1873 issue
seventy-five, a remarkable 60 percent increase. But as the entire area
between State Street and the Depot became more exclusively commercial, it came to be seen that the continued dependence on Main
Street might inhibit further growth. Forty-eight of the seventy-five
blocks were strung out along the central avenue, vitiating, even with
the new streetcars, the center's natural advantage of concentrated

activity.[14] As early as 1866, the *Union* had urged the establishment
of other major streets parallel to Main, so that a functional grid
could develop and spread property values and business activity more
evenly, providing unlimited potential for expansion. In particular,
attention soon centered on a plan to widen and extend Market
Street, then little more than a back alley to Main, into a second
major business street.[15]

The idea apparently came at once too early and too late — early
because the government was not institutionally ready for such a
costly and comprehensive undertaking, and late because the area
was already too developed, and complications from damage claims
and boundary locations would alone have been prohibitive. Finally,
to judge from the many complaints of "building lots for crafty speculators," the old public consensus here proved quite fragile when
private profits for those along Market Street promised to be so visible and tangible, partly because the abuttors included men like
Bowles, Henry Alexander, and other controversial leaders of the
local establishment.* Even though the *Union* charitably cautioned
that it would be foolish to "delay a needed improvement just *because* it will benefit two or three unpopular men," all these obstacles
proved sufficient to keep the project from going through in any
form.[16]

Other downtown efforts met with more success. Dwight Street
was extended almost to the railroad and Harrison was pushed eastward up to the brow of the bluff where Chestnut had emerged as
something of a business street, thus creating an important link between the flats and the slope which helped to extend the center
both horizontally and vertically. One striking project here reflected
the increasing urban character of the city's center: the only substantial home building in the area was near Chestnut, just behind where

*In the final analysis, the area was already too developed to allow change to occur
easily. At one point, for example, when complicated route negotiations and damage arrangements had been laboriously completed, it was discovered that the new Methodist
Church on Bridge Street — right in line with the proposed new street — had been begun
while the talks were going on. It is unfortunate that efforts to restructure downtown
Springfield were not more successful, for the rapid decline of the city's central business
district in the mid-twentieth century is due in large part to Springfield's having failed to
become other than a "one-street town" in its commercial heart. The side streets had remained back streets, filled with warehouses, and they deteriorated swiftly as soon as Main
Street began to falter.

the Museum Quadrangle stands today, and it took the form of two long rows of elegant brick townhouses, built by William Matoon on a new street through his land. Lined with four-story mansards that sported the fancy "swell fronts" then synonomous with Boston urbanity, Matoon Street was promptly hailed as Springfield's Beacon Hill, a sure sign of a promising urban future.[17]

The scope and detail of all these developments — North End, Hill, Mill River, and Center — when taken together, suggest that a substantial revamping of Springfield's image must have been taking place. That Springfield was coming to be seen in a new and more comprehensive way is evident, for example, from the map printed annually as frontispiece to the city directory. Before 1865, it showed only an area within a mile and a half or so from Court Square. But by 1873, the yearly map had become a large fold-out, covering a three-mile circle and including all the new areas of settlement and older neighborhoods in the outskirts — places like the "X," which had been there all along, but had not previously been thought of as part of the city proper.

Another illustration of the new scale of perception was the widely discussed 1870 proposal for a park system. The plan envisioned a belt of park roads, two-hundred-foot-wide avenues with trees, malls, "delaying parks," and walks, that would ring the city. Starting with a riverfront park, the belt would go past Brightwood, loop around back through the Van Horn area to the top of the Hill, near Lake Como, then proceed down across Mill River to what later became Forest Park, back to the Connecticut, and north along the river to the center of town. Only fragments of this dream were ever to be realized, but that is hardly the point: the concept was, at the time, becoming one of the most controlling and influential ideas in the infant science of landscape and urban design, and its early vogue in Springfield provides some measure of the city's urban ambitions, not to say its pretensions. In another sense, the circumferential park loop suggests an effort to comprehend the scattered and diverse sections of the city in one coherent image, to digest the changes taking place in such an unconcentrated fashion. And as with so many of the physical developments here discussed, the new approach shaped the framework of local thinking about the particular question of parks for years to come.[18]

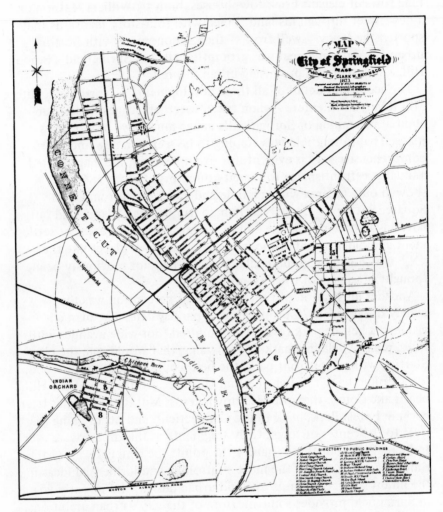

Springfield, 1873

Perhaps the most fundamental feature in common among all these developments was the new manner in which the environment itself came to be perceived and touched by public and private policy. In almost every instance, lots were developed in larger and larger units, projects were more grandiose, plans were projected further into the future and over wider, more variegated areas. The city environment, in short, was being transformed in an increasingly comprehensive and manipulative manner, which not only bespeaks a changing "image" of the city but carries even more important implications, for the light of rational planning, projection, and manipulation could alter the image of a wider range of non-physical community concerns in the same way that it illuminated possibilities for change in the city's physical structure and environment.

That a general physical self-consciousness represents more than an historian's abstraction seems clear when one considers the substantial and sudden turn to imposing architecture that characterized the postwar decade. Here, more explicitly, individuals and groups sought to express through design their sense of what Springfield was, and what sort of buildings were appropriate to it. As a look at the form and dimension of this revolution in local architecture will show, the emergence of a grand style at this particular time, far from being a coincidence, signifies a crucial step in restructuring the city's image, an effort to adopt external symbols of status and to assimilate, through prominent architecture, the many changes in community life. It can almost be said that Springfield was just discovering the social significance of architecture in a growing city.

The dramatic, almost hectic rush to raise elaborate new churches illustrates this point most strikingly. Given the traditional community significance of denominational vitality, when a large number of independent congregations elect to build new churches at about the same time, it is reasonable to say that the decisions represent some form of community expression as well as a desire to better serve the needs of individual organizations. Certainly, the rush was remarkable. St. Michael's Cathedral, completed in 1861, had not only been Springfield's first Roman Catholic Cathedral, but was also the only church raised in the city between 1850 and the end of the Civil War. Within a decade of the war, however, and mostly within six years, twelve major church buildings rose, almost all of them elegant stone and brick structures on a scale of elegance and design previously rare in Springfield.[19]

The financial dimension of the accomplishment has considerable significance by itself. Most of these churches cost over $125,000 with the great Unitarian and South Congregational churches reaching the then imposing sum of $150,000. In all, the total community cost exceeded a million dollars, an expenditure especially remarkable in that it apparently was financed by the congregations themselves without recourse to extensive borrowing. Huge donations from the wealthy and general subscriptions from the rest of the society kept debts low in almost every instance; the Church of the Unity, for example, had $50,000 pledged even before plans had been accepted, and at completion reported "no baleful shadows of unsettled obligations." Such accomplishments suggest vividly the fluidity and dimension of wealth being amassed in Springfield, and the willingness of people to spend it for such community projects.[20]

The planning of these churches shows a symbolic perspective, as well as a new scale. Elaborate architectural competitions were held, as each congregation sought to outdo the others, with entries solicited from important firms in Boston and New York. If the results have only moderately impressed architectural historians, they excited Springfield nonetheless. Most of the grand new buildings were in the prevailing Victorian Gothic form, dark and heavy, still something of a novelty in Springfield. Still extant are the large South Church, and the Memorial Church by the famous Richard Upjohn, with its large square tower, octagonal buttresses, and contrasting shades of local Monson granite, both good illustrations of the period's taste and Springfield's pride.[21]

Church-building reached a peak of interest among Springfield residents with the arrival of a young designer who was to become a pivotal figure in American architecture — H. H. Richardson. At Harvard, Richardson had been a good friend of James Rumrill, soon to be the son-in-law of Chester W. Chapin. Chapin was both pillar and pocketbook of the Unitarian Society, and when a new edifice was contemplated Rumrill secured entry in the competition for his friend, a young unknown just back from several years in Paris. Richardson won easily, and the popularity of his buildings, together

St. Michael's Cathedral, State Street

with his valuable contacts, brought him several other commissions. Within a few years, he had designed six structures in Springfield, the most important works in his early period.[22]

His Church of the Unity, on State Street directly opposite the new city library then under construction, has seemed to some critics "in no way remarkable" in the light of his later work, but at the time it was hailed as "the most ambitious, the grandest, and the most satisfactory attempt at elaborate church architecture ever attempted" in Springfield. More or less Gothic Revival, it stood on a broad plot which set off the large corner tower and gracefully sloping roof. Richardson made effective use of rough-cut local stone, a technique he was to develop greatly later, and featured a large rose window on either side of the church.[23] For decades it was considered Springfield's most beautiful building; in sad and typical fashion, developers demolished it several years ago to make way for a hotel that, owing to a dispute over its liquor license, was never built, and the lot is still

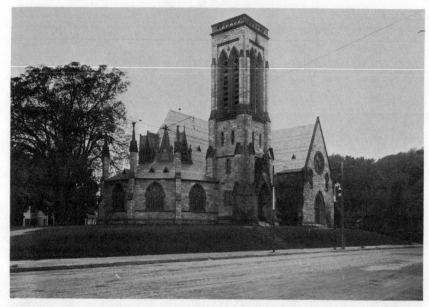

Memorial Church (Congregational), by Richard Upjohn

vacant at this writing. Richardson's other Springfield church still stands. The North Congregational on Salem Street, now a Baptist church, is quite different, a simpler Norman structure of dark, rough-cut brownstone, suggesting in its pitched roof, round arches, tower, and tall stone dormers the Romanesque influence that would be so important in Richardson's mature work.[24]

The location as well as the imposing style of such projects carried considerable significance. With the exception of the Memorial Church, in the North End, and Grace Methodist, built in 1875 after the major spurt of construction, all of the grand new churches rose within a half-mile of Court Square, at the center of community wealth, communications, vitality, and status, where they could symbolize city, and not neighborhood, pride. But on the other hand, there was considerable movement within this central area, somewhat outward but more generally upward. Most of the new churches were located on the bluff or the slope of the hill, overlooking the flats downtown. Five of the major projects, in fact, involved a move directly uphill from old locations. In part, this represented a desire,

especially among wealthier congregations, to move closer to the
homes of prominent members, and to enjoy the status and prestige
that such location could imply.[25] But at the same time, such implications can be easily exaggerated, for the congregations were looking primarily for physical sites as imposing as the projected
buildings, for which the hillside plots proved both most suitable and
most feasible.[26] As it happened, the churches and other public
buildings in this area were transforming it, rather than embracing its
previously residential, almost exclusive character; State Street, near
Chestnut and Maple, was fast becoming, as it is today, a quieter and
more specialized part of the community's center, a focus of public
activity. The city's unusual topography, which made land so close to
the commercial heart seem so much further removed in character
thus allowed the church-builders the unique opportunity to "flee"
the materialistic city at the same time as they celebrated and contributed to its expanded urbanity.

Other important public buildings illustrate similar themes in the
emerging physical consciousness. With $100,000 in public contribu-
tions and leadership from figures like Daniel Harris, the City Library
Association finally succeeded in building an appropriate home, one
of the most ornate and pretentious structures of the period. Designed by George Hathorne of New York, it adopted the fashionable
"Medieval Revival" style, a vaguely Gothic mixture of brick with
stone trim, a tower, and an elaborate stone arch vaulted porchway.
Inside, the main room boasted a vaulted dome, and book alcoves
radiating out hexagonally. Well set back from State Street, opposite
Richardson's Unitarian Church, the library seemed a vivid symbol of
successful community effort, especially considering the long preceding struggle to get it established.[27]

Perhaps the greatest public meaning of all attached to a building
that was not technically a community project. It is almost as if
every aspect of Springfield's changing character was to receive
physical expression; certainly, the great Hampden County Courthouse, the single most impressive building of the period, well symbolized Springfield's new importance in the life and economy of its
region. Richardson designed this structure, triumphing over five
other prominent architects in the competition, and the result represents the most significant work of his early period. It was his first

City Library, by George Hathorne

Hampden County Courthouse, by H. H. Richardson

real experiment in Italian and Romanesque forms, a massive stone building in the shape of the capital letter I, the head on Elm Street facing Court Square, the foot on State Street. Low rounded arches, striking rough-cut gray granite, the magnificent central tower modeled on the Palazzo Vecchio of Florence — all demonstrated what Henry-Russell Hitchcock calls "the major virtues of mass, scale, and distribution, virtues of a very great architect."[28] The only flaw was the lot itself: narrow, deep, and off to the side of Court Square, it hardly provided an elegant setting for the city's brightest gem. Aesthetics alone would have indicated the upper State Street site originally considered, near so many of the other new contributions to Springfield's architecture. It is especially significant, then, that despite these reservations, and a political tangle that would perhaps have made the State Street choice somewhat easier, the building most directly expressing Springfield's new stature was situated so as to reaffirm the city's continued orientation around Court Square, the traditional focus of its institutional life.[29]

Given the central role of business activity in Springfield's rise, the public attention lavished upon the almost thirty business blocks built in these years should not be surprising. Several in particular stood out in the public eye. Another Richardson building, the Boston & Albany Office just north of the Depot, aptly symbolized the tremendous importance of railroads in local prosperity, being a strong work whose five stories of solid granite, mansard roof, and raised main floor reached by double stairway were all "symbols of modernity in the American commercial world." Other good examples of the period were Richardson's Agawam Bank, demolished recently, and Hathorne's Springfield Institution for Savings block, still standing on the north-east corner of State and Main. This typical mixture of Gothic and mansard with stylish cast iron fronting was at the time called the finest public building in western Massachusetts; today it seems a thoroughly modest and ordinary structure, the survival of which, incidentally, is not a very flattering comment on the progress of Springfield's central business district in the present century.[30]

Finally, as objects of public attention, there were the many imposing private homes built in the period. The most sumptuous rose on Maple Street, toward Crescent Hill, such as O. H. Greenleaf's

Downtown in transition

Main Street, corner of Vernon, late 1860's

Court Square, south side, early 1870's

Springfield Institution for Savings, Main and State Streets,
late 1870's

Main Street, 1878

"English Cottage style" mansion with towers and terraces at 275 Maple, which cost the then staggering sum of $40,000. All areas of the city, however, boasted at least a few such homes. On the Hill, candy merchant Horace Kibbe built a grandiose "Greecian and Doric" palace, while other wealthy businessmen built equally imposing homes along North Chestnut Street in ward one. And nearer the city's center, still visible today, the Catholic Church built an ornate mansion for newly consecrated Bishop P. T. O'Reilly, which had twenty-seven rooms, a mansard roof, and plenty of gingerbread, and which earned criticism from some parishioners for drawing away, by its splendor, too much attention from St. Michael's Cathedral next door.[31]

The public interest in all these churches, official buildings, business blocks, and homes was but part of the more general fascination, almost intoxication, with the great variety of smaller projects on all sides. The newspapers filled columns with the details of almost every substantial new building, and the city directory expanded from a modest address book to a large classified reference volume hundreds of pages thick, including long detailed essays on local growth in which all new buildings were profusely illustrated and described. The significance of Springfield's involvement with its own architectural development did not go unrecognized at the time. Just before the Civil War, interestingly enough, the *Republican* had pleaded for a new approach to buildings, for a shared pride in a beautiful city. This, it was argued, offered the best way to bind the classes together, a sort of visual share the wealth plan. And from this, it even followed that "the rich man has no moral right to deny the community that graceful expression of his prosperity which a beautiful home conveys . . . An ugly or mean house becomes a crime against the public." Springfield's problem, the editorial went on, was not poor architecture so much as *no* architecture, and thus no appreciation of its important public role.[32] The postwar period seemingly responded to this call, bringing both the architecture and implicit recognition of the role, not only in the buildings themselves, but in the very absorption in the construction boom. Beyond expressing considerable local pride, all of these aspects can be seen as mechanisms by which the community could retain conceptual control of the rapid and diverse changes taking place in the environment, helping to integrate a myriad of private changes into a common coherent public image.

By 1873, Springfield's image had been drastically altered in every dimension, and the city was almost a new place for less than a decade of physical change. And in these terms, the image it offered its citizens must have been a relatively strong, or "legible" one. Springfield had, by this time, an extremely diverse yet uncomplicated and readily comprehended physical structure. A few major streets, central organizing elements like the river and the Hill, well-defined and differentiated neighborhoods, many architectural landmarks of great public interest, and special focal points like the Armory, Court Square, the emerging district on State Street where the library, Unitarian, and Catholic Church stood — all these suggest that Springfield presented few obstacles to a clearly organized environmental sense for all its people, which perhaps at least partially accounts for the relatively small incidence of visible social disorganization in the rapidly urbanizing community.

More important than a retrospective evaluation of this image, however — most small cities at the time would also rate fairly well in these terms — is the fact of its very emergence. For in a sense these years of physical change heralded the birth of a modern city-image for the people of Springfield, a new and important form of collective self-consciousness, which operated on several levels. Most explicitly, Springfield was viewing itself now as an ascendant modern city, adopting the symbols of that urbanity and seeking to express through extensive public discussion and "public" architecture its pride and its ambitions for the future. More deeply, the concept of such a self-image represents an abstract relationship posited between community and environment, and it could be said that in these years, people in Springfield first began to see themselves, and discuss their collective physical growth, in terms comprehensive enough to permit such an environmental view to stand as a living abstraction. In such a context, the most important fact about this developing relationship was surely its reciprocality. In the face of rapid growth, the abstraction of the city image emerged as one new way to digest and assimilate change. At the same time, such a conception itself generated more change, by suggesting methods, plans, and goals for comprehensive development that were not conceivable earlier.

Springfield's most exciting development, in this sense, was a general mode of thought and action, a rational, projective, manipulative, and comprehensive approach to the physical environment born of a number of seemingly unconnected decisions. This type of response was to be of crucial importance in shaping the way Springfield responded to other less tangible questions it encountered as it grew.

8. Community Change and the Public Interest

Springfield's physical development in the postwar years, a composite of many individual steps and plans, had been a relatively smooth process. But the community's more formal, collective response to the continuing demands of city growth in the same period, its continuing evolution as a public institution, proved to be a much more complex matter. With only a few rough edges, the period divides readily into two parts. From the war's end until 1869 or 1870, Springfield coasted on the consensus and energy of the war years, still catching up with the tremendous expansion generated then. As that momentum gave out, there was a sort of collective faltering in community activity, an exhausted pause, but postwar growth continued to push new problems, demands, and ideas to the fore, and a new burst of activity quickly followed this interruption. Then, even before the depression of 1873, a general political crisis and the realization of just how deeply community relationships were changing led to a new uneasiness, anxiety, sharp conflict, and confusion, all of which fueled the severe near-paralysis of the mid-1870's.

During the war years local government had encountered substantial resistance in assuming new responsibilities, or in redefining traditional ones; only after considerable difficulty had apparent community needs begun to be met by 1865. Considering the complexity of these obstacles, their virtual evaporation after the war seems remarkable. Perhaps because of the easing crisis atmosphere and the somewhat slackened crush of population, the community digested the changes which had been taking place, and accepted as appropriate the approaches for which leaders had battled for years.

This turnabout was most vividly illustrated by the postwar consensus on the accelerated school-building program long advocated by Josiah Hooker and the School Committee. Appropriations rose steadily, and even site decisions occasioned only modest squabbling and even less delay. The first of the new-model houses – large, three-story brick buildings serving five hundred students – rose on North Main Street in 1865, appropriately named the Hooker School, and others on Elm, Oak, Worthington, and Central Streets quickly followed. By 1870 all the city's schools revolved around them: thoroughly graded, each acted as the administrative center for the smaller neighborhood schools now loosely organized in "groups," around the large houses.[1] Explicit hostility to the principle of more centralized and systematic structure both in individual schools and in the complete school program had virtually disappeared, and the schools grew, free from serious controversy, on the strength of their demonstrable new order and efficiency. Between 1864 and 1871, using the measure of available statistics, while expenses rose by 150 percent, the value of school property more than quadrupled, from $80,000 to $365,000. The number of students, rising much faster than the school-age population as a whole, increased from 2,798 to 3,403, and not only enrollment but also attendance and the size of the teaching staff increased dramatically. On the whole, Springfield seemed quite satisfied with its progress, feeling that the demands of extraordinary growth had been met, and Hooker hailed the "gradual and auspicious change in the public sentiment."[2]

The controversy over water supply, like the bitter school debate, dropped from view after the war; the momentum of the earlier period was carried through without much conflict, and seemed to suffice. The city paid for fire protection for private property, and the Aqueduct Company supplied domestic water to some of those without access to suitable wells or springs. By 1870, pipes from the new Van Horn Reservoir had been laid, and the number of families served increased from 1,345 to a claimed 2,500. Impressed with this progress, many in the city felt secure that "their aqueduct can supply Springfield for twenty years to come."[3]

The fire protection system itself continued to develop in these years. More steam engines were purchased and firehouses built, with the department as a whole reorganized into formally structured companies supervised by a Board of Engineers. The most visible change, one particularly interesting in the context of a comprehensive self-image, was the 1868 adoption of a fire alarm "telegraph-box" network throughout the city, replacing the old "system" whereby the City Hall bell tolled out the ward number to which engines should rush in search of the fire. The glamor of the old volunteer companies, through all these steps, moved closer to being totally supplanted by a less personal and exciting, but far more efficient city service.[4]

Still following general lines sketched during the war, many aspects of public regulation and administration showed a similar impulse toward formalization of the easy-going procedures of a smaller community. A comprehensive truck and hack ordinance in 1865 defined zones and regulated fares within them; another ordinance celebrated the center district's urbanity by banishing pigs from its streets; still another regulated privies and licensed night-soil collectors. And looking to its own housekeeping, the city condensed and revised many years of ordinances in the form of a new and more comprehensive code.[5]

In all these matters, and especially regarding property improvements, Springfield embraced, as it had resisted before, the implications of the "true economy" argument. A general understanding emerged that necessity, even more than economy, was involved, that the community had a positive obligation to anticipate its future needs. And because the very intoxication of rapid growth was accompanied by a sharp fear of prospective collapse, the argument for the community's responsibility to insure continued expansion gained special strength, particularly regarding property improvements, the longer the boom went on. "We can't run Springfield like a small village," argued the *Republican*: "The increasing demands of a broadening, elevating, and embracing civilization impose unusual burdens. We must grow by being worthy of growth, and offering the facilities and temptations to the world around to join in their lot with us." Even the *Union*, usually so suspicious of spending, boldly called for the abandonment of "old fogey and conservative notions about improvements" if it were desired to attract "respectable people and business that will fill unimproved land and add to the valuation of all existing property." Springfield had listened long enough, it said, to the "old fossils perpetually croaking about municipal bankruptcy, or harping on the one potent string of robbing the outskirts."[6]

In this spirit, the government turned to the tremendous amount of catching-up needed after the war. Sewer work was particularly imperative. Critics charged that Springfield had "the most abominable drainage of any city of equal size in the country," a charge particularly telling in light of the natural advantages enjoyed by a city that sloped down to a broad river along its entire length. The energetic governments in the first postwar years proceeded rapidly with the plan for large lateral brick drains, fifteen feet underground, leading to the river, such as the one built earlier on Worthington Street. The largest project of all was a sewer up Union Street almost to the top of the Hill, and to this and the other trunks a growing number of smaller drains were connected on a somewhat more haphazard basis. By 1870 authorities pointed to fifteen miles of new sewers, and the dramatic improvement of such soggy, squalid areas as the notorious Ferry Street slum near the Depot.[7]

Road work proceeded at almost as fast a pace. New streets were graded and accepted, and before 1870 the first of the more ambitious structural improvements, the Dwight Street extension discussed above, had been begun. But macadam paving, another innovation of the war years, represented the most extended involvement for the city government at this time; by the end of 1869 almost the entire downtown area had been covered with an improved quality macadam rock surface, as were several important streets in other areas of the city.[8]

In implementing these policies, older if hardly proven ideas governed procedure as well as plan. The city built the new sewers under the 1863 act authorizing assessment of part of the cost on territory judged "bettered," even if not abutting; this usually meant the city paid about a third of the cost. When Springfield accepted a broad betterment law passed by the legislature in 1867, the same approach applied to major street improvements. The concept seemed fair, and since $10,000 of public funds could build $30,000 worth of improvements, it allowed the city to plan more ambitiously.[9]

Such, at least, was the theory. In practice, more extensive work only complicated the old problems of measuring the extent of public obligation. The Betterment Act, while offering no general way of defining this, still attempted to locate it by a quantitative division of costs. The necessarily ad hoc approach provided opportunity for ample confusion, dispute, and frequent litigation. Thus the *Union* argued on one day that the people ought to pay for drainage because such improvements were "demanded by public conscience, morality, and health." On another occasion, the same paper asked, "is it right to require Wards 5, 7, and 8 to pay for these sewers when they get no benefit except as the interests of the city as a whole are advanced, while property in the vicinity is doubled in value?" The endless squabbling in assessing and collecting the private share once public money had been expended, soon began to sap the program's strength, and the momentum behind it. "Let us know where we are going before we have our baggage hauled," complained the *Union*, "The city cannot be called on unless the parties are willing to contribute towards their cost in the manner provided."[10]

In this context, the public began to be alarmed about the increase and cost of public activity. The distance Springfield had traveled seemed all at once very frightening. Total expenditures from 1865 to 1869 had jumped from $182,000 to $418,000; debt was up from $344,000 to $440,000, mostly for sewers, schools, and streets. It was noticed with some alarm that street work had for the first time become the budget's largest item: the $30,000 of 1865 leaped to $140,000 by 1869, when the cost of macadam and the Dwight Street extension were felt. There was a bright side to all this not unrecognized at the time: property valuation had doubled to $24.5 million, while the tax rate dropped somewhat from the 1866 high of $18. Furthermore, as the city replaced demand notes with short-term bonds, the debt found a more secure footing. But these facts, and strenuous efforts to hold down costs, could not sustain the momentum, and as it ran out the community came to take a closer look at what had happened.[11]

There was more to this sudden vertigo, however, than the soaring costs of municipal improvements; in several ways, the more general political and social climate in the nation was becoming increasingly relevant to local affairs. People in Massachusetts had been following the great political issues of Reconstruction with far more interest than controversy. The Republican party retained solid control throughout the state, while the Democrats were weak and fragmented, tainted by a copperheadism that seemed more disgraceful as the war and its anxieties receded from view.[12] Locally, Springfield saw an almost dynastic succession of politically linked Republican mayors, beginning with Henry Alexander, Jr., in 1862. Albert Briggs followed for three terms when Alexander moved to the state senate, and Briggs was succeeded in 1868 and 1869 by Charles Winchester, a young and popular lawyer for whom Winchester Square was named on his untimely death in 1871. The City Council was overwhelmingly Republican throughout the period, and other important party and community leaders, such as Daniel Harris and Tilly Haynes, sat in the legislature.[13]

Paradoxically, however, this one-party domination and the consensus on national issues enabled state and local politics to become especially turbulent. Divisive issues on this level were not lacking, only a strong party framework within which they could be expressed and handled. The result tended to be confusing and unstable issue-politics, with constantly shifting factional alliances making elections, especially for the legislature, highly unpredictable. Temperance was the chief of these issues, stirring up Massachusetts politics again even before the Civil War ended. The battle against the prohibitory Maine Law had been taken up in force both by those wishing outright repeal and those who sought a strict and more realistically restrictive liquor license law. The state police force created in 1865 as a last attempt to enforce prohibition succeeded only in generating tremendous controversy and resentment of state authority, and in the next years, legislative opinion swung chaotically back and forth, opting variously for repeal of prohibition, its reenactment, a license law, local option, beer only, restaurant liquor only, and so forth. Not until 1875, with passage of a strict license law that would last a decade, did Massachusetts achieve a semblance of stability on the question.[14]

Springfield accurately mirrored this situation. Though few in the higher ranks of society publicly called for Free Rum, there was considerable division on the question of licensing, with no clear social or political lines differentiating the friends of prohibition from the foes. The events of 1867 showed what confusion this could introduce in the local scene. The legislature had failed to pass a license law, and demand for repeal of prohibition banished all other issues from the fall campaign. A semisecret club called the "PLL" (Personal Liberty League) sprang up all over the state to fight for an anti-Maine Law legislature, leaning itself to a free-rum position. In Springfield, the prohibitionist *Union* gloated at the pro-license *Republican's* effecting an uncomfortable alliance with the often rowdyish PLL and free-rum copperheads. But after the license forces carried the November state elections, the shoe was exchanged and the issue carried into local balloting, with the *Union* and other rum-fighters now even more uncomfortably working with free-rum forces in opposition to the entrenched Republican leaders so close to Bowles.[15]

Issues like this injected considerable tension and confusion into local politics after the relative harmony of the civil war years. In addition, the general climate in the nation brought forth new questions which had far more local relevance than had the debates over slavery, the war, or Reconstruction. By 1868 the concerns that would later be identified with the Gilded Age had already begun to emerge sharply in terms of political issues involving economy, currency, fiscal integrity, capital and labor, public administration and private corporations, and, more sensationally, bosses, rings, and corruption. The daily press vividly brought all this to Springfield's attention, and Bowles's *Republican* in particular was just beginning what would be a long journalistic campaign against corruption, especially in relation to publicly assisted railroads. This emerging national concern substantially influenced Springfield's 1869 crisis of confidence, and it is somewhat ironic that by contributing to public suspicion of business and political morality, Bowles helped weaken the building policies he supported, and the local Republican "machine" in which he himself was often labeled a boss.[16]

This process first became politically visible in 1869. Mayor Winchester, an otherwise lackluster leader, took the bold step of presenting a realistic budget request that exceeded the previous year's budget by 40 percent, rather than following the usual practice of asking for modest appropriations first, and later obtaining supple-

mental funds when the work had been done and only the bills remained.[17] The shock was sufficient to crystallize widespread weari-
ness with the long Republican succession. Even Bowles's paper
reported "a general feeling that we need a new and vigorous and
economical administration," and few were surprised when a largely
Democratic "Citizen's Ticket" carried the December elections
easily, headed by William L. Smith, well known lawyer, Democrat,
twice president of the Common Council, and twice unsuccessful
candidate for mayor. The Republicans had revealed how played out
was their string by nominating former mayor Briggs, whose three-
terms of spending could hardly answer the call for economy.[18]

Smith's victory margin made his mandate clear. The *Union* saw it
as an "emphatic public condemnation" of past policies, but the judicious assessment of the *Republican* perhaps came closer to gauging
the public mood:

Our habits and our expenditures as a municipality have been entirely revolutionized [in recent years]. This revolution has, as a whole, been inevitable and
just; but in some respects, it has been carried too far. Now there is a natural reaction, both in public capacity and popular demand. There is something of
hesitation in municipal growth . . . We have reached, even passed, the limit of
just yearly expenditure for public purposes, and must enter now upon a season
of more stinted appropriation and more careful administration.[19]

The new government made valiant efforts to carry out this mandate.
Pledging allegiance to "the laws of business and of common sense,"
it cut appropriations by 25 percent in 1870 and held them steady in
1871, Smith's second term, balancing the budget for the first time
in years. Improvements were the special target, with street work
slashed from $150,000 to $70,000, and the $27,000 sewer expenses
also halved. And perhaps most symbolically, the government acted
to reduce the debt, paying off bonds and other miscellaneous debts
rather than refunding them, as usual. Within two years, the total
debt had fallen from $440,000 to $385,000 and temporary demand
debts had been virtually eliminated, with old bonds now falling due
at a manageable $6,000 per year. Smith earned substantial populari-
ty for his program and was easily reelected in 1871, when even the
Republican, which went through the motions of supporting the

regular party candidate, had only warm praise for him. When Smith
moved up to the state senate in 1872, his successor as mayor, Republican Samuel Spooner, praised him effusively and pledged to
continue in his footsteps, a pledge backed by the initiation of annual appropriations earmarked for reduction of the debt.[20]

The pause was refreshing, but it could never last, for the city had
not stopped growing. Though a response to this continued postwar
growth was inevitable, however, few could have been prepared for
the sudden force with which its demands hit Springfield around
1871. Almost overnight, the community seemingly catapulted into
a new era, which altered the framework of most civic issues beyond
recognition. In spite of the deeply rooted impulse to economy, a
host of grandiose projects doubled Springfield's expenditures within
three years. Where a $100,000 increase in debt had been fuel for
bitter argument only a few years previous, the city found itself
blithely floating a million dollar bond issue, sending its total indebt-
edness from $385,000 to $1.1 million in 1873 and, hardly slowed
by the depression, doubling that to $2.5 million in another two
years.[21] How all this happened is the story of profound change in
Springfield. The momentum of growth, the changing self-image, aspects of the external atmosphere, particularly in other cities — all
helped restructure the community's approach to public policy.

To look again at a traditional civic responsibility, years of sustained growth in Springfield's schools could not but bring about
more qualitative changes in attitudes towards the actual role of education in the community. With the passing of the one-room schoolhouse, traditional ideas about curriculum and secondary education
were doomed also. But such changes were slow in coming; in the immediate postwar years, a critic has written, "both high school officials and the community continued to favor the traditional
curriculum of the old time grammar school and the New England
academy." The lower grades had remained in the grip of "the cult of
spelling" while the high school, a classical training ground for the
few going on to college, could hardly be considered a part of a
general education program for the community.[22]

The new graded system that had emerged in the large schoolhouses, however, necessarily implied a more systematic approach. In
1866, as the Hooker School opened, a twelve-year course of study

was developed, approaching schooling as a continuous and integrated process from primary to high school. This impulse to systemization, so much in the mainstream of the period's school reform thought, was linked closely to newer ideas about the purposes of high school, which posited a close tie between broadened middle-class education and continued community growth. This aspect of educational reform has been associated, throughout New England, with dynamic, urbanizing communities, and it should not be surprising that it emerged in Springfield during the city's most prosperous and promising years. By 1869, the high school had embarked on a long series of curriculum changes felt to be "absolutely necessary to furnish a more complete and thorough education." A fourth year was added, and officials defined the broader goals that they conceived the high school to have: "More distinct reference must be had to the wants of those who are to engage in mechanical, mercantile, or manufacturing pursuits, just as we now have a preparation for college and the professions. The High School [must be] the People's College, providing *all* our citizens with the means of educating their children well."[23]

The question of a new high school building became the vehicle by which community response to this redefinition could be expressed, for once such goals were accepted, the need for a new building was self-evident — the existing high school occupied a few rooms in the old central-district schoolhouse shared with primary grades, and spilled over into makeshift quarters in the City Hall basement. This situation proved disturbing or not depending on what one thought the community place of the high school should be; there was substantial opposition from those who felt an expanded high school would still serve too small a portion of the community to justify the substantial new cost all would have to share.

After a good deal of pressure and study, the government finally decided to build, arguing that secondary education was crucial to a modern city and that a community of 4,200 school-children could not limit itself to high school quarters holding well under two hundred students. After many delaying difficulties, the elaborate $100,000 structure finally rose next to Unity Church and opposite the library, a thoroughly modern four-story building including twenty classrooms, a large lecture hall, laboratories, and workshops.[24] As with so many other transitional steps for the community, once the decision had been made it came to be popular, rapidly accepted as natural, appropriate, and obvious. Springfield took pride in its high school as another badge of its promise and urbanity, and the building's completion coincided with the rounding out of an important phase in educational reform. All schools were fully graded and coordinated, teacher's salaries raised to make them professionally competitive with other cities, the forty week September to June school year adopted, and the high school now offered three programs – Classical, English (practical), and General (in between the others). By the opening of the new buildings in 1874, city leaders hailed "a rapid transformation on the subject of popular education."[25]

Similar themes found far more dramatic illustration. Until this time, public responsibility for drinking and domestic water had not seemed necessary. Water supply, yes, but only for property protection in fire emergencies; the community did not acknowledge that the public might need similar emergency protection in case drought, contamination, or sheer human growth rendered normal supplies inadequate. The matter was just not seen in such terms.

It is hard to say exactly why things changed so suddenly around 1870, for no crisis existed, nor were normal needs particularly pressing. But all at once, the question of a more broadly conceived water supply appeared as a major issue. The most important factors in this seem to have been the internal perspective of the broadened self-image and the external identification it encouraged with municipal developments elsewhere. As conceptions of the city's physical scope broadened, the existing aqueduct system came to seem more and more unacceptable. The entire Hill area, over 1,450 families, lay above the line of the Van Horn Reservoir, thus out of reach of the aqueduct pipes. As the local perspective broadened in time as well, projecting Springfield's evolution into a more crowded and complex urban center, continued reliance on wells and springs, especially on the Hill, appeared as a thoroughly short-sighted security. And finally, as Springfield came to view itself as a major ascendant city, the important steps toward water systems being taken at the time in Hartford, Worcester, Boston, and other familiar cities became all the more controlling, and Springfield's own eventual need to face the same problems became that much more inescapable.[26]

In the fall of 1871 the city began to search for "the most feasible plan for supplying the city with water." A noted hydraulics engineer hired as a consultant, Clement Herschell, told Springfield once again that local wells and springs offered no hope, and he included in his report much comparative data from other cities and an appendix by the state assayist that showed the aqueduct water to be dangerously near the point of contamination. Herschell suggested that Springfield's path lay in pumping water by steam, from any of the several points along the Connecticut or Chicopee Rivers, up to the reservoir where gravity could feed most of the city.[27]

With interest building, the new 1872 government took up the question, this time intrigued with a new idea: why not pump water directly into the pipes, supplying the city by steam pressure rather than gravity? This was the plan of the famous Holly Company of Lockport, New York, successfully implemented, it was claimed, in Buffalo, Indianapolis, and many small cities, a number of which were inspected by Springfield councilmen. The idea seemed promising and the estimated cost of $500,000 fell a good bit below Herschell's projection.[28] But while the committee deliberated, the situation and, in fact, the nature of the discussion changed rapidly, for many were becoming concerned about the governmental as well as the technical implications of assuming the broadened responsibility. Such a level of enterprise, they argued, could not be best handled by a political committee that changed with annual elections. Again following the example of other cities, Springfield's leaders secured a state law creating a Board of Water Commissioners, an almost independent body of five that would be popularly elected for staggered three year terms, enjoying broad powers to direct and finance construction of a water system. Expenditure of $1 million in thirty-three-year bonds was authorized, and municipal purchase of the old Aqueduct Company required. That the move was seen locally as a constructive one, enabling Springfield to cut through political tangles efficiently and provide a needed service, is indicated by the four-to-one referendum vote accepting the act.[29]

Members of the superceded City Council viewed the new board with a suspicion that seemed confirmed when, though they were still studying the Holly System, they learned that the commissioners favored a plan depending not on rivers, but on distant rural water-

sheds.[30] A major feud began to emerge, when suddenly nature interrupted, presenting the city with a severe and sudden drought as if to
warn it to concentrate on the matter at hand. On June 20, the Aqueduct Company, then involved in the sale of its property to the city,
had embarrassingly to inform the purchaser that "we can see no
reason why the city will not be short, if not entirely out of water in
the next sixty days." At this point the City Council asserted itself,
declaring that "the demand of the city for a supply of water beyond
the apparent ability of the Aqueduct Company to furnish is so
urgent as to warrant extraordinary measures." It was fortunate for
Springfield that the situation did not become quite as desperate as
had been feared, since months of fumbling and mistakes in the emergency plan of pumping from the Garden Brook near the reservoir
succeeded only "in getting an engine too small for the pump, and a
pump too small for the pipe, and a pipe too large for the supply of
water in the brook." Equally disappointing was pumping done sub-
sequently from the Connecticut River at Brightwood. The drought
thus had several results: it discredited the idea of pumping, it
showed the limitations of City Council efficiency and expertise, and
it effectively ended the dispute between the council and the water
commissioners, turning public attention to the more comprehensive
solution now so obviously needed.[31]

In 1873 the commissioners held yet another investigation, with
public hearings and professional testimony. After showing once
again that "wells or springs flowing through a thickly populated city
should be abandoned," the board went on to conclude further that
both science and common sense were "averse to the use for domestic purposes of water from streams below large towns or manufacturing villages." Having eliminated the nearby rivers, the board
turned to rural sources and finally selected the watershed of Broad
Brook in Ludlow, seven miles from Springfield. Engineers recom-
mended a huge 445-acre reservoir there, from which, it was promised, a limitless supply of pure water could flow by gravity to all
areas of the city. Having the power to act on its own recommendations, the board did so; by the onset of the depression, the city had
purchased the Aqueduct Company for $250,000, sold the first
bonds for the million dollar waterworks, and actually taken the first
steps in construction.[32]

It would be several years before the system was in operation, and experience would reveal serious problems in the site chosen. Nevertheless, the community progress before 1873 was quite significant. A new definition of social needs and a new sophistication in understanding environmental problems had become generally accepted. Moreover, Springfield had begun to experiment with new administrative concepts in its efforts to fashion comprehensive and effective long-range public policy. In dealing with the very tangible and immediate water crisis, Springfield was moving as well into a new world of ideas concerning finance, government, politics, and the public interest.

Since most of the physical expansion described in the previous chapter occurred after 1870, it is not surprising to find the improvement activity, which had precipitated the 1869 pullback, once again a focus of attention, and a good index of changing attitudes. Rather than respond to random petitions, the city was now trying to plan work more comprehensively and projectively, and as the quantity of work increased, it discovered that even individual improvements had to be coordinated and planned; it made no sense to pave a street one year only to dig it up again for a petitioned drain the next, when both could be done at once. The new complexity and the sheer burden of all this work had clearly outgrown the administrative capacity of the City Council's committee system, and more basically the determination of public and private costs, on which so much of the program was administratively and conceptually based, was threatening to break down completely. "Betterments turned to Worsements," moaned the *Republican* when, in a case growing out of the Maple Street widening, the State Supreme Court held that a technicality voided the city's betterment law and all assessments under it. Though the government was able to obtain a retroactive loophole-plug from the legislature, the case had caused a sharp panic and had made clear the need for a more reliable policy system.[33]

The City Council turned to an institutional remedy then in great favor in other cities: sewer street and sidewalk improvements would be handled by a board of "three able and discreet men," conversant with the technical and legal questions involved, especially concerning betterments and assessments. They would investigate proposals, draft plans, and make recommendations, although final power would be reserved to the council. Faced with a spreading administrative breakdown, the city government saw the new Board of Public Works as a way of separating administration from obstructive politics, hopefully promoting thereby efficiency in the former and broader vision in the latter. When this and several other changes were formally installed in municipal law by an 1873 revision of the city charter, the new concepts received a somewhat symbolic as well as strictly legal legitimacy.[34]

The more substantive side of this development, paralleling developments in city thinking on the water question, can be seen in the way Springfield was approaching the question of sewers. Here too, one step implied and actually forced the next, for a more general, abstract image of the city had many practical implications. Once water supply came to be seen as not only a matter of fire protection, conceiving of sewers merely as drains to improve property also appeared as an increasingly inadequate approach. Once the commitment to *pure* water had been made, the city physician noted in 1872, the removal of *impure* water became a public responsibility as well. The connection was made even clearer by the dramatic emphasis then being given to sewage problems in the overwhelmingly thorough reports of the state's Board of Health, and in large cities elsewhere in the nation. Once again, there was a crucial concatenation between a problem's emergence in the general culture, and Springfield's arrival at a point in its own development where it was becoming imperative to deal with the same problem.[35]

This altered perspective made itself felt when the new Board of Public Works came to consider the question, securing the services of Phineas Ball, one of the state's most noted sanitary engineers. The system of lateral drains to the river, so comprehensive and modern in 1866, was judged in 1873 to be hopelessly inadequate, even harmful. "With the growth of the city," wrote a later mayor reflecting on these years, "the distance to which lateral drainage could be carried proved altogether insufficient." In addition to the fouling of the entire riverfront by the drain outlets, critics scored the continued dependence on the Town and Garden brooks for drainage through the city's center, brooks which as common sewers "carried corruption and miasma to every door, the receptable for all the worn out tin and earthen ware, hoop skirts, baskets and the like,

together with all dead animals smaller than the horse." When much
of the already meager flow was diverted to the reservoir in the 1872
crisis, the danger of relying on the brooks became even more apparent.[36]

The Board of Public Works and Phineas Ball proposed instead a
huge trunk sewer, large enough for cleaning men to walk through,
which would run north to south, the entire length of the city, "falling continuously from the Chicopee line to the foot of York
Street." It would completely "obliterate" the Town Brook by absorption, and would discharge at only one point on the river, safely
below the city. All major and lateral drains would lead into it, thus
tieing all of Springfield into one complete system. The plan occasioned great controversy, hardly surprising considering its scope,
novelty, and projected expense, and critics raised many arguable
technical objections to it.* The depression set in before a decision
had been reached, putting the matter off for several years.[37] But
perhaps more important than the delay and ultimate modification
of the plan was the drastically altered framework in which it was
even discussed. Not only did the idea represent a far more comprehensive and general approach to sewage and the physical city, but
also a considerably enlarged view of the governmental role in relation to public responsibilities. The community seemed generally to
accept the board's view that "the truest function of a municipal
government is the preservation of the public health, and in no other
way can this object be so effectively accomplished as by an efficient
system of public sewerage." As the city physician had said: "There
are ways of destroying lives quite as effective as shooting. All this
means sanitary reform."[38] What had started, then, as an extension
of traditional public aid for property improvements had begun to
change quite fundamentally into a new type of public service, a
transition with conceptual, administrative, and political implications
for the community that reached far beyond the sewer question itself.

---

*Some experts said that given Springfield's topography, a long sewer could not slope
enough to prevent wastes from settling and decomposing within it. There were also fears
about carrying waste from the entire North End through the heart of the city, even if
many feet underground. The later compromise called for the trunk to start from the Hill
and then branch north and south, following both branches of the old brook, discharging
into the river at two spots removed from the center of the city.

A similar judgment can be made of the other developments — streets, schools, water, and administration. The processes of self-conscious city-building and public institutional change remained generally similar to those observed before 1865, but the pace and scope had been altered quite fundamentally. The two opposing triangles of forces are still relevant in generalizing about the dynamics of this change. The triangle that represented change and progress was strengthened on all sides. "Necessity" as the city grew more complex and interdependent, seemed greater and increasingly manifest; more important, perhaps, the concept of what was necessary changed even more than the objective demands of increasing density and growth. Second, the influence of outside events and experience counted for much more than it had previously. City problems were matters of ascendant interest everywhere, and Springfield's new self-consciousness as part of a broad urban change made the content of this discussion increasingly important in local thinking. Third, the basic perspective and influence of local planning leadership were widened by the adoption of the Board of Water Commissioners, the Board of Public Works, and other administrative innovations.

On the other hand, the triangle of forces that previously restrained those seeking to redefine the scope of public activity had weakened considerably. Widespread consciousness of urban problems, combined with generally sustained faith in prosperity and the city's momentum, reduced fundamental objections to the new ideas and programs being proposed. Given the greater momentum of public activity and general public support, particularistic tangles of conflicting interests offered less obstruction than in previous years. Finally, the handicap of sheer administrative and political inability to make decisions and policy had been greatly relieved.

All the forces at work in these developments had become, in the postwar years, mutually reinforcing to a remarkable degree, with the result that not only did the government's role increase dramatically, but there was also the beginning of a more fundamental transformation in the way Springfield conceived of and conducted its public affairs. Earlier, with the community reducible to the association of taxpayers, public policy had been little more than the intersection and sum of private interests, privately perceived. But underlying all the small steps surveyed in this chapter were several themes which, taken together, suggest the emergence of a new way of seeing the

meaning of government — they suggest the notion of the public
interest, an abstract projection of collective needs and goals not at
all reducible to the sum of constituent private interests.

This broad conception was implicit in the comprehensive scale and
systematic planning of new public improvements; it was somewhat
more explicit in the broadening areas of collective responsibility, as
in schools, sewers, and water supply; it was most directly embodied
in the new administrative concepts. By setting up the new administrative boards, Springfield moved further away from the traditional
faith in government by the amateurs and politicians on the City
Council. Springfield's leaders were beginning to argue, in the more
general terms then gaining rapid favor in the country, for a more
bureaucratic and administrative interpretation of democracy, for
the concept of a public interest that needed to be lifted above the
obscuring particularism of daily politics and that could best serve
the people by paradoxically being occasionally removed from direct
contact with them. In Springfield, then, what would later emerge as
the full-blown Progressive concept of the public interest had its
roots not so much in the more purely political and social power
struggles often noted elsewhere, but rather in the step-by-step responses of those governing the rapidly changing city. Many of these,
pushed forward by the logic of their search for comprehensiveness,
order, and efficiency, were coming to believe that to govern a more
complex urban community required a separation of politics and administration that would at once insure the competence of the latter
and the democracy of the former.

The transformation at this point was hardly complete; much of
the conceptual change was only implied, and attention focused instead on the specific policies involved and their implementation. In
this, much could be and was glossed over. While some traditional
concepts had been visibly changed, others had merely been
stretched and extended to fit the contours of a new environment.
Especially in the critical areas of property improvements, Springfield avoided coming to grips with fundamental questions of public
and private roles; despite administrative improvement and a wider
planning perspective, these and other questions were still approached on an ad hoc basis, with their public meaning remaining
ambiguous. Beyond this, also not well perceived, lay the much

deeper question of what pushing public obligation past property-
related questions did to the fiscal assumptions of a government
based on property, and, in fact, to the social assumptions of a community based on property. In the midst of one debate in 1873, the
Republican gave a hint of these emerging questions by using an argument which could not have been used much earlier:

At the same time, it must be realized that though the mass of the people are
not taxpayers, they also have claim to conisderations which are not to be
measured by the amount of money they contribute to the public treasury.[39]

But if the articulation of the public interest could thus become
more general and abstract, in actuality the concept also became, by
the same token, less tangible and more vulnerable to attack as traditionally enshrined property value came under pressure. This is what
was happening by 1873, when after several years of rapid growth
and enormous spending, another crisis of confidence built up, far
more profound and extensive than the one which had produced the
brief pullback of 1869–1870. A new complex of factors produced
this crisis, of which the depression that began in 1873 was only the
final and most critical element. And just as the postwar period had
changed Springfield culturally as much as materially, so too would
this general depression crisis prove to be not only an economic collapse, but a more profound cultural and intellectual confrontation
with the unresolved implications of community change.

Hesitation and Hard Times, 1870-1880

Part Four

Heartaches and Hard Times, 1576–1590

9. Suspicion, Confusion, and Crisis

America's unleashed economy was generating a truly enormous amount of energy, the direction and control of which gradually became the age's major concern. At first the nation viewed unrestrained growth with unrestrained optimism and confidence. But even before the overheated economy collapsed in panic, hesitation about its direction began to build on many levels. Directed energy, of course, means power, and especially in the worlds of business and politics, the new forms and quantities of power, some falling into unscrupulous hands, bred conflict among groups and increasing concern for the cohesion of the national community. At first subtly, then blatantly, a mood of suspicion, insecurity, and nervousness colored a succession of public issues.

Springfield, busily rounding out more than a decade of breathless growth, proved particularly susceptible to this mood, for reasons which go to the very heart of the way in which the city had been changing. Springfield became increasingly sensitive to national issues and the experience of other cities because its own development raised similar questions; in fact, the two contexts of experience helped crucially to define each other in local eyes. Moreover, the new perspective proved profoundly disturbing because it questioned not only the implications, but also the deepest assumptions and relationships upon which growth had been championed by local leaders. For them, to lose confidence in the momentum and promise of local change was to discover the inherent ambiguity of the quest for the public interest which had been both the vehicle of their substantive leadership and the justification for their community power; it was to sense that their very assumptions had become a threat to themselves in particular and the community more generally. In three areas especially — railroad expansion, local politics, and, of course, the depression itself — Springfield's experience turned its most aggressive boosters and builders into sour, suspicious, and cynical critics of recent change, a process that throws valuable light on the broader meaning of this change itself.

In a burst of exuberant activity, the number of miles of railroad track in America doubled between 1865 and 1873, and the excitement involved far more than dramatic projects like the transcontinental railroad. In cities and all over the country, the drive for new rails, whether small spurs or major trunks, assumed epidemic proportions as one community after another fought the contagious fear of being left behind. The result, Edward C. Kirkland has written, was "a second era of public assistance to railroads so extravagant and so generous that the pre-war years were but a diminutive forerunner." Anxious to realize the seemingly unlimited opportunity beckoning on all sides, "impatient communities fell with a shout upon the possibility of tapping the finances of state, city, or town."[1]

At first, Springfield's response to all this was defensive, for it was well served by existing connections that since 1848 had included major roads north, south, east, and west. These railroads, furthermore, had been diligent in warning off new competition. But after the war, the local perspective on community needs began to change, partly as a result of the growth of the existing roads. After years of squabbling, Springfield's Western Railroad and the Boston & Worcester finally agreed, in 1867, to become the Boston & Albany Railroad, on its formation the wealthiest corporation in Massachusetts. Though Springfield held the main office and the road was tightly controlled by its president, Springfield's Chester W. Chapin who had headed the Western, the B&A soon looked outward, and before 1880 had close ties to the New York Central system. Similar impulses toward consolidated arrangements took Springfield's southern connection, never under local control, even farther away, as the New Haven and Hartford, with Springfield its northern terminus, merged in 1872 into the New York, New Haven, and Hartford, soon one of the East's railroad giants.[2]

These stirrings helped awaken Springfield businessmen to the tremendous ferment, opportunity, and potential threat in new railroad
developments, and they suddenly erased twenty years of compla-
cency by making their city the state's "biggest plunger" in the great
race for more rails and the power they promised.[3] Local enthusiasts
saw three general objectives in such expansion. First, new links to
relatively isolated contiguous areas would bring them within Springfield's economic orbit, while delay would lose them to Hartford or
Worcester. Second, prompt action could place Springfield athwart
the new through routes taking shape, particularly south to Long
Island Sound, enhancing its commercial power enormously. Finally,
new routes would compete with existing railroads, thus insuring
lowest possible rates and extending the competitive advantage of
local business.

Two specific proposals emerged in 1869, each promising to serve
all these ends at once. The first (see p. 182) was for the Springfield
and Farmington Valley Railroad, a route to the southwest intersecting, probably at Tariffville, Connecticut, the old "Canal Railroad"
from New Haven to Northampton. The project would not only tap
a prosperous valley, but would connect with the Connecticut Western Railroad, then a promising through route to the Hudson and the
west; in addition, it would open a second, competing route from
Springfield to New Haven and New York City. The other project, a
new venture to the southeast called the Springfield and Longmeadow Railroad, would similarly offer a variety of advantages
through its connection to other routes at Stafford Springs, Connecticut.[4]

The two companies had little difficulty circulating their stock subscriptions, but required even more aid and turned to the city, obtaining charters that permitted Springfield to invest in each up to
1½ percent of the city valuation, and to guarantee a portion of railroad bonds as well. The total possible municipal investment could
reach $1 million under these terms, with $600,000 of it in common
stock, and thus the required referendum, by which the city accepted
the charters and gave the council authority to invest, was of very
great consequence. "Never," urged the *Republican*, had Springfield
faced a question "fraught with so important consequences as this
will be," for the new rails would fix whether Springfield "shall con-

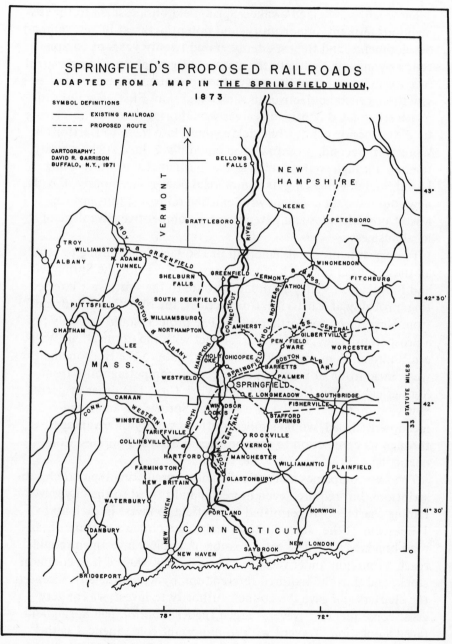

Railroad lines, Springfield, 1873

tinue to be a pleasant suburban city or become a great inland business center," while failure to grasp the opportunity would "give notice to Hartford, Northampton, and Holyoke that she gives up the race for supremacy." In this instance the newspaper unquestionably spoke for the community, for in an unusually heavy turnout for a special election, seven eighths of the voters endorsed the plan. It was striking evidence of the continued importance of what Carter Goodrich has called the "spirit of improvement" in American economic development, the degree to which "public and private roles were almost always thought of as cooperative rather than competitive." This cooperation had always assumed the primacy of general economic growth as a community goal; now, the new scale of growth and the regional role to which Springfield aspired made extensive new railroad development seem that much more a public imperative.[5]

But the enthusiasm and momentum began to fade almost from the moment of the referendum's triumph. Getting the railroads built proved to be difficult — in the Farmington case ultimately impossible — because the roads crossed state lines and opposition both from and within the Connecticut legislature, particularly from Hartford interests, succeeded in repeatedly stalling and frustrating final approval and construction. Springfield, fortunately, had refrained from actually buying the authorized stock in anticipation of such problems. But though it thus lost no money, the cost in community momentum and confidence was considerable; three years after the excited discussion and public commitment, Springfield had nothing but frustrated dreams to show for its effort.[6]

This frustration had the additional and more profound effect of making many in Springfield that much more sensitive to the general economic and moral problems that the surge of public assistance to railroads was raising elsewhere in the state. Massachusetts was rapidly finding that the old concepts governing public assistance to private corporations could not be that easily fitted to the contours of the railroad age, where the corporations and the interests behind them were often much more powerful than the public bodies to whom they were supplicant. The sudden revival of large-scale public involvement in corporation affairs produced many confusions and conflicts, in which public aims and private power became hopelessly entangled.[7] In the General Court of Massachusetts, the play of private pressures, of course, was nothing new — getting a corporation charter had long been a matter of "At the worst . . . corruption, at best unprincipled log-rolling." But the proposed huge doses of state money for railroad projects with complex regional implications made this old game far more serious, and its results of immediate interest to local communities facing parallel questions.[8]

Two major questions in particular obsessed the legislature in these years and both, significantly, were of more than indirect importance to Springfield. The first was the perennial Hoosac Tunnel issue, the matter of state aid for the "Great Bore" through Hoosac Mountain that was to open a vital alternate route across northern Massachusetts to the west. From the start, Springfield had been deeply involved in fighting the project, one that would parallel its own east-west route, but opposition involved more than just particularism, especially as time went on. State construction, attempted from 1862 to 1868, was thoroughly bungled and the entire Hoosac story became one of "inertia, false starts, and incompetence." Furthermore, the controversial matter of a flat $5 million grant in 1868 to private contractors to finish the job coincided with the notorious Fisk-Vanderbilt "Erie War," in the shadow of which all railroad dealings tended to seem somewhat sordid.[9] The second question, aid to the fledgling Boston, Hartford, and Erie Railroad, reinforced this mood even more clearly. Here too Springfield businessmen had their own reasons for fighting the project, which envisioned a new major western route across southern New England, but they were soon joined by more general public sentiment when the road fell into the hands of Jay Gould and the Erie Ring. The road squandered millions of dollars in successive state grants, obtained through powerful lobbying despite a rising outcry, until the governor vetoed a final appropriation in 1870, declaring that Massachusetts could no longer "be disgraced by silent acquiescence in the course of deception, peculation, and fraud practiced by the company." The issue had a sustained impact on public opinion throughout the state, but especially in Springfield where the *Republican*, its voice as an independent anticorruption journal becoming more defined, reprinted in full the official debates and reports outlining the road's manipulation of public funds and its inordinate power in the General Court itself.[10]

Profound doubts about the protectability of the public interest when dealing with powerful corporations were thus generally on the rise as Springfield struggled with its own frustrated commitment to railroad expansion. Suddenly, a new turn of events threw much of this into sharp relief. The Athol & Enfield, a new Massachusetts railroad linking the Vermont Central to the new through route to New London, requested local aid for an extension of its tracks to Springfield.[11] Though similar in its goals to the other plans, this proposal produced not enthusiastic approval, but rather an intensely bitter conflict, dramatically revealing the reciprocal and mutually reinforcing relationship between local interests, and deepening the disillusion with public policy both locally and generally.

The Athol road was the personal project of a local businessman named Willis Phelps, soon to be called the city's greatest benefactor by some, and its Boss Tweed by others. Whatever else may have been involved, Phelps did not represent the brash young challenger to an entrenched old guard so often pictured. At the time, he was sixty-five and had been in Springfield since his teens, when he and Chester Chapin shared a garret while employed as wagoners at the river piers. He made his fortune building railroads throughout New England and as far away as Kansas, and over the previous thirty years he had held many public offices and had been active in the Methodist Church and civic organizations of various kinds. But the solid citizen had his enemies: identified with Hill interests tied to the Democracy, he had often clashed with the Court Square establishment, and his blunt and aggressive personality kept old animosities alive.[12]

Phelps's new project represented something of a direct threat to local railroaders, in particular Daniel Harris and Chester W. Chapin. But in the increasingly suspicious atmosphere, a number of other factors helped account for the mixed reaction his proposal received. The existing stretch of the Athol road could not, the State Railroad Commission had found, "be said to be either well or thoroughly built, nor could it sustain any considerable traffic and continue safe." Second, questions surrounding the route seemed to involve a more than usual number of speculative windfalls, and even the *Union*, a staunch supporter, acknowledged that there was "more than one cat in the meal." Finally, Phelps produced a quick storm of controversy by the methods he employed in getting a charter from the legislature, by the terms of the seemingly binding referendum it provided for, without recourse to the city government, and by the amount of the grant itself, described by critics as three times what the sixteen-mile link should cost. The *Republican*, early on, termed the entire proposal a "transparent job, impudently lobbied," and it was not alone in this feeling.[13]

But the bulk of the community, at this time, did not see it this way, for the long-frustrated desire for new rails was too strong to be denied by the sudden trepidations of previous boosters. In the spring of 1872, well over the required three fifths approved the subscription in a referendum, and after the government voted the $300,000 the new link was swiftly constructed. It was opened by the end of 1873, renamed the Springfield, Athol, and Northeastern, the first addition to the city's rails in twenty years.[14] The fact that many called the opposition to Phelps merely a defense of existing interests masquerading as concern for the public virtue only made defeated foes that much more embittered and sensitive; when Phelps came forward with another plan for public support in 1873, they immediately joined in battle. Among Willis Phelps's many hats was the presidency of the Springfield and Longmeadow Railroad, the southeast extension so enthusiastically and generally endorsed in 1869. Now, with the Athol road breaking the logjam, Phelps requested that the long-delayed stock subscription be made, promising that this action and some minor route changes would win speedy cooperation from Connecticut.[15]

While no one questioned the general aims of the plan, the city government was increasingly hesitant about the details. Many felt the route had been plotted more for quick profit than effective service, that it hardly required the $150,000 requested, that it was a shaky speculation furthered by questionable practices, and that a Connecticut veto was still likely. Its friends argued that Phelps had proved that he could deliver railroads for Springfield where others had made only promises; the road enjoyed in addition substantial support from Hill interests, since the proposed route ran past the Armory area on its way to the downtown depot, thus offering the first direct rail service to the southern and eastern portions of the city. After much discussion, the city council finally denied Phelps's petition, an action which, far from closing the question, precipitated a savage debate that raged through the summer and fall of 1873 in the press, the council, the legislature, and on the streets, finally becoming the dominant question in the December local elections.[16]

The hostilities of the Athol dealings and the general anxiety fueled by the economic panic that had begun in September were all culminating in this fight over the Longmeadow Railroad. Then, just before the election, an unruly caucus blocked the expected mayoral nomination on a nonpartisan slate of the popular James Thompson, reputedly because of his opposition to the road. Phelps was reliably reported to have directed the move, and was quoted as saying "You can't have him. You can't have anyone who is opposed to the road." This was the final straw for the *Republican*, and Samuel Bowles lashed out with an editorial unprecedented even in the paper's long history of uninhibited polemics. "TWEEDISM IN SPRINGFIELD" screamed the headline, followed by text no less inflammatory, concluding:

Mr. Willis Phelps is the Boss Tweed of Springfield. He openly bids for a city "job"; he goes to the Legislature and lobbies through a bill . . . with the help of votes he buys, he openly carries an election. As contractor, he says how much he will take for the job, as the city he gives it to himself. Every dollar which the city through indifference or corruption permits to pass under this all-covering thumb is an incitement to new demands, a temptation to new crimes, and the very measure of their consummation.

A few days later, Bowles was even blunter:

Mr. Phelps proved himself in the Athol transaction a public robber and a public corrupter, and he is now repeating the exhibition in the most audacious and flagrant manner. Having spoiled the city of $200,000 he is now using that money to despoil her of another sum nearly as large.[17]

Phelps matched the figure with a $200,000 libel suit, removing the charge from public view until it later came to trial, and leaving the Longmeadow issue in center stage. That few shared Bowles's indignation became clear when the voters returned a council favorable to the railroad; but that more shared his suspicion of the plan was illustrated by the continued vitality of debate throughout

1874.* Finally, however, reassured by a new state law clarifying procedure for such municipal subscriptions, both the council and a public referendum approved the $150,000 investment. The *Republican* could only grumble about jobbery and public irresponsibility, for the community still clearly wanted more railroads and was willing, as the *Union* argued, to give Phelps an admittedly excessive profit in order to get them. And once again, he produced results. By early 1876 the renamed Springfield and New London was in operation, the city's second and last accomplishment of this railroad era.[18]

Lest anyone forget what the fuss had been about, Phelps's libel suit came to court just as the last thorny details of the new road's opening were being worked out, and it completely captured public attention for weeks. The presence of the famous Richard H. Dana as chief counsel for his friend Bowles, together with the growing general interest in questions of railroad politics, shady and otherwise, created nationwide interest in the case. Bowles based his defense not only on the general privilege of the press, but on the specific truth of his charges, a tactic making for dramatic testimony. He strenuously sought to prove that Phelps had betrayed the democratic process at every step. A supposedly packed caucus had sent his son John to the legislature in 1872 to push through the Athol bill, the referendum for which the family then managed to carry at home. Then, it was alleged, another controlled caucus sent another son, Henry, to the legislature to get another bill for the Longmeadow road; when this failed Willis Phelps turned to dumping Colonel Thompson and rigging the 1873 city election. To support all these allegations, Bowles and Dana produced a succession of local politicians and ward workers whose colorful testimony offers a sharp picture of political practices in the period. Though there was little solid evidence of outright bribery, Bowles made a good case that an enormous amount of questionable lobbying, caucus packing,

---

*Bowles's wrath was not confined to such public forums, nor to polite points. In 1874 he wrote to the president of Amherst College, as one of its trustees, protesting the awarding of an honorary degree to Phelps's son, John. "Had I been present when the name was suggested," said Bowles, "I should have felt obligated to say that he was not fit for the honor of Amherst. He is a notorious liar; he is a vulgar, coarse, brutal fellow, a corrupter and a briber of voters; he has been treated by his family physician for venereal disease since he was a married man." Samuel Bowles to (illegible), n.d. but sometime in 1874, Bowles Papers, Box II, Yale University Library.

Samuel Bowles   Chester W. Chapin

Willis Phelps   Daniel L. Harris

and general power politics had been employed in obtaining official and popular sanction.[19]

The judge's decision was somewhat ambiguous: Phelps was awarded a token $100 because Bowles had not proved that further plans to "despoil" the city had been afoot, as charged. However, Phelps's dealings were termed "improper, illegitimate, and corrupting," which is what Bowles had sought to demonstrate. For the most part, this all was taken as a victory for the *Republican*. As one of Bowles's close friends wrote, hardly able to contain himself on hearing the news: "Good Enough! The victory is yours in everything but the skin of a technicality. Old Phelps would sooner have taken one hundred hot burning coals on the top of his pate than that award of $100 . . . God save the Springfield *Republican*! Bully for you, Sam Bowles!" To others, however, the token award represented a moral victory, and the *Union* pronounced Phelps vindicated as "an honest man, honorable in every public and private relation, as he has always appeared."[20] Beyond all this, the real meaning of the trial lies in the fact that both sides, in a sense, did not disagree about what Phelps had or had not done, but only about the meaning and culpability of his acts. The trial's revelations exposed only the political facts of life, and opinion divided as to how reprehensible was this type of behavior. The fact that Phelps remained influential, even running well as a candidate for mayor in 1876 and state senator in 1878, shows that most of the community did not find it very much so; in any event, the ends more than justified the means, as the two new railroads seemed to prove.

This very fact, however, renders the position of Phelps's enemies more significant than their relative isolation might indicate. Precisely because the community had broken with the reformers when Phelps proved able to deliver the goods everyone so much wanted, as these results themselves became cruelly disappointing, public opinion became equally if not as dramatically sour. It did not take long for this to happen. The Athol road was a dismal and almost immediate failure, and its physical and financial condition rivaled each other in shoddiness; when the financial structure proved the weakest, the city's stock was foreclosed in the interest of the bondholders, which meant Phelps, exactly as critics had originally predicted. Weak and faltering, the road fell into the hands of the

B&A, with which it was supposed to have competed. Phelps's Long-meadow road fared only slightly better, for the through routes it joined never amounted to much, and it too was soon controlled by those it had promised to rival. And as these dreams were evaporating, the censure of Chester Chapin for his part in a minor stock manipulation seemed to confirm that the once bright promise of local railroading had become as sordid and depressing as so many other aspects of life in the increasingly gloomy 1870's.[21]

However one evaluates the motives and impulses that first turned Bowles and other railroad boosters against the notion of continued public subsidy of expansion, their opposition thus proved to be a harbinger of more general attitudes in the community, as more and more people came to feel a similar suspicion, disillusion, and frustration at failing to harness private power for the general community interest. Not only did the city have very little to show for its $500,000 investment, but the loss on years of invested energy, commitment, and spirit was proving to be even more substantial.

Similar forces were at work in the political sphere, reflecting and generating a considerably darker view of community affairs. In this, the backdrop of state politics figured significantly. Massachusetts politics in the 1870's approached a state of total chaos, as the Republican party's wartime stranglehold gradually loosened and finally disappeared. Almost every volatile aspect of this situation found representation in the remarkable person of Benjamin F. Butler, notorious Civil War general and the fulcrum of Massachusetts political life in the next decade. From his seat in Congress and in successive runs for the governor's chair, Butler brought to Massachusetts a new type of personal political machine, a state-wide network of carefully controlled local organizations fueled with generous doses of patronage, and a new type of political approach. Openly contemptuous of the "respectables," he appealed directly to the workingmen, the Irish, and the veterans, and won their loyal support. It is hard to say what about Butler most offended nearly all traditional leaders – his radicalism on reconstruction, labor reform, and soft currency, or his outrageous glee in sneering at the polite politics of the gentlemen, but in any event he came to inspire in such circles a most passionate hatred.[22]

After his humiliating defeat of the proud Richard H. Dana in
1868, and a rapprochement with President Grant giving him enormous patronage power, Butler came to be viewed as not only a contamination, but a real threat.[23] When he moved for the gubernatorial nomination in 1871, "Butlerism" became a statewide issue with
important ramifications in Springfield. Here, the local caucus for
delegates to the nominating convention was overwhelmed by Butlerites, commanded by the General in person, who won a stunning
two-to-one victory in the raucus session. Though the state convention turned down Butler's bid after a fierce battle, which the *Republican* termed "the most brilliant victory ever gained over
corruption and political harlotry," his local victory had deeply stirred Springfield politics. The *Union* exulted that the "ring" controlled by Bowles and his friends had been shattered, but even they
were somewhat uneasy on discovering that Butlerites controlled the
city's Republican committee, incongrously allied with prohibitionist
stalwarts. Whatever side one took, all could see that new forces were
at work in local affairs.[24]

For some, the events helped precipitate a drastic decision. Deeply
disillusioned with the quality of public life and policy under President Grant, Samuel Bowles finally decided that the Republican
party itself was past saving, and he joined with other state figures
like Dana, F. W. Bird, and Lyman Trumbull in abandoning it in
favor of the Liberal Republican bolters gathering around Carl
Schurz of Missouri.[25] The decision was a very difficult one for
Bowles, but once it was made he committed himself forcefully to
the effort and played an active role in the 1872 presidential campaign mounted by the new party. At its Cincinnati convention he
and three other powerful editors became known as the "Quadri-
lateral" for their strenuous efforts to keep the movement true to its
reform purposes.[26]

Few in Springfield were ready to go quite this far, and the cru-
sading *Republican* found itself isolated as never before: during the
exciting Grant-Greely race, many people cancelled subscriptions,
postmasters refused to deliver the apostate journal, and when
Bowles dissolved a twenty-year partnership with publisher Clark W.
Bryan, for business reasons, the latter took several of the office
staff, bought the floundering *Union*, and turned it into an immedi-

ately popular spokesman for Grant and the G.O.P. The election it-self confirmed the pessimism Bowles had masked behind his vigor-ous editorial campaign, for Grant's 70 percent of the statewide vote equaled his 1868 support, and in Springfield he did almost as well, solidly carrying every ward. Other Liberals fared no better than the hapless Greely.[27]

Subsequent events however, as with the railroad question, showed Bowles to have accurately presaged the drift of community opinion in the spirit if not the letter of his protest. In 1873 Butler made an-other try for the gubernatorial nomination. The script was almost exactly the same, especially in Springfield where the Butlerites again captured the local caucus before being defeated at the state conven-tion, but the fighting was considerably more bitter this time around, for opposition to Butler had spread widely among loyal Republicans who had held no sympathy for the aristocratic renegades of 1872.[28] Moreover, the sweet victory could not hide the fact that the fabric of state politics was continuing to disintegrate. Massachusetts saw some free-swinging battles when both of the state's seats in the United States Senate fell open upon the successive deaths of Henry Wilson and Charles Sumner. The temperance issue, reaching one of its periodic climaxes in 1874, completed the chaos.

Most Republicans had supported substitution of a strict license law for prohibition, and they were stunned when their leader, Governor Talbot, vetoed just such a bill. When the prohibitionist minority secured his renomination by a timely bargain with the Butlerites, matters came to a head. The triumph of this small fac-tion together with the Grant administration's daily more sordid ap-pearance made the reformers' old charges seem more substantial. With disaffection rising and the state election pictured as "a battle royal between the Machine and the People," the Republicans found themselves defeated for the first time in twenty years, and as a measure of vindication for the "respectables," Butler lost his con-gressional seat in the same election.[29] This "Democratic Revolution of 1874" signaled the end of coherent party lines for several years: poor Massachusetts soon boasted Regular Republicans, Independent (Butler) Republicans, Greenback/Butler Democrats, Regular (Anti-Butler Brahmin) Democrats, Independent Greenbackers, Prohibi-tionists, and Labor Reformers. Butler himself spent the next years in a gradual swing to the Democracy that would make him governor at last in 1882, while his enemies took advantage of the same fluidity, urging the perennial man of public virtue, Charles Francis Adams, upon whatever party would honor itself by taking him; the *Republican* argued that "the nearer the two parties come to resemble each other at the foot, the more probable and easier becomes an inverse exchange of qualities at the head."[30]

In this context, the reform outcry against corruption, machine politics, and politicians in general struck a more responsive chord than it had in 1872, exemplified in Springfield by an important race for Congress in that election of 1874. The Democrats nominated Chester Chapin and the Republicans Henry Alexander, a former mayor and the city's most experienced politician, who had apparently engineered his own nomination through adroit caucus management and secret deals. To his enemies, Alexander had always seemed a puller of strings; in the atmosphere of 1874 this became a more widespread impression, putting Samuel Bowles to a critical test: Alexander was not only a longtime friend and political ally, but also his brother-in-law. In a moving letter the editor sought to convince Alexander not to run, warning him that though "it would be the great personal grief of my life to be the instrument of this . . . the *Republican* will be obliged to oppose you openly and vigorously." Bowles was true to his word, and the paper abandoned Alexander dramatically: "Behind Mr. Alexander are the worst practices and the worst tendencies in local politics – the professionals, the vote-mongers, the rings, and the jobs. The defeat of Henry Alexander will be the best day's work for the cause of political reform, honest caucuses, and clean nominations." This time, the public heartily endorsed the *Republican*'s rejection of the Republicans: the *Union* seconded Bowles, the revolt spread throughout the district, and the voters sent the well-respected Chapin to Congress by a wide margin.[31]

A further aspect of this political turmoil helps to explain the changing tone of community politics; related to the crisis of issues and politicians at the top was a new thrust from the bottom. The new political atmosphere inspired the foreigners in Springfield – that is to say, the Irish – to take the first steps down the road to power. The immigrant vote, assiduously courted with favors, had long been an important factor in local elections. But in the Springfield of the 1870's, the Irish began to demand not only a larger share of the political pie, but a larger role in its cutting. This was done by an impressive effort to increase the number of Irish voters, a powerless minority's prime resource. In 1873 Irish leaders formed the Jackson Naturalization Club, soon the center of their political influence. The club identified and assisted qualified aliens in becoming citizens, often paying their poll taxes; by 1875 it claimed to have tripled the Irish vote, a claim that official figures suggest was not exaggerated. Between 1865 and 1875, statistics show, with every other contemporary source indicating that change began really in 1872 or so, Springfield's foreign-born electorate grew by 200 percent, from 441 to 1,307, or from 9 percent to 19 percent of the total electorate, not far below the foreigners' 25 percent share of the population. Where only 20 percent of immigrant males could vote in 1865, 35 percent were enfranchised in 1875. And within these figures, there could be no doubt which ethnic groups were the agents of change – in Springfield as throughout Massachusetts, only the Irish had more voting-age males naturalized than not, surpassing even the English and Scots in this respect. Although only 60 percent of the eligible immigrants, the Irish accounted for over 70 percent of Springfield's naturalized voters.[32]

Standing on this base, the Irish rallied behind their own leaders and began to demand power within the Democratic party. These leaders ranged from the respectable – Hugh Donnelly, a young lawyer and war veteran who had been valedictorian at Springfield High School – to men more closely fitting the period's stereotyped image of Irish politicians, such as James O'Keefe, president of the Jackson Club who proclaimed the new era in a slugfest with a party chief at an 1874 caucus, or Philip J. Ryan, who operated a Catholic bookshop and emigration agency, or "Dave" Power, the epitome of the tough, brawling, efficient ward organizer.[33] The Butler excitement fueled their efforts, and caucuses became frequently embroiled in their challenges of checklists, chairing, and vote counting; by the close of the decade, the Irish generally controlled almost half the seats on Springfield's Democratic City Committee.*[34]

The Irish influence at this point should not, however, be over-emphasized, for their real drive for power did not come until the 1880's. At this time, insurgent activity was a function of the state-wide disintegration of party discipline, and of the issues surrounding Butler's forays in state politics, rather than a developed response to community change in Springfield. Even after the Democratic sweep of 1874, when Hugh Donnelly was elected alderman and three other Irishmen chosen for the Common Council, the new challenge did not visibly affect the issues, the discussion, and the conduct of local government as it later would. But it was a harbinger of change, and the implied potential shook the traditional leadership. Where the railroad issues had convinced many that the community was being victimized by greedy exploiters and by its own ambition, political disorganization at both the top and bottom raised the more ominous specter that government itself was losing its traditional identification with the respectable, responsible, tax-paying portion of society.

This vision was all the more frightening in presenting itself at a time when these very people had been busy extending the power and role of their government, secure in the assumption that their particular perceptions of the public interest found general acceptance in the community they believed themselves to embody. A challenge to their control thus implied a challenge to these assumptions, and the political turmoil of the 1870's, by suggesting that political power might be turned against them and the community by those less responsible, made them fearful and suspicious of the public role they had championed. Values, policies, and aims both past and present were, in this and other ways, coming to be seen in a new light; with this process well under way, economic depression provided the final pressure necessary to create a genuine and explicit crisis in the community.

*The old Democratic leadership at first attempted to head off this surge by offering the Irish greater representation on the ticket, running, for instance, Springfield's foremost Catholic, P. T. O'Reilly, bishop of the diocese, as a candidate for School Committee in 1871. The ploy was unsuccessful, and, interestingly, the attempt to secure Irish votes occasioned more comment at the time than the fact of such a high prelate running for an office concerned with public schools.

When panic dramatically shattered the nation's financial equilibrium in September 1873, few in Springfield, as elsewhere, grasped how prolonged and acute an economic setback had been initiated, though most expected some sort of commercial and industrial slowdown to follow. The first months seemed to confirm expectations that the panic had set off only a transient "slow fever." Money became tighter, some employers missed payrolls, a few workers were laid off, and trade dulled, but the problems seemed less serious than elsewhere, and local bankers decided, as a group, to keep their doors open in a show of confidence. Both local papers saw inflated currency as the "grand underlying cause" of the trouble, and demanded an immediate return to gold specie, but there was little sense of urgency in their appeals; everyone expected that spring would revive the chastened and hopefully enlightened economy.[35]

The situation was a good bit more complex. Massive national overinvestment in railroads had triggered the crisis, which then thrived on generally flooded consumer markets and overproduction. It set in motion the spiral of shaky credit, surplus goods, reduced demand, crushing debt, and stagnation that is the now familiar pattern of major recessions. Early in 1874 the *Republican* observed with surprise that there had "not been as yet the first sign of the usual spring trade, but [rather] a halting hand-to-mouth policy characterizing all business transactions." In July, it noted "Here is our midsummer, and the business activity which we were to witness eludes us again." By the first anniversary of the crash, people had begun to realize that far from being simply elusive, the expected vitality had fallen victim to a serious and general prostration. While the situation never became, in Springfield or elsewhere, particularly desperate, the depression made up in tenacity what it lacked in force, breeding a frustration which became increasingly pronounced as the economy undramatically settled into a seemingly unending torpor. Despite occasional and deceptive remissions, the depression was to hobble Springfield, and the nation, almost until 1879. Instead of being struck down by the sort of blow it had feared and expected since the Civil War, Springfield found itself caught in a slowly tightening vice, and the pressure helped to make explicit the anxieties, questions, and conflicts that prosperity had obscured.[36]

The depression did not hurt all sectors of the economy evenly or simultaneously. Heavy industry felt the strain first: mills slowed to a crawl, railroad and other machine production was hard hit. The Armory work was cut back in stages, until in 1877 an observer described the plant as being in a state of "perpetual sabbath." For most large manufacturers, however, the worst had passed by 1874 or 1875 as they adjusted to the new conditions, while an opposite pattern characterized smaller businesses and manufacturing. Able to absorb the initial shock due to their size and diversity, they found this advantage becoming a handicap; the cumulative pressure of one dull season after another began to take its toll of small businesses operating close to the margin. Hampden County saw thirty-four failures in 1875, seventy-eight in 1877, and twenty-nine in just the first two months of 1878, the peak of the epidemic; some called "the bankruptcy business the only brisk trade" in Springfield. Many other firms, in addition, were forced out of business though managing to avoid actual bankruptcy, and the embarrassing failure of so many local people, including prominent, conservative businessmen like D. H. Brigham underscored the situation's gravity for those less directly threatened.[37]

Declining property values made the final years of the slump especially gloomy. At the start, builders and speculators had taken advantage of falling prices and put what available capital there was into land; property values continued to rise, hitting a $31 million peak in 1875. But this could not last, and the inevitable fall should not have been as surprising as it apparently was. In the winter of 1875, one of the city's leading real estate dealers, auctioning off choice properties to unload his debts, found he could get only $200,000 for land previously valued at well over $300,000. Another auction in 1876 saw property earlier rated at $160,000 and then "realistically" reappraised at the depression level of $120,000 bring only $85,000 when offered for sale. Main Street became dotted with empty stores whose tenants could not meet steep rents even as reduced by desperate landlords, and the situation was not much better elsewhere in the city. By 1878, property value had sunk to $23 million, the lowest point since 1870 and a clear sign, in a society where rising valuation was held to be synonomous with community health, of real trouble.[38]

Jobs and income were of more immediate concern to most people, of course, and the picture here also varied through the depression. The worst unemployment seemed to have come early on, when the larger plants and the Armory laid off hundreds and the completion of city public works begun earlier released many more into the labor market. In addition, young men from hard-hit country towns continued to stream into Springfield, hoping that the city still meant work, as it had for years. At one point in 1874, it was reported, a grocer's ad for a wagon man brought 112 applications. Conditions provoked protest in 1876, when several hundred workingmen jammed City Hall to demand more job-creating public projects. It was a strange meeting, in which the men were supported by prominent community figures like Reverend M. C. Stebbins, and scolded by Irish leader "Dave" Power, who was driven from the platform when he urged the jobless to go back to the farms they had come from. A delegation, mostly Irish, met with the mayor, and the council set up a special committee to study unemployment. Little apparently came of this, but in any event the situation eased substantially by the fall, and reduced hours and wages became more of a problem for workingmen than lack of jobs. Good statistics are scanty, but all indications are that wages fell sharply, far more so than prices. Between 1875 and 1877 alone, for instance, wages dropped more than 15 percent, which gives some idea of how substantial the decline for the entire depression must have been.[39]

For all this, however, it cannot be said that the prolonged depression created substantial social distress in Springfield. As Robert Wiebe has said of the national situation, it was the country's longest depression, but "in human terms it proved one of the mildest." It was more a business depression than anything else, and its main effect was to interrupt the rhythm of business activity and the community growth so dependent on it. "In a nation geared to promotion and expansion," Wiebe noted, "stagnant years had traditionally carried a special frustration," and the observation holds particularly true in explaining the meaning of the depression in cities like Springfield.[40] Before the first hints of revival in 1878, the city had been brought to a near standstill in terms of the sustained growth so much a source of local pride and energy in the postwar years. As shown by the mute but dramatic statistics of the 1880 census, the population had increased by only 25 percent in the decade, to 33,340, and by only 7.4 percent since 1875, more than a halving of the previous ten year's rate and only one sixth the increase of the five-year war period. The growth rate was now no greater than that for all of Massachusetts, suggesting that emigration to Springfield had become negligible. And for the first time, not only the percentage but also the absolute number of foreign-born dropped, from 7,713, or 25 percent in 1875 to 7,533, 22.3 percent in 1880. Most of this decline came in wards one, two, and three, working-class areas with many boarding houses and less permanent households, and most of it was registered among the Irish; perhaps many took Dave Power's advice after all. One final statistic confirms this picture of a city grinding to a halt — the number of dwellings in Springfield increased between 1875 and 1880 by only thirty-six, an insignificant rise of under 1 percent, a particularly revealing figure in a community even then beginning to advertise itself as the "City of Homes."[41]

Such a downturn would have been traumatic at almost any point in time, but it was particularly so for occurring at what must have seemed the worst possible moment. Springfield had recently committed itself to the most expensive and extensive public projects in its history — the railroads, the water works, the trunk sewers — little realizing that the rising slope of prosperity was about to become a precipice. As the first tremors of the depression shook the community, local leaders began to grasp the fact that no matter how bad the situation might become, they could not avoid massive spending and rising debt in the next few years because of these commitments. Though the large projects provided something of a cushion in insured jobs for workingmen and contracts for builders, for a community almost obsessed with traditional notions of fiscal integrity, the specter of soaring debts and municipal bankruptcy precluded much sense of consolation. And the debt did increase, from $1.1 to over $2 million between 1873 and 1875, sums whose frightening meaning can be appreciated when it is remembered that $400,000 had seemed extravagant and unbearable only five years earlier. A feeling of deep frustration and helplessness resulted, making every day of the deepening depression seem that much darker.[42]

As with the collapse of railroad visions and the growing turbulence of local and state politics, the economic collapse produced — at first for those in leadership roles and then more generally — a feeling that community affairs had slipped dangerously out of control. In each of these instances, there seemed to be vivid local counterparts for the villains, scandals, corruption, collapse, and general peril so dramatically visible in American national and urban life in the crisis years, a congruence that fueled and partially explains the mood of sharp bitterness and cynical disillusion that grew in Springfield. But there was more substance to the emergent crisis in local life. The community shared a growing feeling of victimization, but was unclear and divided, from group to group and from issue to issue, as to the nature of the problem — whether Springfield was falling prey to predatory outside corporations, political bosses, Irish or establishment, general economic forces, or the extravagance of its own ambition and that of its leaders. More and more, however, these questions took explicit form in a re-examination of local governmental affairs. To assimilate growth and promote progress, it has been shown earlier, the role, scope, and rationale of public affairs had undergone substantial transformation. With growth and progress now stilled, the confused community turned to this transformation with grave criticism and misgivings, seeking to understand the problems it seemed to have produced.

10. A Disturbing Self-Examination

Throughout the country, matters of currency, debt, and spending regularly functioned as vehicles for public anxiety about the direction American society seemed to be taking; it is not surprising that so much of Springfield's response to its own problems also focused on fiscal aspects of local affairs. Just as the national crisis was often apocalyptically pictured as retribution for corruption and profligacy in both public and private life, the retrenchment that became the theme of Springfield's public life assumed some of the aspects of a religious crusade. Like the depression itself, this response developed slowly but inexorably.[1]

At the end of 1873, sensing the chaos at hand and concerned about rising debt, a large number of citizens led by the editors of the *Union* mounted an unusual nonpartisan drive to draft Samuel Bowles for mayor, believing, as they said, "that party politics should not have a continuing influence in our municipal elections and desiring a vigorous, intelligent, purely economical administration of city affairs." Despite wide encouragement locally and throughout New England, Bowles declined the offer and the next choice, Colonel James Thompson, backed down in the Willis Phelps incident. This produced a partisan campaign even more free-swinging than usual, turning largely on the railroad issue and personal pique, at the end of which Springfield voted out its Republican government and elected the entire Democratic slate, headed by John M. Stebbins, an established lawyer.[2]

On taking office, Stebbins acknowledged the broader concern that had animated the Bowles draft effort, declaring resolutely that "the times and the people call for retrenchment, and for decisive and continued action in that direction." But his efforts proved to be sporadic and ineffective, especially so considering the expensive on-going projects to which the city had previously become committed, and it seemed that public pressure for economy was also fading in the face of this momentum. This made the 1874 election that much more significant, for the voters surprisingly and decisively rejected Stebbins's bid for the customary second term and elected Emerson Wight, who had promised a vigorous fiscal retrenchment. That this Republican victory followed by only a month the "Democratic Revolution" that had swept Springfield and all of Massachusetts made all the clearer the community mandate for fiscal reform and conservatism — taken, in this context, to be almost synonymous.[3]

Wight had been in Springfield since 1840, and had been active in civic affairs while making a fortune in lumber, building, and real estate, including the downtown workshop blocks. In a youthful rail-road accident he had lost both legs at the knee, but as with other public men before and since, the handicap became something of an advantageous political symbol. Thus his wooden legs were often re-ferred to in his campaigns as the literal mark of a man who could be relied on to "put his foot down" loudly and unflinchingly. Wight left no doubt as to how solidly he stood on his principles, and his inaugural address provided the opening sermon in his retrenchment crusade:

In the last fifteen years the tendency of states, counties, municipalities, and individuals has been STRONG and SWIFT toward EXTRAVAGANT expendi-tures, and undue confidence in a continuing prosperity to meet the outlays of the present . . . Springfield's leaders acted in accordance with the wishes of a constituency which felt RICH and expected to be infinitely RICHER. But we are no longer living in the gushing season of an UNNATURAL and UNEX-AMPLED prosperity, and our official lot has fallen upon a time of REACTION . . . Whenever retrenchment is practical, it MUST BE MADE. The city must live within its INCOME. I would not spend a dollar which we are not prepared to raise by immediate taxation. A short corner in our career MUST BE TURNED. The period of inflation has passed. The DAY OF RECKONING is at hand.[4]

Both newspapers hailed the new administration as the "front of a local revolution," and something of the excitement Wight's call aroused is indicated by an unusual petition, signed by several hundred businessmen and citizens, urging the City Council to follow his lead. This it was to do, and with enthusiastic support Wight was to carry his message through a second, third, and even as the spirit faded, an unprecedented fourth term.[5]

Behind Wight through most of this time stood another figure, who proved to be an even more powerful driving force in the retrenchment campaign. This was former mayor Daniel Harris, who had returned to government with Wight and served on the Common Council until poor health forced his retirement in 1878. Having seized on the cause of retrenchment with almost fanatic intensity, Harris embodied at every meeting the belief that only total frugality could save Springfield from bankruptcy and ruination. This was a position not without its irony, since Harris had been turned out of office in 1860 for spending too audaciously on public projects. Nevertheless, he nostalgically contrasted his administration with subsequent developments, pointing at "the plain fire companies now superseded by grand and costly fire departments with showy equipment," "the poor housed and fed in hotel style," and the old-fashioned schoolhouses replaced by "costly palaces, with their four stories, lofty staircases, and salaried janitors." Harris's abrasive, forbidding personality eventually helped tire the public of retrenchment and reform, and even at the campaign's height, it often proved hard to take seriously what the *Union* once called "his wild dream of restoration of affairs to the rural basis of 1860."[6]

But the crusty ex-mayor was more than an old man resentful of what time and change had done to his world, and he played more than a gadfly role. Harris dominated the government for the three years he served on the council, directing a relentless attack against appropriation requests, refusing to consider any exceptions to the strictest economy, and often waging personal vendettas against those who found his rigor excessive. Perhaps his most constructive contributions, though, were in research: he worked prodigiously to amass financial facts and figures illustrating the need for reform, and became something of a national expert on the matter. In the fall of 1876, he presented his work to the Saratoga meeting of the American Social Science Association, an influential young group providing for Mugwump businessmen, Brahmins, and gentlemen scholars what one student has called "a crucial point of contact among the nation's middle-class dissenters."[7] Whatever the influence elsewhere through this forum, Harris's paper called "Municipal Extravagance" had quite an impact on people in Springfield, who were considerably embarrassed to have the details of what Harris termed "high carnival" in local affairs held up to such public censure. It was one thing, moreover, to speak vaguely if earnestly of extravagance, and quite another to be informed that Massachusetts cities had grown by 47 percent the previous decade, but that taxes had leaped 95 percent, and funded debts by over 400 percent, or from $35 to $84 per capita; Springfield's $86 figure represented a 633 percent jump. Local taxes, it worked out, showed a 450 percent per capita rise in the fifteen years since 1861, far above the statewide rate of increase. Whichever way the columns were arranged, they put solid substance behind the retrenchment invective.[8]

Action by the state soon reinforced this message. The legislature passed a bill strictly regulating municipal debt, a first step in state control of local finance in Massachusetts and one that reflected, the *Union* observed, "a deep and universal anxiety. If our towns and cities cannot practice self-restraint, then they must be restrained." In complying with the law, Springfield found it could eliminate most of its outstanding demand notes, and fully fund its debt so that only $70,000 above interest would fall due annually, a manageable level. Even if circumstances did not permit a more drastic reduction, prodding from Boston helped the city bring its indebtedness under control.[9]

In the day to day running of city business, however, it proved more difficult to turn intention into accomplishment. As the unsuccessful Mayor Stebbins had noted in frustration, the citizens "complained of taxes in the autumn, only to insist on more costly improvements in the spring." Under Wight and Harris, the problem was a little different. "The Mayor preached economy from the pulpit, and the people shouted Amen from the pews," but when it came time to sacrifice, everyone claimed exemption from the obligation. Each year's salary ordinance offered consistent illustration of how difficult it was to actually implement retrenchment: with various departments and interests each trying to avoid the fall of the ax, and Daniel Harris singlemindedly resisting all efforts at compromise, decisions proved almost impossible to reach. After observing months of sputtering debate on the 1875 salary bill, for instance, the *Republican* predicted whimsically but accurately that "there will go up a faint, wavering cry, the limp little corpse will be flung under the table, and the next reform will be called on."[10] The annual appropriations bill was similarly intractable but far more substantive, and therefore more complicated politically. Thus the seeming immunity from retrenchment that their political influence guaranteed the police and fire departments encouraged others to view their own cutbacks as inequitable; in such a climate, even symbolic steps such as the mayor's ban on all-night street lighting were roundly criticized as more inconvenient than economical, and timorous in the absence of bolder attacks elsewhere.[11]

The education issue perhaps best illustrates the real difficulties of cutting back public activity in a complex city. The mayor, opening his attack in 1876, pictured a "startling degree of extravagance in school operations" and offered detailed statistics showing a tripling since 1861 of the "cost per scholar," to a $27 level, the highest in the state. Teacher's salaries would have to be cut, he vowed, and janitorial, repair, and even heating costs drastically curtailed — in all, a "prompt and radical pruning." Springfield's recently modernized schools had by this time become objects of pride to the community, however, and the mayor's attack met immediate resistance even from enthusiastic retrenchers. "He gets the wrong pig by the ear most extraordinarily," snapped the *Republican*, which saw politics at the root of the mayor's demands; "The schools," agreed the *Union*, "ought to be the *last* to suffer in any scheme of reduction."[12]

The School Committee and the superintendent rushed to the defense of their system, asserting that it had actually been "most moderate in its ratio of increase, and most economical in its administration." They disputed the mayor's arithmetic and statistics on per capita costs, and argued, regarding teachers' salaries, that "true economy by no means consists in cramping the energies of skilled labor, which if not sufficiently compensated in one position readily seeks another." The battle became a nasty one, particularly since the School Committee controlled salaries and the City Council controlled school appropriations, but its substance is not as important as the general problems it represented, for similar arguements could be and were put forward by most administrative departments asked to economize. The results proved representative also, when all the shouting was over and compromise cutbacks settled on. Faculty salaries were scaled, with modest reductions in the lower grades, while more substantial economies were obtained from lowered administrative costs. By 1879 school expenditures were down $40,000 from the 1874 peak of $126,000. The mayor expressed his satisfaction, and the School Committee acknowledged that the quality of education in Springfield had probably not suffered much by the belt tightening.[13]

Similarly, the accomplishments of the retrenchment were more impressive than the protracted wrangling might indicate. The city slashed basic appropriations from $614,000 in 1875 to $270,000 three years later; total expenditures, an index of real economies rather than good intentions, peaked in 1874 at $781,000, and then quickly tumbled below $500,000, remaining there until the revival of prosperity in 1879. The debt had been brought under control, property valuation had been scaled down realistically, and the tax rate itself, the most visible and meaningful criterion for most citizens, fell from 1875's $17.20 to $11.00 in 1878, Wight's last year in office.[14] Such results, though, had not been produced primarily in the tangled debates about schools, salaries, and other administrative costs, however much time was donated to these matters. Rather, the real retrenchment came in the complex matter of property improvements, where the depression brought some different and significant questions to the surface.

The financial statistics themselves show the extent to which the crisis was thought to be centered in Springfield's relationship to property improvements. While the government reduced administrative costs modestly, drastic cuts proved the rule in improvement spending, especially street work. The $126,000 expended in 1875 shrunk to $30,000 the next year, and through 1876, the peak year of Wight's effectiveness, the street department accounted for over 60 percent of the government's total saving. Seen another way, the figures show that this largest category of municipal expense fell from a substantial 23 percent of the total outlay to around 5 percent.[15] Of course, this could happen largely because economies were easier to effect in such matters: the improvements were rarely of immediate necessity, and petitions from even well-placed property owners could be turned away more easily than appropriation requests from departments. But the improvement reductions involved more than the trimming back of luxuries: the turnabout gradually became a general attack on the principle as well as the cost of public involvement in property improvements.

The traditional approach in such matters did not allow for any clear distinction between public and private interests, and the city generally had considered each request for community assistance on an ad hoc, more or less informal basis. These concepts and mechanisms bore a tremendous weight as the quantity, scope, planning, execution, and public meaning of property improvements grew. Even before the depression, communities like Springfield had generally begun to recognize what Carter Goodrich has called in a somewhat wider context the "failure to develop a workable theory of the limits of public promotion. From Gallatin's day on, the advocates of internal improvements were able to present general arguments for government action . . . But for how much expenditure? . . . How are the diffused and inappropriable gains to be estimated? And how much of a direct financial loss − in general or in the specific case − should the public authority be prepared to sustain in order to secure these advantages for the community at large?"[16] With the onset of the depression, the overburdened improvement spirit began to dissolve in suspicion and doubt, forcing its former adherents to search for new ways of understanding the public interest, and new mechanisms for furthering it.

Some of the specific improvement issues of the depression period show this conceptual crisis in bold relief. Most important was the collapse of the never very efficient damage and betterment assessments, the machinery erected to apportion public and private costs in improvements. The depression helped bring about this mechanical breakdown, for as much as debt frightened the government, hard times gave individual property owners additional incentive to evade assessments for improvement work already completed or in progress, and the search for loopholes to void betterments or to increase damage awards apparently continued to present few challenges to the diligent. The Board of Public Works, set up previously to solve the problem of uncollectable assessments, found that it had merely shifted the quibbling from one room to another, and the situation soon reached intolerable proportions. In late 1875, over one hundred suits for assessment relief were meandering through the courts, and this at a time when the city had paid out $137,902 in project damages while collecting only $29,000 of the $80,000 thus far levied in betterments. The courts, as usual, almost invariably held that some technical or procedural flaw voided the assessment, as in December 1876, when a judge dismissed $30,000 owed the city for work done on Fort Pleasant and Sumner Avenues. "Altogether disastrous," the *Union* called the city's self-victimizing improvement policy, while Mayor Wight later noted that "it would argue dull scholarship if we had failed to learn that we cannot now be too cautious." In this respect, a City Council committee suggested that all street openings be discontinued " . . . excepting when the abutters shall become legally bound in advance to accept a certain stipulated sum as damages, and to pay without litigation a specific amount for betterments."[17]

But the government did not have to be losing money to sense how impossible it had become to weave public decisions from the tangle of private interests and practical problems. Anyone casually walking up Springfield's Main Street today, through the railroad underpass and into the North End, would hardly guess that it could have required over twenty years of genuinely ferocious controversy to build that underpass and the adjoining railroad terminal. The matter, which had first arisen in the 1860's, unhappily reached one of its periodic climaxes during the depths of the depression, when patience was scarcer than profits.

The Boston & Albany had proposed to replace the dilapidated old Union Depot on the west (river) side of Main Street with an elaborate new terminal on the east side — stretching back toward Chestnut (the eventual location). The idea quickly became linked with a plan to eliminate the grade crossing at the depot by passing Main under raised tracks. Speeding trains presented no hazard here; rather, the problem was the continual blocking of Main Street owing to the switching of engines and the making up of freight trains in the adjoining yards. One 1872 watcher counted the gates go down

sixty-six times between 11 AM and 3 PM, and on most days the
street was closed as often as it was open. Everyone agreed that the
nuisance was "monstrous and accumulative," and should be eliminated. But as so often, consensus on ends proved irrelevant to the determination of means.[18]

From the start, the city and the railroad could not agree on how
the work was to be done, who would do it, and how it would be
paid for. Coordinating the tracks of the several connecting railroads
to a raised depot grade presented formidable engineering problems,
but they paled before the obstacles of more particularistic pressures.
Adjacent hotel and store owners feared being stranded above a
street sinking down into a gloomy underpass; Daniel Harris objected
to the expense of raising his own railroad's tracks; and any number
of less well-placed citizens raised other objections, not the least of
which was a general fear that horses would panic when trains rum-
bled overhead — such underpasses being still something of a novelty.
The issue came to a head in 1874, so totally confusing all observers
that to unravel matters here would seem to betray the spirit of the
historical record. The city offered to lower the street six feet if the
tracks were raised eight, while the railroad insisted that it would
only raise its tracks the six feet, that the street would have to sink
eight. Meeting after meeting was held, filling hundreds of hours with
elaborate legal and technical testimony, so that both newspapers
took to heading their accounts of the proceedings "How Not To Do
It." In addition to everything else, nobody could say who had final
authority to make a decision in the matter. The buck was tossed
from the City Council to the Board of Public Works to the county
commissioners, then back again in reverse order, and finally to the
state supreme court, where a lawsuit, two petitions for certiorari,
and a bill in equity all arrived simultaneously. When the smoke
cleared, things stood pretty much as they had at the start of the
year.[19]

As silly as it seems now, Springfield was not amused. The city
could solve less complex problems, including grade eliminations at
Bridge and Chestnut Streets, but the Depot underpass and terminal
would have to wait, as it turned out, through fifteen more years of
wrangling. For a community frustrated in so many ways in the
1870's, the inability to thread this maze proved vexing in the ex-

treme. The depression forced it to back away from several near compromises when costs loomed as prohibitive, and the confused authority further underscored the city's ambiguous relation to such improvements.

In this context another sad experience provided even sterner lessons. For many years, efforts had been made to end Springfield's dependence on the 1816 covered wooden toll bridge that, aside from ferries and the railroad trestle, was the city's only link to the other side of the Connecticut. There had been a series of attempts to have the old structure declared a free bridge by the legislature or, failing that, to have a new free public bridge built at either the North or South ends. In 1872 the General Court once again had a batch of petitions to these effects before it, when suddenly everything began to backfire for Springfield. The legislature surprisingly authorized *both* a North End crossing and the freeing of the toll bridge, at city expense; the next year's session, for good measure, threw in the Agawam Bridge at the South End. The city government was appalled, even amidst predepression vitality, and confused: it had encouraged the idea of a bridge, but never dreamed that developers had the political power to win authorization of all three projects. And now, since bridges crossed town lines, the matter was in the hands of the county commissioners; however the costs were apportioned, Springfield's share was sure to be an enormous burden made even heavier by the deepening depression.[20]

When the commissioners ordered construction in 1876, Springfield sought unsuccessfully to block the action in court, enraged by the failure of authorities to wait until the depression had eased and charging that speculators in Westfield, West Springfield, and Springfield's own suburban areas had forced "these monuments of reckless extravagance and official folly" on the community. The city eventually had to pay $73,000, or 65 percent of the South End Bridge costs, and $140,000 of the $165,000 spent on the more expensive North End span. Fortunately, these obligations did not fall due until conditions had eased somewhat, and the general stimulus the construction gave to employment and trade did much to coat the pill. Nevertheless, there was considerable bitterness even after both bridges opened in 1879. Once again, the city felt victimized by its own efforts, manipulated by political and property interests, and confounded by forces and authority beyond its control in its efforts to reduce debt.[21]

All this, then — the bridges, the depot underpass, the betterments, the railroad subscriptions of the last chapter, the general depression — all produced in Springfield a profound disillusionment with public improvements, particularly among those who had once supported them vigorously. As early as 1872, the *Republican* had begun to feel that benefitted property should bear the full cost of improvements, whatever the indirect public benefit; by 1874, the *Union* joined it in the belief that private gain could no longer justify public subsidy. Wrote the *Republican* in 1875:

We are not blind to the fact that a respectable proportion of the municipal debt is represented by improvements and public works necessitated by the rise of large towns into cities . . . but a much larger proportion of it is due to the persistent pushing forward of private interests as public ones. In the interest of real estate development, we have laid a heavy burden upon our manufacturing, mercantile, and laboring interests.

This, of course, still left the chief problem — distinguishing between legitimate and spurious claims to the public interest, a conundrum that led the newspaper to declare in frustration that local government ought to be limited to fire, school, police, and other basic administrative responsibilities, foreswearing all contact with any property developments whatsoever.[22]

Springfield was hardly alone in feeling such revulsion; as Robert Wiebe has shown, improvement and development questions were central to a profound "crisis of the communities" in many cities and towns during these years.[23] But the process by which the audacious liberal city-builders of the 1860's had become the fiscal conservatives of the 1870's also offers more particular insights into Springfield's urban evolution. For curiously enough, there is something more of continuity than change in the halt to building and spending, a conceptual progression and extension easily obscured by the dramatic reversal of fiscal priorities. The years of building involved a progressive enrichment of the concept of a public stake in the city's growth, and a progressive differentiation, at least abstractly, of public and private interest. With the depression era's loss of confidence and stability, city leaders sought to effect a similar differentiation in fact as well as in theory between public and private; they felt the need, in other words, to express in policy the fact that Springfield had outgrown more traditional conceptions of community and government purpose. The efforts to limit public activity can thus be seen, in at least one sense, as ways of clarifying and thereby strengthening that newer sense of a public sphere, whatever the more tangible sources and implications of the impulse.

In this respect, it is not coincidental that one can identify at work in this context the same opposed triangles of forces that were observed in the prosperous years, though to opposite effect. The triad of mutually reinforcing factors that had moved the community toward innovative development – a belief in imperative needs, strong leadership from respected leaders and informed experts, and the influence of experience in the world beyond Springfield – these now operated to restrict spending and ambitious public involvement. And the forces that had resisted an expansion of activity earlier – the play of particularistic pressures and politics; the opposition to outside ideas and advice; and the inefficiency of political and administrative machinery – all these served to impede disengagement and retrenchment, ironically sustaining the same momentum they had initially sought to restrict. Perhaps the reversal of Daniel Harris's roles in 1860 and 1875 was not so paradoxical after all.

During these same years community leaders directed a great deal of attention to the structure of city government itself, an explicit acknowledgment that the depression crisis touched something deeper than finance or municipal policy. In this, once again, the outside context played an important part, for it was becoming apparent to almost every observer that something was dreadfully wrong with America's large cities, that they possessed some fatal flaw that was already leading some critics to anticipate Bryce's later judgment that city government represented democracy's signal failure in America. The large cities, struggling with titanic problems, spent much of the seventies involved in the first phases of a reform movement that would culminate in the Progressive era a generation later, and far from the least important aspect of this response was the transmission of the reform perspective to many smaller communities. As late as 1871, Springfield had still viewed the affairs of the great cities with some detachment. Both papers generally referred to New York simply as "The Metropolis," and they frequently contrasted its problems, particularly in the wake of the Tweed scandals, to the "traditional education in self-government" guiding New England communities like Springfield. According to these lights, the problem of local government seemed simple: "As long as the people of a city respect themselves, care for their neighbors, fear God, and take an affectionate pride in their city, they will see that it is well governed." But the depression served to redistribute more equitably the anxiety of urban problems, so to speak, helping people in Springfield complete the process by which they regarded their community as a true city, sharing the problems as well as the promise of urbanity. More and more, Springfield looked outward to this general urban context to understand the roots of the local crisis.[24]

Most of the reform discussion at this time identified as the central flaw of municipal government the general absence of clearly defined and visible responsibility in decision making. City governments had become patchwork nightmares, shrouding the inner workings of both politics and administration. The resulting curtain not only prevented the people from seeing what was happening behind it; by also cutting off government figures themselves from public needs and public surveillance, it more or less encouraged them to serve more particularistic priorities, helping to produce city governments generally characterized by inefficiency and incompetence at best, and outright corruption at worst.

This analysis found fertile soil in Springfield, for it centered on the very problems just emerging from the city's own experience. "We are just discovering the difference between a city and a town," concluded the *Republican*. In a town, "everyone knows everyone," and public decisions are open and informal. But because of the complexity of decisions in a city and the welter of pressures that could obscure the public interest, an urban community "requires long terms of office; it requires unity, and intelligent system; it must subject the magistracy to more clearly defined and more precisely located responsibility, by which the public power is in reality confirmed, rather than enervated."[25] In other words, just as Springfield's imposing new churches and public monuments made its rapidly changing cityscape more coherent and comprehensible, so too, its leaders argued, new institutions were needed to give the abstract concept of the public interest greater substance, power, and visibility in the hectic marketplace of city government.

In Springfield, as in other cities, the drive for charter revision became the vehicle for these ideas. From the time Boston wrestled with a proposed new charter in 1875, Springfield heard talk of restructuring the local government, and when the Mayor appointed a committee in 1877 to study the matter, it ended up drafting an entirely new charter for the city. The plan, largely the work of the committee's head, long-time Judge of Probate William Shurtleff, was comprehensive indeed. First of all, it reorganized the city's ward structure to take account of growth since the original divisions of 1852, providing for nine redrawn wards with a city council of nine aldermen and twenty-seven common councilmen. It also spoke to the general desire to end the disruptive and inefficient annual turnover of almost the entire government, by expanding the mayor's term to two years, and by setting up an odd system whereby two of each ward's three councilmen would be elected for annual terms, with the third chosen for a two-year tenure. Thus, at each December's balloting, one third of the aldermen and two thirds of the council would come up for election.[26]

More fundamental was Shurtleff's effort to effect a thorough separation of executive and legislative authority so that responsibility might be consolidated. In the legislative sector itself, a specific allocation of responsibility to separate committees in each branch sought to eliminate the confusion inherent in the 1852 charter's joint committee procedure. The mayor, under the new system, would relinquish his seat on committees and at the head of aldermen, becoming an executive officer only. This hardly meant a reduction of his role, however. In addition to the lengthened term of office, the new charter gave him added authority over appointments and administrative decisions, and though a two-thirds vote could overrule him, the new mayor was to have the type of final, responsible executive power so generally felt to be lacking under the 1852 structure.

The heart of the proposal lay in the rationalization of administration. The new charter set up four consolidated administrative boards to advise the mayor and conduct the business of government: overseers of poor and health; fire and police commissioners; commissioners of public works; and a board of finance. Each five to seven man board would include the mayor, the relevant appointed officials, and at least two "citizens" appointed by the council. The reorganization, an extension of the steps toward bureaucratization taken earlier on an ad hoc basis, intended to provide for comprehensive planning and execution of public policy, with all ambiguities of authority removed. The city, it was hoped, would thus be able efficiently to decide what to do and then actually to do it; and if it were not done, with the workings of official power made clearly visible the public would at last have what the *Republican* called "the ability to say to somebody: *Thou* art the man!"[27]

The community seemed proud of Judge Shurtleff's work when he unveiled the new plan. At a number of large public meetings, people discussed it enthusiastically, and the City Council, approving it unanimously, sent the charter to Boston where it cleared the legislature with only one dissenting vote. It then returned to Springfield, needing only a referendum approval to become the city's basic law. As the *Republican* observed, the new charter was the latest thing, and put Springfield in the forefront of modern city thought: "It embodies and applies to Springfield all the best results of recent municipal experience and study here and elsewhere." And in fact, its significance lay precisely in this lack of uniqueness, in the charter's being a representative product of a new reform era. This made the results of the referendum all the more startling, for on June 18, 1877, the people of Springfield overwhelmingly rejected the entire plan by a more than two-to-one ratio.[28]

Community leaders were stunned, and at first they could only attribute the results to the "sinister influences" of entrenched interests and the apathy or overconfidence of "respectable citizens." These factors did have enough relevance to make interpretation risky, since only 1,700 votes had been cast, and peripheral yet passionate issues such as Mayor Wight's strong hand in liquor law enforcement had figured heavily in many pre-election meetings. But as the reformers had to recognize, it was important to take opposition to the new charter at face value, for opponents were often just as concerned with fundamental principles. They rejected, most basically, the very elements that were the charter's main reason for being — the consolidation of administrative authority, the independent executive branch, and the two-term mayor. All these they feared might put too much power in the hands of a governing elite, placing them beyond the reach of the people. They found the concept of public interest that the charter embodied altogether too vague and abstract, resenting its implication that the people needed to be protected from themselves. On the contrary, the difficulties of the depression era apparently convinced voters that they most needed protection from government itself, even at the cost of efficiency and system.[29]

Disappointed and bitter, community leaders continued to argue against such viewpoints even after the decisive vote. Claiming a fine distinction — perhaps too fine — between strength and power, they asserted that the charter gave the government more of the former while more firmly checking the latter. The *Republican*, offended that some had seen partisan and economic interests behind the charter move, decried the fact that "there are people who seem to find it impossible to believe that their fellow men can interest themselves in public affairs for any but base or purely personal motives." All in all, Wiebe's general comments on the reform movement well epitomize the situation in Springfield: "The theory [of reform through bureaucratic rationalization] was immediately and persistently attacked as undemocratic, an accusation that never ceased to sting its defenders. Sensitive to the traditional suspicion of an overweening government, uneasy as they trod so close to elitist rule, they still believed they were only modernizing, not destroying, democracy."[30]

It would seem as if very different concepts of the nature and purposes of city government were emerging within the community. And yet, to understand this split, which would not become fully explicit and mature for some years, it is important to recognize the extent to which it grew from attitudes and values shared rather than contested. For one thing, the same basic impulse moved all elements in the crisis-era community — a growing fear of the tremendous power and the potential for its accumulation generated by postwar America and, particularly, the modern city. In this sense, the retrenchment drive, the charter reform, and the charter rejection as well all represent efforts to bring under control forces that were felt to be running wild over the community. More fundamentally, the developing idea of the public interest figured crucially in all aspects of the debate. Just as the concept of public benefit had become progressively differentiated from private interest, and could no longer support continued high levels of spending for property development, so too, for others, the public meaning of community leadership had become similarly abstracted from any particular social context, and faith in traditional leadership, always dependent on the accepted blending of public and private roles, could quickly give way to distrust. Thus, rather than finding in the charter reform a confirmation of the public power, critics of community leadership saw the plan as enshrining only another, more powerful and potentially more dangerous form of particularistic private power.

There is a powerful irony in all this, for it suggests that the shared articulation of the public interest concept itself led to lesser, rather than greater, consensus in the community — that, in fact, the weakening of the traditional link between private and public provided an important way for incipient social tensions and grievances to begin to find the forms and terms of political expression. The depression years thus brought Springfield more than a crisis of finance and public policy; the period represented something more than a crisis *for* the community. In ways then only beginning to become clear, it represented a crisis *of* community, of the changing meaning the concept held as Springfield grew from town into city. There were, however, aspects to this transformation more positive than the fear and suspicion of the retrenchment crisis, and yet just as central to an understanding of community development. These involved discovering the shared social needs and concerns of an increasingly urban community, and it was to these, in the last years of the 1870's, that Springfield directed its attention.

11. Community as Interdependence

The later depression years brought significant changes in the way people in Springfield understood questions of social needs and policy, including the assumptions about community structure underlying them. In a number of ways these changes represented the response of traditional forms and concepts to the demands of urbanization, rather than their supplantation through the social conflicts generally associated with city growth. Rather than seeing a discontinuity forced from below by a challenge to traditional leadership, or a struggle for power in the face of a disintegrating sense of community cohesion, Springfield witnessed a more subtle and in many ways more interestingly complex evolution.

Whatever anxiety the depression generated, it did not call forth an explicit sense of social crisis in the community. The working classes did not suffer the sort of hardships one would now expect in such a prolonged industrial breakdown, and they said and did little to challenge the business values that had always governed the way the community understood the needs and problems of workingmen. In fact, Springfield remained remarkably isolated from the tide of militant unionism rising elsewhere in the country. The most ambitious local labor activity during the period followed solidly traditional lines, involving the formation in 1874 of the "Sovereigns of Labor," an organization that sought to become something like an urban Grange, providing fellowship, discussion, and cooperative organization. Explicitly rejecting the concept of divergent class interests, the Sovereigns recruited members from all ranks of productive enterprise, even including some merchants and manufacturers, in accordance

with the old ideal of the "community of all producers." Although
the organization enjoyed some initial success in Springfield and a
number of other New England cities to which it spread, it soon
faded, and had disappeared by decade's end.[1]

If Springfield's workingmen did not reflect the ferment found elsewhere, it is unsurprising to find that ideas about the labor movement and the relation of the classes had not changed very much in
other sectors of the community. The 1877 riots were roundly condemned by all, and some took the opportunity to denounce the
labor movement in general, calling the demands of unions and labor
reformers "shocking rubbish and rank communism." But the overriding tone of the local response to a decade of labor agitation
seemed to be one of detachment. On all levels, people in Springfield,
in contrast to their concern with national issues of government extravagance and municipal corruption, apparently found the issues
not yet directly relevant to local life.[2]

In most ways, then, older concepts of class harmony and social
leadership continued to hold sway in Springfield, and these found
expression, very often, in quite traditional terms. Thus the temperance crusade remained a powerful focus of local life, embodying and
shoring up faith in the community's moral consensus. In fact, developments in the perennial battle against Rum enabled it to become, if anything, less a source of conflict and more a focus of
unity and affirmation. The 1875 repeal of prohibition in Massachusetts, and the subsequent enactment of a strict license system, enabled a much wider constituency to unite behind the moderate if
vague principle that too much liquor was a bad thing, and this
helped keep the politically treacherous business of actually granting
the licenses from becoming too heavily charged with social tensions
and conflicts.[3] The temperance reform, in turn, became part of a
broader emphasis on individual moral reform that, as in the past,
had explicitly religious overtones and leadership. Local clergymen,
including a number of Catholic priests, were quite active in this
cause. In addition, abstinance crusader Francis Murphy and evangel-
ist Dwight Moody, who had much in common, drew huge audiences
and enthusiastic responses when they appeared in Springfield. The
modern city had not quite yet supplanted the old-time religion.[4]

The passion of these efforts suggests that deeper currents of

change were astir beneath the surface of the community. Two men
who entered Springfield's life around this time, helped the city to
sense these stirrings, and they themselves embodied the new social
concerns involved; both were destined to become major figures in
American life and thought. The first represents particularly well the
continuity between newer urban outlooks and the more traditional
religious and moral focus of the community. Washington Gladden
was fairly well known when he accepted a Springfield pulpit in
1875, having already taken the first steps along a road that would
make him one of the most significant preachers of what came to be
known as the "Social Gospel."[5] From his first sermon as minister of
Springfield's North Congregational Church, he wasted no time in establishing himself as the voice of this new spirit in the community.
He reorganized his parish structure to attract a more socially diverse
congregation, abolishing pew rentals in the process, and he began to
speak widely on a variety of social questions, both in and out of the
pulpit. In 1878 he launched a monthly magazine called *Sunday
Afternoon*, a deceptively informal sampling of light family reading
on religion and society that included contributions from such figures as Lyman Abbott, Charles Sumner, Charles Loring Brace, and
Edward Everett Hale, and announced its quite serious aim of discovering "how to mix Christianity with Human Affairs, how to
bring salvation to the people that need it most . . . How to keep our
religion from degenerating into art, or evaporating into ecstacy, or
stiffening into dogmatism, and to make it a regenerating force in
society."[6]

Gladden was never to approach the Christian Socialism of the
more radical Social Gospel thinkers like Walter Rauschenbusch, and
in his Springfield days he still stood a long way from even that
moderate belief in corporate social responsibility that marked his
mature thought; it was not until he moved to a pulpit in Columbus,
Ohio, that he began to think deeply about municipal reform and the
labor movement. Nevertheless, he had begun to deal with such
topics while in Springfield, giving a series of lectures shortly after his
arrival that were later republished as *Working People and Their Employers*, and which have been called the Social Gospel's "most important discussion of this issue prior to 1880." Gladden later acknowledged that the book was "not quite so sympathetic as it ought

to have been towards unions," arguing as it did that cordiality and integrity did more for class harmony and justice than strikes or government regulation. "I fear I did not recognize so clearly the responsibility of the community for the relief of [unemployment] conditions," he went on, "I am not proud of the achievement, but I am not sorry that I made the endeavor."[7] In appreciating his influence in Springfield, this last point is probably the most important. Gladden's ideas themselves were not yet sufficiently out of step with prevailing attitudes to offend many people, and perhaps because of that his audacity in claiming, for example, that a manufacturer's treatment of his workers could be a matter to which Christian precepts were relevant and a clergyman's attention appropriate, had that much more of an effect in turning community attention to social concerns. His stature and influence in Springfield grew almost from the day of his arrival, and the fame he later won in national life probably surprised few who had known him at the time.

In contrast, the other young man who in these years suggested new directions for social thought in the community displayed less prominently the talents that would eventually lead to international acclaim. In 1872 a quiet, frail, solitary, and serious young writer from nearby Chicopee began to grace the pages of the Springfield *Union* with brilliantly literate book reviews, essays, and editorials. In these early writings, Edward Bellamy showed the intense concern with the social and economic implications of industrialism that was to culminate later in *Looking Backward*, one of the century's most significant books by almost any measure; even as a twenty-one year old in 1871, he had shocked a Springfield lyceum by warning his respectable audience that they faced a socialist uprising of "the toiling masses of the world" if injustice and oppression were not eliminated. To a remarkable degree, in fact, the basics of his mature thought had taken clear shape by the time poor health forced him to leave Springfield in 1877 for several years. And if he differed from Gladden in this respect, his meaning in the life of the community was quite different as well. His mostly anonymous newspaper writings attracted Bellamy little personal notice, and their general influence can only be called indirect at best. But if Gladden's role was of practical importance to the community at this time, then

Bellamy's certainly had symbolic importance, pointing to a range of concerns that, sooner or later, would force themselves more directly to Springfield's attention.[8]

This blend of traditional leadership and values, widening social awareness, and incipient conflict appears most vividly in an examination of Springfield's understanding of its public welfare obligations, at any time a good index of a community's social values. From the beginning, charity in Massachusetts, following the English tradition, had been organized around the towns, and not the county or state. Communities were obligated to support those paupers with a legal settlement in the town, and the state reimbursed them for aid given to vagrants. Few challenged this arrangement, though over the years local assistance had become less "helping one's own" than an effort to reduce the nusiance of beggary and the menace of crime; pauperism, in any event, was taken to be a fact of community life about which little could be done except to comfort the afflicted and ameliorate the effects of their misfortune on the community at large.[9]

The depression of the 1870's placed tremendous pressure on this old system, as did, indirectly, first efforts to help on the state level: by reducing residence requirements in order to combat vagrancy, for example, the state enabled more paupers to qualify in the communities, thereby increasing proportionally the burden of the towns. Local systems very quickly approached the point of collapse as the depression lengthened.[10]

In Springfield, where even before this crisis the welfare system had grown cluttered and confused through years of only partial adaptation to vastly altered circumstances, public charity took three forms, all of them strained to the limit by the middle of the 1870's. The almshouse, which housed infants, orphans, the aged, helpless paupers, and even the "school" for incorrigible truants, was crowded with three times its normal number at the depression's peak.[11] At the other end of the welfare spectrum was the sixteen-foot square "tramp room" in the City Hall basement, where vagrants could obtain two nights' shelter and morning meals, so that they would not resort to the nuisance of backdoor begging. But despite precautions, the overwhelmed tramp room itself quickly became a nuisance during the crisis years. Springfield's role as a railroad center made it a natural basin for thousands drifting the countryside in search of work or, as many townsmen liked to think, "with no higher objective than living upon the bounty of others." The city dispensed as many as 8,000 nocturnal doles during peak years, far fewer than the number of tramps who had appeared looking for help.[12] The third category of public assistance was the most important and controversial. From the 1860's on, in order to relieve pressure on the almshouse, Springfield and most other cities had turned more and more to the partial assistance known as outdoor aid, at first in the form of groceries or coal, and later including medical expenses, payment of rent, and even outright cash grants. As with the other forms of charity, the number of recipients increased dramatically, from five hundred annually before 1870 to over two thousand a few years later. But because this aid was proportionally more expensive, the increase alarmed the community a great deal more. While almshouse costs had risen by 50 percent between 1870 and 1876, and the total welfare budget had doubled, outdoor aid quadrupled from $5,000 to $20,000. In the economy-sensitive city, many began wondering whether the able-bodied on outdoor aid were not exploiting the public's benevolence; characteristically, Springfield's reassessment of the nature of that benevolence began with the property-owner's concern for extravagance and the tax-rate.[13]

At the end of 1876, Mayor Wight, backed staunchly by the unswervable Daniel Harris, opened a campaign to bring the Pauper Department under control. Although much of the debate which followed sank into an unseemly political squabble over the practices of the salaried almoner, one D. J. Bartlett, this dispute — which dragged on for years — did not completely obscure the broader questions. A. B. Harris, obviously his father's son, presented a dramatic statistical report in 1877 that fully wakened Springfield to the depth of its problems. In 1872, his figures showed, every thirty-fifth person in the city received some form of relief; in 1877, it was every thirteenth person, and every twenty families purchased coal for the twenty-first. In addition to such vivid statistical representations, Harris showed that the costs of all this were highly disproportionate to Springfield's population and the actual incidence of pauperism, with the result that the per capita costs placed the city close to the top in state rankings. Few may have wondered with A. B. Harris "how long it will be before we shall have here in Springfield the worst species of communism," but the investigations convinced many that the dole had gotten wildly out of hand, and that something substantial had to be done.[14]

Aroused community leaders were not content to leave the matter in the hands of the squabbling politicians. What Springfield needed, they felt, was a vastly more efficient and well organized system for ministering to the poor and, closely related to this, an understanding of the nature of the poverty problem itself that would be more relevant to the conditions of the modern city. In finding a vehicle for these purposes, Springfield looked to other large cities, and became one of the first to adopt the sort of semipublic agency then being pioneered in Buffalo and Philadelphia. Thus, in the midst of the Bartlett tangle late in 1877, the Union Relief Association was formed, championed by a number of community leaders from many callings — Samuel Bowles, former mayor A. D. Briggs, Washington Gladden, and, particularly, Mrs. Clara Leonard, the wife of a lawyer, locally prominent in her own right for charity work and later more prominent in state-wide reform, eventually becoming the first woman to serve on the Massachusetts Board of Health.[15]

The Union Relief, as it was generally called, worked on several levels. Although some direct charity was provided from the dues of the hundreds of members, the organization served more basically as a clearing house for public and private charity, examining and visiting recipients, referring cases, and coordinating diverse programs. It also functioned unofficially as a supervisory and investigatory body for the welfare system, far exceeding in thoroughness the efforts of the city government in this respect. The first Union Relief report was particularly influential and showed the short path leading from investigation to reform: following the revelation of deplorable conditions in the almshouse, the Union Relief mounted a successful campaign to remove all children from it, where they lived in daily contact with the senile, diseased, and degenerate, placing them instead in foster homes.[16]

But the association concentrated its main attention on the outdoor aid program, where the need for efficiency seemed most paramount. Largely as a result of its efforts, a new system of visiting and investigating applicants and aid recipients was developed, involving both salaried and volunteer agents and fully integrating official city procedures and private benevolence. By 1879 costs had fallen considerably below what the returning prosperity would alone have suggested, and the government proudly reported that "smaller appropriations do not necessarily mean lessened efficiency."[17] For the reformers, however, efficiency had less to do with bureaucratic arrangements than with the underlying approach to the problem, and probably the most significant contribution the Union Relief made to the economy was the discussion it generated concerning the nature of poverty and, particularly, the way poorly directed charity could make the problem worse, whatever its intentions.

It was generally recognized that the depression created real problems for most working people, and that "wages paid to the laboring classes have been so reduced that it is impossible for them to accumulate a sufficient amount to maintain them in idleness, and as soon as reverses come upon them, they are obliged to rely upon charity." Nevertheless, most people believed, as no less sensitive an observer than Washington Gladden wrote for the association, that "a very large proportion of this money is obtained by the unworthy and the vicious poor." If aid was to help those who really needed it, indiscriminate giving had to be eliminated — not only because it strained resources, but because far more basically, it was no favor to those "able-bodied whose poverty is a result of their own vice, indolence, or improvidence." As a City Council committee concluded, "It is not a kindness to the poor to give with an unstinting hand. This leads them to the lower depths of poverty, shiftlessness, and distress. Free outside aid in this city has increased pauperism, and is continually spreading the disease." And it was a disease, plainly, not merely the concern of the afflicted themselves: the entire city, said the mayor, suffered from the public sustenance of a class of dependents "whose poverty will be as detrimental to our morals as it is to our treasury."[18]

Accordingly, most discussion of welfare policy focused on the qualitative dimension of charity, rather than the objective circumstances of the poor themselves; since the main problem appeared to be differentiating the worthy from the unworthy poor, a rational-

ized system more capable of drawing a clear line would be inherently more just to the poor and beneficial to all, at the same time as it
was more efficient and more economical. It was, in this sense, a central policy of the Union Relief that "real charity may consist in
withholding alms," and hence the strong programatic emphasis on
investigation, visitation, and the strict limitation of outdoor aid.[19]

The community significance of all this is made plainer by yet another dimension of the "new charity," as it was often called. Just as
reformers held the attitude of the poor to be more significant than
the mere fact of their poverty, so too did they feel that the very
concern shown by a benevolent community would be of more value
to the worthy poor than the actual material assistance dispensed.
The effort to get orphans out of the poorhouse and into respectable
homes, the emphasis on putting the indolent back to work, and especially on visitation to every aid applicant by a charity agent or
volunteer — all aimed at increasing the exposure of the poor to the
life and values of the community, the ultimate cure, so it was
strongly believed, for indolence and vice. As the Union Relief said
at one point, the chief need of poor people was "occasional contact
with, and the genuine personal interest, sympathy, and moral support of those who are more fortunately circumstanced and better in-
structed." As this concern indicates, Springfield's leaders saw the
problem of poverty as stemming more basically from the social patterns of the modern city than from the economic patterns of modern capitalism. As Roy Lubove has written of the "new charity"
more generally, "The charity organization ideal was to reestablish
the patterns of social interaction of the small town or village, where
the primary group exercised powerful social controls. The charity
society was an 'artifice,' designed to restore the 'natural relations'
which the city had destroyed."[20]

It is somewhat difficult, from today's perspective, to appreciate
the spirit of these developments and attitudes, and the general excitement they generated within the community. The compulsion to
weed out the unworthy poor seems to mistake seriously the nature
of poverty in industrial society, and one is tempted to cynicism by
the concern of the comfortable for those whom they would aid by
withholding material support, thereby inculcating virtue in the poor
by conveniently reducing the taxes of the rich. The concern for

community cohesion — which, as Lubove notes, involved a romantic impulse linked to a passion for bureaucratic, scientific efficiency — this concern can be read as a defensive, fearful, paternalistic response to the threat of social change, an effort to preserve hegemony rather than an effort to construct a more equitable and viable community for a new age.[21]

The very validity of these criticisms, then, serves to obscure somewhat the meaning the charity experience held for Springfield as a changing community in the 1870's. In the first place, whatever its failings at the time or retrospectively, the citywide associated charity organization was fast becoming one of the period's most exciting and influential ideas, a major milestone in the development of modern social work and community welfare policy. Not only had Springfield joined this new movement quite early, but with local leaders such as Bowles, Harris, and Mrs. Leonard active in prominent reform activities and groups like the Social Science Association, the community had good reason to feel itself among the pioneers of a new era for community welfare. When the *Republican* observed in 1880 that "the condition of the poor and the reorganization of public and private charity [has become] a universal topic of discussion all over the country," it could modestly add that Springfield was "a little beyond the first novelty in such matters."[22]

In this context, people generally regarded the new attitudes as major humanitarian advances, and in some senses they were, for the new doctrine proclaimed the community's ability to control an aspect of its environment — in this case a social condition — which had previously been accepted as an immutable fact of life. At last, it was sincerely held, an attempt was being made to strike at the sources of poverty. As the Union Relief noted, "The ruling bent of the time is to go to the root of things, to deal with pauperism and vice where they are engendered. The world is waking up to see the enormous waste of philanthropic effort which has resulted from the simple mistake of beginning at the wrong end." This attitude, in large part, helps explain why the work of the association was conducted and received by the community with an exuberance and optimism quite removed from the otherwise grim and frightened tone of the retrenchment crusade.[23]

In this context, it also becomes appropriate to take the concern with community relations on its own terms. Whatever the interpretation, it certainly was true that in different ways both prosperity and depression had helped isolate and detach the poor from community life and the power of traditional values and leadership. Faith in the integrative power of visits and social contacts was, certainly, naive. But it embodied the notion — as did, more generally, the charity movement in Springfield — that problems whose roots lay in the disintegration of older community social patterns had become the responsibility of the public at large in a modern city, not really out of the fading sense of neighborly concern, but out of a newer belief that the welfare and stability of the entire community, and everyone in it, might literally depend on how those problems were met.

This dual perception of interdependence and increasing social distance had far-reaching implications, which come through somewhat more explicitly in those areas of community concern related to public health. Before 1876 Springfield had not even had a Board of Health as such — the aldermen merely assumed that title and the few special powers it conferred whenever they came to consider occasional nuisance complaints or responses to epidemic threats. But when, after years of entreaties, an independent board was established in 1876, under the aggressive leadership of the City Physician, Dr. David Clark, the advantages of concentrated executive administration over the unsystematic if earnest workings of the City Council were quickly demonstrated. Together with the Union Relief Association, the board was responsible for a dramatically heightened awareness of health questions, and it helped offer informed and sophisticated leadership in coping with them.[24]

One of these involved the city hospital, which had been founded in 1867 to serve those otherwise self-sufficient citizens who, during serious illness, could "not have at home that care and attention which they need at that time."[25] Yet, perhaps because the idea of a public hospital still seemed somewhat alien in smaller communities of the period, it was greeted with relative indifference; the facility treated fewer than fifty patients a year, usually two or three at a time, and these generally the aged and senile. In such circumstances, people during the depression years began to wonder why the public was paying $4,000 a year to subsidize an institution that seemed to be serving at the most a symbolic function. Although its managers promised that "with a better understanding of its benefits, the Hospital will be more largely patronized and made more nearly self-supporting," it quickly became fair game for retrenchers in and out of government, who demanded its closing.[26]

The hospital did not handle charity cases, which were treated in the almshouse, but nevertheless the Union Relief investigated it along with other welfare agencies, to important effect. The 1877 and 1878 reports by Clara Leonard condemned every aspect of the beleagured institution's operation, finding it disorganized, unprofessional, and thoroughly mismanaged in the performance of even the small role it had been playing. Citing in particular the absence of any medical board of control, the Union Relief concluded that "in fact, it has no claim to be called a hospital at all. It is a boarding house, where the inmates may or may not be ill." At the same time, the association also reaffirmed the need for a genuine hospital, and pleaded for the reform of a facility "diverted from its legitimate mission." Surprisingly, given the mood of the period, the combined endorsement and condemnation virtually ended demands for closing the hospital, and turned community attention toward reform.[27]

Acting on suggestions by the Union Relief and the city physician, the 1879 government reorganized the hospital thoroughly, setting up a board of trustees — to include the mayor, city physician, and three women — separate from the Springfield City Council. The board, in turn, would select a medical staff, a rotating group of twelve community doctors who would receive no fees for their supervision of the hospital. The pauper sick, previously receiving the dubious ministrations of the wretched almshouse infirmary, were to be cared for along with paying patients, and several free beds for those unable to pay for needed services were provided. The restructuring, perhaps regressive in the sense that it made the hospital seem more a charity than a general institution, was in every other respect an important advance, and the mayor soon pronounced the institution to be "no longer an invalid's boarding house, but rather a well-equipped and well-managed hospital, one of the necessities of a city of our size." Faced with the choice of abandoning the ludicrous old facility in the name of imperative economy, or moving to a broader understanding of urban needs and responsibility, Springfield significantly chose to accept the added burdens. It was probably not a choice the community would have made at a very much earlier point in time.[28]

Still, the hospital, like the charity reform, touched few citizens directly; the more important redefinitions of public responsibility came in other areas, such as water supply and public sanitation, that involved the entire community. Springfield had been long in moving from a view of water supply as property protection to conceiving of it as a public utility. Just as the depression began, the city had committed itself to a comprehensive reservoir-aqueduct system for domestic and sanitary needs as well as for fire protection. Attended by great interest in the community, the huge reservoir at Ludlow had been dug, dammed, and slowly filled, the new pipes had been laid, and by 1875 the auxiliary pumping from the Connecticut could be ended. Springfield was now relying solely on its expensive new waterworks, built at a then imposing cost of over a million dollars.[29]

As the next years showed, winning public acceptance proved more difficult than constructing the facility. City councilmen, jealous of the independent and often haughty water commissioners, continually sniped at the project and its operation, while much of the public remained embittered and skeptical after the long years of policy debate. The basic difficulties underlying all these problems, though, were physical. Almost at once, a thick green growth came to cover the million dollar reservoir, and from the million dollar pipes flowed, more often than not, cloudy, smelly, and strange-tasting water. At first, people hoped the condition was temporary, the result of decaying tree stumps in the reservoir bed, and a prominent expert from the Massachusetts Institute of Technology declared after a brief investigation that the water quality would "improve as time passes, and need not awaken the slightest anxieties." A year later the embarrassed expert returned, and conceded what many had feared from the start — that decomposing bacteria caused the problem, and that it would in all likelihood remain endemic, particularly when summer heat reduced the flow of fresh springs into the reservoir. The condition, in fact, eventually did become so bad that Springfield was forced, shortly after the turn of the century, to build an entirely new system, ironically choosing a Westfield watershed site rejected in the surveys of the 1870's.[30]

Although the situation in the depression decade was not as bad as this later development might suggest, the water was distasteful enough to disillusion many with the system. People on the Hill, in particular, continued to rely on their private wells, notwithstanding the frantic warnings of city and state authorities that the clear, fine-tasting water there was deceptively contaminated to a dangerous level, while however discolored, the Ludlow water actually proved to be quite pure. By 1876 public displeasure had become manifest to city officials: although the new pipes covered all of the Hill's ward five, only 95 of its 1,250 families had bothered to have their homes connected. Throughout the city, of 6,200 eligible families only 4,239 were subscribers, and these, for the most part, had only faucets; city water filled only 1,800 waterclosets and 613 bathtubs in Springfield.[31]

This situation had direct financial implications, since the city counted on water-rents to pay the annual interest on the bonds which had built the system, and its operating expenses as well; the $50,000 that came in 1875 and 1876 hardly sufficed. Because of this, and also owing to an understandable desire to see some value result from such a controversial investment, the city worked hard with mixed results to improve the works and win public acceptance of the system. The number of takers grew by only 600 in the next four years, and receipts rose at a sluggish, if steady, pace. Backbiting and recriminations between the City Council and the water commissioners, meanwhile, worsened each year. Finally, in an effort to tie the water administration more closely to the city's executive system, the government replaced the independent board with a new executive body, consisting of the mayor, two citizens chosen by the council, and the city engineer. This change — part of a piecemeal adoption of ideas from the rejected 1877 charter, though supported by foes of that move — represented an inevitable and popular reorganization, for whatever the value of the commissioners' independence during the planning and construction of the waterworks, it proved less advantageous in the department's daily operation within a complex political and administrative context.[32]

And as it turned out, the reform seemed to mark a more general turning point in the utility's troubles. Even though the water itself remained murky, with the turn to prosperity and a new decade, receipts rose, administration became more satisfactory, and people be-

gan to find the idea of bathtubs, faucets, and toilets in every house
less strange. Efforts to make the best of a bad situation had, by
1880, at least produced a more general understanding and acceptance of the matter of public water supply. As with the city hospital,
pressure and problems had led to a search for solutions, rather than
a retreat from public involvement. The city, of course, had no
choice concerning water supply: faced with the need to obtain
greater public support, it extended its commitment to the public
importance of a general water supply for the community. But again,
the contrast with the improvements crisis is significant, for where
the frantic search for a clear line between public and private spheres
led, in that matter, to a reduction of the public role in what had
been a mixed enterprise, in questions more directly touching the
shared needs of all people in a complex urban environment, the
same pressure and a similar process produced an opposite and more
positive response, and this in regard to the water supply, which had
initially combined public and private roles just as ambiguously.

As attitudes moved in this direction, however, many vestiges of
the old dualism still remained. Thus, although the water board
argued, in opposing a proposal to meter water, that scaling cost to
consumption would encourage "those who most need to use water
to refrain from the free use of it," the mayor at times could operate
under different priorities: anxious about deficits, he once threatened
to be guided in the extension of piping solely by considering "which
streets promise the best rentals."[33] The implied conflict between
these conceptions of the role of a public utility became more explicit still in a closely related area — the city's new sewers.

Quite obviously, every increase in the water piped to Springfield
homes made an improved system for removing waste water that
much more imperative, and in any event the inadequacy of earlier
storm drains was every day more glaring. According to the description of the city physician: "You find damp and wet cellars, yards in
which are thrown the refuse matters from the home, and often
mixed with animal excrement; shallow water-closets whose contents
overflow the surface of the ground. Especially in the hot months
and after warm showers, these substances undergo rapid decomposi-
tion, filling the atmosphere with putrid and noxious vapors." The
city had adopted a comprehensive drainage plan amidst great

controversy, just before the depression. Major brick trunk sewers
were to follow the line of the old brook down the hill, dividing at
Worthington as had the stream itself. One trunk was then to go
north, curving to the river at Brightwood, while the other, completely obliterating the Town Brook, was to go south through the center
of town to a York Street river outlet. Smaller trunks and individual
street drains would feed the whole city's sewage into these branches.[34]

Technical questions, reduced appropriations, and betterment problems slowed progress on the system during the depression. Moving
cautiously, the city began construction from the ends of the plan,
moving in toward the center of town where conflicts of interest
were certain to be many — the north branch, as it developed, stalled
at Carew Street for five years when the city and uncooperative abuttors reached an impasse. By 1880, however, the trunk lines had
been virtually completed, and attention could begin to shift to the
lattice of smaller drains that would eventually include every city
street.[35]

The dimensions of the work made the shift from a property-drain-
age to a sanitation system — and the attendant problems — apparent
to all. With a sense of excitement, wonder, and some fear, Springfield recognized it was taking part in the revolutionary development
of sanitary engineering just then transforming public health concepts
in all major American cities. People found the idea of the huge
trunk sewers somewhat hard to adjust to, awed by the fact that beneath their streets ran "Rivers of Death, black, hidden, and hideous,
slowly winding their sluggish current through the city . . . full of the
foulest gases, vapors, and death." Hyperbole aside, the new methods
did create special problems, chief among them the accumulation of
sewer gases. And with the homes of the city quite literally tied together and each connected fixture potentially a chimney for the
vapors, a great deal of attention had to be given to traps and ventila-
ting devices, to say nothing of public reassurances about their effectiveness. So swiftly were cities becoming sophisticated in such
matters that a local expert commented in 1879 that a house with the
most advanced plumbing of the 1860's "would now be considered
almost unfit for human habitation."[36]

There were immediate political and philosophical consequences of the new trunk system as well, paralleling the water-rent question. Traditionally, the city had charged property owners a flat fee, above costs, for the privilege of connecting houses to the street sewer, usually around fifty dollars. These receipts, an important source of revenue, seemed justified because of the advantages any householder gained through such improvements to his property. It was not considered unusual or inappropriate to delay construction of a street drain "until the abutters are ready to pay entrance fees sufficient to justify the city in the construction of the smaller sewers," for without such commitment the city had no assurances that the sewers, once built, would be used.[37]

The rationale underlying this approach came under attack in the late 1870's, particularly from Dr. David Clark, the forceful city physician. In 1877 he demanded that the city reduce or even abolish the fees in order to stimulate the installation of drains. Fees covered only one fifth of the cost anyway, he pointed out, and to let them constitute a barrier for the poor who were in greatest need of better sanitation represented the narrowest economy. Further, Clark argued that the health of the entire community required that entrances be made compulsory whatever the fee. Individual choice and property rights simply could not apply in a situation where no person, however complete his own facilities, could be safe from contamination by virtue of his neighbor's inability or reluctance to provide drainage: good sanitation was by definition a communal condition, and it required a community standard to obtain it. Concluded Dr. Clark, "It is our obvious duty to give all, both rich and poor, every facility to breathe pure air, and protect them from disease and death."[38]

If the community was not ready to accept the need for mandatory entrances in 1877, at least the idea of reduced fees to promote wider use in the poorer sections of the city stimulated considerable discussion and interest. By 1879, a petition demanding a drastic reduction of fees was presented to the City Council, signed by hundreds including many taxpayers whose burden could only be increased by such a move. After stalling for a year, the council ordered a trial reduction to twenty-five dollars, and a thorough restudy of the entire sewer administration.[39]

The experiment proved somewhat successful, tripling the annual number of sewer entrances, but it in so doing brought the government squarely up against the conceptual dilemma it had been trying to avoid. As a special committee put it,

In a sanitary point of view, and as drains for the surplus water in the streets, the whole of the citizenry are benefitted. But as a matter of convenience for house drainage, the sewers are a special benefit to the parties entering. An entrance to them has come to be a necessity to many, and a convenience that would be cheap at a much larger fee than has been charged. As it is of great importance to the health of the city that the citizens of the thickly settled portions should avail themselves of sewer privileges the fee should not be so high as to discourage entrances. But it should not be so low as to work an injustice to those taxpayers not directly benefitted who would bear a large portion of the cost.

This, of course, provided no guideline at all, however well it expressed both ends that the policy was expected to serve. The cautious council, turning away Dr. Clark's arguments, still committed to the concept of apportioned benefits and, therefore, apportioned costs, proceeded to set the fees back at the higher level.[40]

The decision showed once again how difficult it was to move from the assumptions that had guided past policy. Although the concept of clear community priority in health matters had thus not been fully accepted and embodied in policy, it had at least altered the framework of discussion significantly and permanently. This, as Dr. Clark concluded, represented important progress regardless of initial results. The new questions, he declared, were the "offspring of a deeply felt public necessity," and represented "the principle, which is coming to be generally recognized, that the protection of the public health by the government is as truly a right of the people as the protection of persons and property against violence and fraud. It is not a mere sentiment of philanthropy, but a principle sanctioned alike by just reasoning and public economy."[41]

Public health as a community concern was itself an idea as old as New England, but Springfield had begun to discover that urbanization gave it a quite different meaning. The density and complexity of life in this setting implied that responsibility for the basic conditions of health and welfare, which had always been an individual or family matter, would necessarily become a community obligation, although the forms for carrying out that responsibility were by no means well defined. More generally, the emerging practical necessity for such public authority was linked to the emerging awareness of how dependent the people of an urban community were upon each other, and upon the institutions expressing that interdependence, precisely because the effects of any individual's weakness or irresponsibility now clearly extended well beyond the confines of his own life, necessarily if inadvertantly touching all those around him.

It is far from coincidental or paradoxical that this perception and its ethical and political corollaries bacame most explicit in precisely those areas where a traditional sense of community cohesion seemed to be weakening. The process of urbanization has always generated both centrifugal and centripetal effects, for the more individuals are driven into isolated, specialized roles and particularized identities, the more dependent they become on others, in both practical and spiritual ways, for the sense of competence and completeness that has been lost. Thus, while the pressure of the depression crisis brought Springfield to question and criticize traditional values of public and private benefit that had been overextended, it also led to important new concepts where the instability of traditional ideas about social harmony and individual responsibility seemed to be creating a dangerous vacuum. These two dimensions can be understood in quite similar terms, for they are both central to the changes that had been taking place in the nature of community, changes that it is now possible to define and evaluate in general terms. This can best be done by examining Springfield in 1880, as the city left the crisis years behind and turned optimistically once again to the future.

12. An Urban Community: 1880 and Beyond

"We are assembled under favorable auspices," announced Mayor Lewis J. Powers in the address inaugurating his second term in January 1880. "The dawn of a returning prosperity to our land, noted last year, has so far advanced that we can no longer doubt its reality."[1] Powers' very presence in office gave evidence that Springfield was passing out of the storm and into a new era. Emerson Wight, until the end of his fourth term in 1878, had continued to ride the hobbyhorse of retrenchment with a singleness of vision that carried him far from the public sentiment. His friends urged him to step down, to make the termination of his leadership fittingly correspond to the end of the depression emergency he had been called upon to fight; less gracious advisors suggested that his austerity crusade had become a "squeezed lemon." Wight spurned the advice, however, and after securing a fifth nomination discovered in the election that his friends had been correct: the people were tired, and voted for a change. The *Republican* called it regrettable that in voting out Wight the community appeared ungrateful for his service, but added that there were things to do, and "economy is not the whole of the law and prophets."[2]

Powers himself embodied a new spirit. He was a Springfield native who had risen from poor newsboy to wealthy businessman through a series of bold strokes during the 1860's, building up an enormously successful wholesale paper operation, complete with manufacturing and retail subsidiaries. While accumulating these riches almost literally out of rags, Powers emerged as one of the most glamorous young businessmen in the city — handsome, a noted sportsman,

238

civic-minded, and politically prominent. At forty-two, he was Springfield's youngest mayor, probably the most popular, and in many ways just the tonic everybody needed after years of depression. As one contemporary remembered, "The Wight administration had been of a Puritan tone, and the Powers regime in contrast was a Cavalier type."[3]

The dawn of a new era was signaled in other ways by the passing of several men who had been closely identified with the old days, among them Henry Alexander, Jr., and the formidable Daniel L. Harris. But the 1878 death of Samuel Bowles represented the deepest loss. Bowles's life, like that of Daniel Harris, spanned the period of Springfield's growth from town to city, a critical period as well in the life of a nation that was just beginning to know and appreciate this remarkable man. Bowles was truly awesome, matching a personality of tremendous power with an overriding integrity acknowledged and respected even by his worst enemies. There can be no question that had he been granted more than only fifty-two years, and these plagued by ill health and frequent prostration, apologies for his present obscurity would not be necessary. Springfield, at any rate, recognized the dimension of its loss, and mourned Bowles at his death as the city's leading and most deservedly famous citizen, if not its most popular. The appointment of his son as editor — the third Samuel Bowles to run the famous paper — somewhat softened the shock to the community.[4]

But Springfield did not linger over the loss of Bowles and other old leaders, or over the sad years just passing. The city looked ahead, and its mood became suddenly exuberant and exciting once again. There had been, in the crisis-obsessed city, no Fourth of July celebration of the nation's centennial in 1876, but in 1879 the awakening community more than made up for this with tremendous festivities, prefaced by months of elaborate fussing and planning. The mood was sustained afterward, and community life assumed a gay rhythm and pace not seen since the war years. Springfield joined gleefully in the spate of fads and fixations that captured the nation and characterized the times, from marathon walking races to more elevated concerns: Sarah Bernhardt played Springfield on her tumultuous first American tour in 1880, and hundreds camped overnight on the sidewalk to get tickets for her already legendary *Camille*. The nation had also discovered Gilbert and Sullivan, with the catchy lyrics from their first major hit, *Pinafore*, quoted to some vaguely connected purpose in almost every speech or article. The famous D'Oyly Carte Company appeared in Springfield at the time, and the glittering lighthearted optimism of their performance well characterized the end of Springfield's depression mood. Beyond such special attractions, a new bounce characterized the city's social season. The crisis years had not been empty, witnessing, for example, the formation of the important Connecticut Valley Historical Society. But with recovery came a flood of new social and sports clubs, musical circles, and a revived interest in community activities. Indicative of this was the excitement attending the opening of Gill's Art Building at Main and Bridge — here were Springfield's first galleries, including a complete art supply store, housed in an elaborate building itself exciting for being, in 1879, one of the first major building projects downtown in years. In all these developments, of course, the symbolic meaning of these cultural stirrings counts for more than their actual importance, or the degree to which they actually represented interests throughout the community, because after so many years of stagnation, such traditional signs of general energy were hailed by almost everyone as genuine harbingers of returning good times.[5]

Beyond the fact of recovery itself — business and building revived so suddenly in 1879 and 1880 as to seem "miraculous" — there was a special exuberance that stemmed from the expectation that a dazzling new era was about to open all over America.[6] No better symbol of this sense can be found than the revolutionary telephone, which made its Springfield debut in 1879, only a short while after it had been commercially introduced to the nation. At the outset, Bell's device was taken as simply a better, more flexible telegraph, a means of connecting two set points. The first phone in Springfield connected the almshouse to the Overseers of the Poor in the City Hall, and soon there were several private lines, with parties strung out on each like railroad stations along separate stretches of track. Almost immediately, however, Springfield picked up from New Haven the idea of a central exchange routing calls among incoming circuits. Two companies with competing city lines and exchanges were shortly in operation, a rivalry part of the national battle between the Bell Company and Western Union for control of the new industry; with the consolidation that gave Bell control, Springfield's two systems merged. By the end of 1879, there were over five hundred subscribers, and lines to Boston, Albany, and many nearby towns and cities. In just a few months, what began as a novelty held to be useful mainly for doctors, police, and some merchants had been generally recognized as a revolutionary innovation in general communications, and the revolution, significantly, was one Springfield had been able to join at the same time as the nation's largest and most sophisticated cities, a vivid indication of its place in this fraternity, and of the increasingly rapid diffusion of new ideas and technology among the members of the group.[7]

Among so many signs of resumption and return, the telephone was far from the only indication that the city of 33,000, about to enter another period of rapid and dizzying growth, had traveled quite a distance from its town origins, and that the new cycle of prosperity would be a very different one for Springfield. But to show, at the close of a long survey, only that Springfield was a different place for thirty years of change could hardly be held adequate justification for having led the reader into such intimacy with the streets, sewers, politics, and people exhumed here from a perhaps deserved obscurity; it is necessary, rather, to show that the years surveyed also define a qualitative change conferring importance on the community's experience. And it can, in fact, be said that by 1880 the city outwardly changed by its cycle of boom, soaring aftergrowth, crash, and recovery, had become in the process a fundamentally different community, whose people had developed important new ways of looking at themselves and their environment. By 1880, this is to say, the transition from town to city had been completed in all important respects. Therefore, while the biography of a city, like that of an individual, offers no fully satisfactory stopping place in midpassage, 1880 offers an appropriate point to pause in order to assess the nature of this transition and the process by which it had been made.

The nature of the traditional community could be understood in large part by studying Springfield's political system and traditions, and reference to this framework is probably the best way to summarize the city's change in more general terms. In the 1840's local partisan politics had been a sort of furious public game, a smoke-screen of activity behind which local affairs themselves remained remarkably unpoliticized. Government was quite limited, concerned for the most part with the interests of the taxpayers and run by and for them. The public business was not much more than the overlapping of more particularistic concerns, and the formulation of policy was thus not considered a matter for which political expression was required. At the same time, by affirming traditional harmony and inclusiveness, politics played the important role of helping to keep the deferential community of taxpayers at once open and cohesive. The occupational composition of the Board of Aldermen in the 1850's well suggested this community of association in which public and private life were virtually indistinguishable.

By 1880 it all had changed dramatically, however gradual the steps. As Springfield grew, city government inevitably became involved in community life in many new ways and on a vastly different scale. In this context, the problems and issues generated by rapid growth became sources of systematic and frequently bitter political conflict. These changes all deeply affected traditional attitudes, as another look at the Board of Aldermen shows. The merchants and tradesmen, 27 percent of the aldermen through the 1850's, rose steadily to 42 percent in the 1870's. The manufacturers enjoyed a comparable rise, and the two groups together, accounting earlier for fewer than half the seats on the board, now represented an overwhelming 75 percent. Moreover, to these businessmen public service had apparently become less ceremonial and more serious: the length of the average tenure among them was now two and a half annual terms, a doubling of the period of service in the first years of city government.

When one recalls Dahl's postulated three-dynasty cycle, it becomes especially interesting to note that these gains were not registered at the expense of the supposedly distinct social, financial, and professional establishment. Far from being driven out as the businessmen moved in, the lawyers, bankers, and insurance men also increased their representation, from 12 to 18 percent. Proportionally, they stood in almost exactly the same relation to the businessmen throughout the thirty years considered. Thus, the structure of what may broadly be called the community elite in government

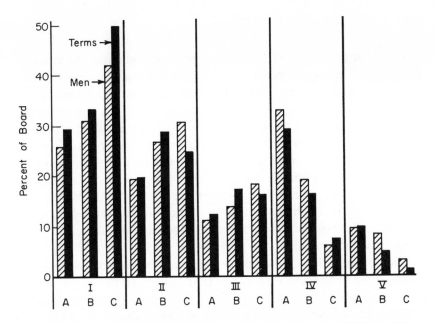

Composition of the Springfield Board of Aldermen, 1852–1880

	Group I Merchants, Tradesmen	Group II Mfgrs., Builders, RR execs.	Group III Professionals, Bankers, Insurance	Group IV Artisans, Working- men	Group V Farmers
A. 1852–1860 52 men serve 72 terms	14 men 26.9% 21 terms 29.2%	10 men 19.3% 14 terms 19.4%	6 men 11.5% 9 terms 12.5%	17 men 32.7% 21 terms 29.2%	5 men 9.6% 7 terms 9.7%
B. 1861–1870 48 men serve 81 terms	15 men 31.2% 27 terms 33.3%	13 men 27.1% 23 terms 28.4%	7 men 14.6% 14 terms 17.4%	9 men 18.8% 13 terms 16.1%	4 men 8.3% 4 terms 4.8%
C. 1871–1880 33 men serve 80 terms	14 men 42.4% 40 terms 50%	10 men 30.3% 20 terms 25%	6 men 18.2% 13 terms 16.3%	2 men 6.1% 6 terms 7.5%	1 man 3% 1 term 1.2%
Total 133 men serve 233 terms	43 men 32.3% 88 terms 37.7%	33 men 24.8% 57 terms 24.5%	19 men 14.3% 36 terms 15.4%	28 men 21.1% 40 terms 17.2%	10 men 7.5% 12 terms 5.2%

hardly changed at all, while the level of its participation increased strikingly. The big losers, of course, were the workingmen. By the 1870's, their 33 percent had evaporated; only two of the thirty-three aldermen in that decade, serving only six of the eighty terms, were artisans or workingmen. This seems to have resulted more from the businessmen's awakened interest in serving rather than from any conscious purge of the workingmen, but the result was the same: the virtual elimination of this traditional presence. It is a significant and ironic paradox that the fading of the informal old deference politics, reputedly characterized by homogeneous leadership, was thus accompanied in fact by a marked decrease in the social diversity of officeholders.[8]

The politicization of the businessmen can be understood in several ways, some of them more obvious than others. In the first place, as it became more active government became much more important to substantial businessmen and property-owners. They feared the rising taxes and the soaring public debt, on the one hand, while on the other they were attracted by government's increased ability to improve their property and promote their prosperity. Because of this, because so much money and power had come to be at stake in public decisions, local affairs now required their more active participation. As Mayor Powers commented in 1880, "Springfield is a mere business concern, and it should be run by business men."[9]

But this is only part of the story, and perhaps not the most important part. To picture the businessmen as suddenly acting out of particularistic motives is to forget their earlier combination of public and private roles, and to overlook the actual processes described in preceding chapters. For as the city grew, the public meaning of government had increased just as significantly as had its implications for private property. The expanded role of the business elite, or so it seemed from their vantage point, stemmed as much from a desire to meet the increased burdens of public responsibility as from a desire to further their own interests. Public and private interest, public and private responsibility — to the old elite, given their understanding of leadership, there was little difference.

The more this traditional formulation was extended, however, the more unsatisfactory it became to all concerned. While growth was steady and shared, the conflict remained implicit, but in the crisis of the 1870's, confidence was virtually destroyed and suddenly the concept of the public interest appeared to be cut hopelessly adrift in a sea of particularistic currents, an abstraction that in justifying almost anything had come to mean, so it seemed, almost nothing. Public and private remained, as always, inextricable, but although the spheres remained mixed now the concepts were differentiated, and the vastly increased importance of community decisions made their tandem relationship seem inherently dangerous from a variety of perspectives.

Traditional community leaders responded with the retrenchment drive and charter reform, all in an effort to protect what they held to be the integrity of the community and its government. Others in the community responded, increasingly, by coveting the power that frightened them, their traditional deference eroded by the very notions of public interest championed by the elite. Appeals to this standard, poorer people began to realize, could support expenditures for their neighborhoods and property as logically as for the traditionally favored interests of those with a greater stake in society — an abstractly defined sword could cut both ways. It all depended on what form and substance was given to the justificatory standard, and this, they were just coming to see, depended in large part on who was perceiving the needs and defining the terms.

In the 1880's this new consciousness was to become explicit, in a sharp departure from tradition. The businessmen, for example, after several false starts and much exhortation from the mayor, formed a Businessmen's Association composed of hundreds of merchants and manufacturers, a first step toward a Chamber of Commerce and an institutionalized, politically powerful voice for the business community.[10] At the other end of the spectrum, Springfield began to see sustained, serious union organizing for the first time, which soon produced several aggressive craft unions and, by 1890, a Central Labor Union among the city's trades. Even at the decade's start, the new spirit had been both recognized and significantly crystalized by the appearance of the city's first working-class oriented newspaper, under notable auspices. In 1880 Edward Bellamy emerged from his Chicopee study and with his brother Charles founded the *Penny News*, which was soon enabled, by a warm reception, to become the *Daily News*. As Springfield's first penny paper, moreover, it could be easily purchased by those whom it sought to reach. Edward Bellamy, as it happened, soon retired to devote all his time to his writing — shortly to result in *Looking Backward* — and under Charles the *News* gradually lost its initial brashness, becoming more tame and conventional. Nevertheless, its existence signaled new pressures and attitudes, and a focused self-consciousness within the various ranks of society.[11]

In this atmosphere, it would not be long before Springfield witnessed a local version of what was then becoming a general pattern in American municipal government — the political challenge and then the accession of the rising immigrants and working people whom Dahl termed the ex-plebes. This had been foreshadowed in the 1870's, but before traditional leadership could be overturned, the ideas and assumptions reinforcing that leadership throughout the community had to be supplanted, and this was the process virtually completed in Springfield around 1880. Workingmen were only temporarily eliminated from government, for as the idea of public interest with which the businessmen consolidated their power became more abstract, it began to function less as a guideline to policy and more as a conceptual umbrella in the shade of which conflicting groups could struggle for power. A new framework for legitimized, self-conscious interest-group conflict seemed to be emerging, a far cry from the consensual, anti-political tradition of New England community government. In the sense that politics can be defined as the systemic expression and management of conflict, Springfield stood on the threshold of what we would recognize as fully urban-style politics. And ironically enough, this new style owed perhaps most to those people and values it was shortly to overturn.

When recast in only slightly broader terms, these observations about the changing nature of politics help to explain the more general meaning of community growth, both in Springfield and in relation to larger questions that have concerned American historians. Robert Wiebe's *Search For Order*, for example, the most impressive of several recent efforts to conceptualize the period covered here, stresses that these years saw a turning from the local, immediate community to more formal and cosmopolitan identifications transcending the community — from the horizontal to the vertical orientation in society, as others put it, or even from the classic *gemein-schaft* to *gesellschaft*.[12] But this study of Springfield suggests that the local orientation could remain hugely significant, and central to the processes of change. It was not that the idea of the local community was disappearing, but rather that it was changing quite basically. Seen another way, to the extent Wiebe is correct the point is perhaps not so much *which* level of society people identified with, but rather the nature and quality of that relationship, on whatever level.

In this sense, by 1880 the changes in Springfield foreshadowed in Part One had taken place. Traditionally, community was severely limited functionally and institutionally, yet seemed to express, in both symbolic and actual ways, a strong sense of cultural cohesion and an intimate association among the people. Over the years, this combination was substantially reversed. By 1880, with relationships becoming more formal and people seeing themselves more fundamentally in terms of interest groups, the community was in the process of disintegrating as a real feeling of association. But at the same time, the growing public functions of government and the accumulating results of rapid social and physical change were giving to the community a new meaning: it was becoming more important and comprehensive as a symbolic expression of interdependence. Community, in other words, was changing from an informal, direct sensation to a formal, perceived abstraction. As such, the emerging idea of community had considerable power and inspirational reach. But it also had the inherent weaknesses of any large abstraction: however potent a symbol, by itself it was cold and empty. It needed to be defined and interpreted in real terms; it had to be embodied in real institutions and policies; above all, it had to be realized through a process that touched the very real world of economic interest and political pressure. In a variety of ways, the emerging abstract quality of community — as with the notion of public interest in government — proved crucial to both the process of change and to the nature of the new urban community being produced.

This all bears directly on the question of the sources of conflict and change in the urban community. Much recent research on American cities has tended to see the forms of conflict — political, cultural, social, or ideological — as virtually reducible to the variations and stresses in the social fabric of the urbanizing community. Samuel Hays, for example, in his work on municipal progressivism, suggests quite necessarily that we look past the high-minded rhetoric of reformers and urban boosters to discover the more particularistic social meaning of their crusade, the structural determinants of their perceptions and their prescriptions. Thus, the drive to rationalize and centralize local government appears as the elite's way of reinforcing itself against real or potential threats, and thus could take on more or less explicitly antidemocratic overtones.[13] The story traced in preceding chapters, however, throws a somewhat different light on such questions, and suggests that we limit outselves unnecessarily by regarding community-building steps in such exclusively structural terms, for the experience of sharing in and overseeing community growth could generate structural conflict as much as it reflected it. In Springfield, traditional leaders found themselves facing crucial decisions just at a time when the entire nation was recognizing what a profound challenge the urban environment presented to its resources and, more basically, to all sorts of traditional assumptions. These leaders were groping for the answers to half understood questions, searching for ways to preserve what they understood to be their democratic traditions while also serving the modern city's need for competent service and constructive policy. The anxieties involved in this search were distinct from, and in Springfield's case prior to, the perception of conflict between social groups. In the same sense that the abstraction of the public interest figured centrally in the emergence of political conflict, so too the actual process of building new institutions provided a new framework for community, in which social conflict and change would be able to depart even more drastically from tradition.

This becomes more understandable when one recognizes how much this search, and indeed almost every physical, social, and even economic step in the building of the city was affected by the emergence of an abstracted conception of community. Whether one speaks of the process of bureaucratic development, the search for the "True Economy," the spreading of the railroad net and wholesaling reach, the shaping of the physical image of the community, the very scale of perception and building, the institutional expressions of social diversity, or simply the projective scope of planning and anticipated growth, time itself being perhaps the greatest abstraction — all of these involved the replacement of informal and intuitive responses by a progressively more informed, comprehensive, and abstract perspective on the city's growth. More to the point, the process bears directly on the problem of understanding the mechanisms by which options are defined and change takes place; it speaks both to the deeper sources of change and its products. For if nothing else, the chapters above should have made clear the ways in which urban change in Springfield built upon itself, in a complex and constant interaction. Cause and effect, stimulus and response — distinctions like these have proven more a hindrance than a help in understanding the building of the city. The taking on of each new responsibility, the planning of each new project in business or government, the crossing of each new threshold of debt or taxation, the abandonment of each out-moded social form — every step involved a more or less conscious rethinking of what was appropriate to the changing city, and each new development, institution, or assumption thus produced became part of the context against which subsequent questions were measured. Add to this the influence of similar processes in other cities and in American society generally, and something of the complexity of Springfield's urbanization can be appreciated. The triangles of forces employed earlier are themselves but hugely oversimplified models for expressing this pervasive interaction among people, ideas, forces, needs, interests, and contexts, between all of these and the framework that conditioned how they were perceived and understood. Is it any wonder that people turned to abstractions when the profound energy of rapid growth made this complexity seem chaotic?

However one understands the general nature of urbanization, then, the process of actually building a city and an urban community involved at its heart the dynamics of conceptual change. Before there could be a meaningful response to growth there had to be understanding; before there could be understanding there had to be perception. In order for a new type of community to be produced, there had to be a new type of approach, and the evolution of progressively more abstract understandings both determined and grew out of the perceptions, the understandings, and the responses that shaped the city. By 1880 the urban community itself was little more than an abstraction, a symbol in the minds of the people. In the years this study covers, Springfield traded an immediate sense of community for an exalted and abstract one, as have most American cities in the past century. If the benefits of this trade were to prove thrilling and encouraging for several generations, its price was even at the time beginning to become apparent. It would only be fully revealed later, however, when the monumental intractability of so many urban problems showed how deep their roots lay in the very nature of the American city, and in the processes by which it had been built.

Notes
Index

Notes

All the local sources referred to in the notes, unless otherwise mentioned, can be found in the local history collection of the Springfield City Library where, for the most part, they are excellently catalogued and easily accessible. Official city governmental sources, both printed and manuscript, are located in the vault of the Springfield City Hall. With the exception of property assessment data, destroyed by fire many years ago, these records are quite complete.

A great many of these materials, official and general, are also available in the excellent collection at the Massachusetts State Library, State House, Boston, Massachusetts. The official Massachusetts state papers and reports are, of course, located there, but the Springfield Library has served as a repository and holds a full set of the official state documents cited in this study.

The newspapers that figure so centrally in the notes are all available, in original, in the Springfield City Library or other local libraries, and they are in generally excellent condition. Some explanation should be offered about the way the *Springfield Republican* was examined in research. The *Republican* usually came out in both daily and weekly editions. The latter was a digest of selected items, and of little research use. But in some years, a semiweekly or triweekly edition was also published. Unlike the weekly, these included all the items from the daily paper, omitting only advertising, filler, and other insignificant matter. Because these midweek editions were physically easier to handle, they were used for research where possible, with spotchecks frequently made in the daily editions to prevent important material from being overlooked. Since files of the daily *Republican* are more generally available today, in Springfield and elsewhere, anyone seeking to use the footnote citations in this study should remember that items in a given issue of the *Tri-weekly* or *Semi-Weekly Republican* may have originally appeared in the *Daily Republican* on the given date, or on several preceding days.

There is a complete file of the *Springfield City Directory* in the City Library. Although the title and imprint of this commercial publication often changed from year to year — *Bessey's Springfield Directory, Springfield City Directory and Business Advertiser*, and so on — it was generally referred to, after 1852, as the *City Directory*, and is so cited in these notes.

The following forms of abbreviations have been used in the notes:

SR   *Springfield Daily Republican*
SR²   *Springfield Semi-Weekly Republican*
SR³   *Springfield Tri-Weekly Republican*
SU   *Springfield Daily Union*
M-Ald.   Records of the Mayor and the Board of Aldermen (MS, City Hall vault).
MR   *Municipal Register of the City of Springfield for 18––. Containing its Charter, Officers, the Organization of the Government, Address of the Mayor, Ordinances and Reports of Various Officers and Committees* (Springfield: imprint varies, 1852–1881).
Mass. AR   *Acts and Resolves Passed by the General Court of Massachusetts in the Year 18––* (Boston: State Printers 1848–1881).

Introduction

1. *Encyclopaedia Britannica*, 11th ed. (Cambridge, Eng., 1910–1911), VI, 400–401. Many of the points developed in this preface are discussed in greater detail and with more thorough documentation in my recent article, "L'histoire urbaine Américaine: Réflexions sur les tendances récentes," *Annales: Economies, Sociétés, Civilisations*, 25 (July–August 1970), 880–896. Mimeographed copies of the original English version of this article are available on request from the author.

2. Charles Tilly, "The State of Urbanization," *Comparative Studies in Society and History*, 10 (October 1967), 100–113, 103–104 quoted.

1. The Traditional Community, 1840–1860

1. Much of the background material in this chapter is available in a number of good local histories, and the text will not be annotated unless specific reference seems called for. Among the most thorough and reliable of these histories are Mason Green, *Springfield, 1636–1886* (Springfield: C. A. Nichols, 1888) and Alfred M. Copeland, *Our Country and Its People: A History of Hampden County, Massachusetts* (3 vols.; Boston: Century Publishing Co., 1902); Harry Andrew Wright, *The Story of Western Massachusetts* (4 vols.; New York: Lewis Historical Publishing Co., 1949) is a collection of excellent monographs on local topics. Charles H. Barrows, *The History of Springfield for the Young* (Springfield: Connecticut Valley Historical Society, 1911), is surprisingly sophisticated and helpful. For an early and thorough survey, see J. G. Holland's famous *History of Western Massachusetts* (Springfield: Samuel Bowles, 1845). Henry M. Burt, *The First Century of the History of Springfield* (Springfield: H. M. Burt, 1898) reprints the official town records for that period. *Papers and Proceedings of the Connecticut Valley Historical Society* (4 vols.; Springfield: Published by the Society, 1876–1907) deal almost exclusively with topics from the town's history in the seventeenth and eighteenth centuries.

2. Harry Andrew Wright, *The Genesis of Springfield* (Springfield, 1949) is a pamphlet discussing this period, and correcting many of the mistakes of the standard local works. Most of its information is also in his *Story of Western Massachusetts*. Barrows, *History for the Young*, is particularly good on geology and topography. See also Louis Seig, "Concepts of Change and the Historical Method in Geography: The Case of Springfield, Massachusetts, 1630–1880," unpub. diss., University of Minnesota, 1968, chap.iii, pp. 55–75.

3. Again, Wright's pamphlet, *Genesis of Springfield*, is best on this. See also Seig, "Historical Geography: Springfield," chaps. iv, v, pp. 76–127.

4. In addition to any standard work for all these events, see the particularly thorough treatment of King Philip's War in Mason Green, *Springfield*, and Holland, *Western Massachusetts*.

5. The best modern discussion of this period in a broader context than local history is Robert J. Taylor, *Western Massachusetts in the Revolution* (Providence, R. I.: Brown University Press, 1954), especially pp. 52–74 on the pre-revolutionary days, and pp. 128–167 on Shays's Rebellion. Taylor stresses Springfield's conservatism as one of the older established towns along the river. Later it was one of the few towns in western Massachusetts to ratify the Constitution. But his conclusion that Shays's Rebellion was basically a class conflict is unconvincing and seems not to follow from his own evidence. For an interesting account of the rebellion seen from a local perspective, see William L. Smith, "Springfield in Shays' Rebellion," *Papers of the CVHS.*, 1 (1876–1881), 72–90.

6. Richard D. Brown, *Urbanization in Springfield, Massachusetts, 1790–1830* (Springfield: Connecticut Valley Historical Museum, 1962, pamphlet), pp. 5–9; Copeland, *Hampden County*, II, 19–20.

7. Timothy Dwight, *Travels in New England and New York* (London: William Baynes and Son, 1823), I, 283–286.

8. Jesse Chickering, *A Statistical View of the Population of Massachusetts from 1765 to 1840* (Boston: Little and Brown, 1846), pp. 8–9, 24–38, 43–49, 73–80; John F. Sly, *Town Government in Massachusetts* (Cambridge, Mass.: Harvard University Press, 1930), pp. 110–111. See also Adna F. Weber, *The Growth of Cities in the Nineteenth Century* (New York: Macmillan Co., 1899), p. 37. For a modern statistical analysis, see Jeffrey G. Williamson, "Antebellum Urbanization in the American Northeast," *Journal of Economic History*, 25 (December 1965), 592–608.

9. This question is the focus of Brown's paper, *Urbanization in Springfield*.

10. In addition to standard local histories, see Felicia Deyrup, *Arms and Arms Makers of the Connecticut Valley*, Smith College Studies, 33 (Northampton, Mass: Smith College, 1948). The basic history of the Armory is Derwent Whittlesey, "The Springfield Armory: A Study in Institutional Development," unpub. diss., University of Chicago, 1920. See also Constance Green, "A History of the Springfield Armory," incomplete, unpublished, and undated manuscript study, Springfield City Library.

11. Brown, *Urbanization in Springfield*, p. 28. For a specialized but disappointing analysis of geography's role, see Lester Klimm, *The Relation Between*

Certain Population Changes and the Physical Environment in Hampden, Hampshire, and Franklin Counties, Massachusetts, 1790–1925 (Philadelphia: University of Pennsylvania Press, 1933).

12. In addition to the local histories, see Margaret Martin, *Merchants and Trade of the Connecticut River Valley, 1750–1820*, Smith College Studies, 24 (Northampton, Mass.: Smith College, 1938), pp. 16, 93–99, 170, 186–188, 203–204. See also Vera Shlakman, *Economic History of a Factory Town: A Study of Chicopee, Massachusetts*, Smith College Studies, 20 (Northampton, Mass.: Smith College, 1935), pp. 24–28.

13. Brown, *Urbanization in Springfield*, discusses the point of gauging local investment, see especially pp. 9–18.

14. Charles Dickens, *Notes on America* (Greenwich, Conn. 1961; first published, 1842), 91–92. Martin, *Merchants and Trade*, p. 197.

15. See the very helpful study by Thelma M. Kistler, *The Rise of Railroads in the Connecticut Valley*, Smith College Studies, 23 (Northampton, Mass.: Smith College 1937), and the invaluable work by Edward C. Kirkland, *Men, Cities and Transportation* (2 vols.; Cambridge, Mass.: Harvard University Press, 1948), for thorough study of these developments.

16. See also the 1836 map in Mason Green's, *History of Springfield*, p. 436. This and the other basic local histories discuss this neighborhood development adequately.

17. Sly, *Town Government*, pp. 103–108, 112–115. Horace G. Wadlin, "The Growth of Cities in Massachusetts," *Publications of the American Statistical Association*, n. s. 13, vol. 2, (March 1891), pp. 159–160. The other cities incorporated before Springfield were Worcester, 1848, Lynn, 1849, and Newburyport, 1851. See also Chickering, *Population of Massachusetts*, pp. 24, 44–49.

18. Charles Francis Adams, Jr., *Three Episodes of Massachusetts History* (Boston: Houghton Mifflin, 1892), II, 965–967. See also Sly, *Town Government*, pp. 111–112.

19. On Cabotville (Chicopee) development, see Shlakman, *Factory Town*, pp. 65–68; and Thaddeus M. Szetela, *History of Chicopee* (Chicopee: Szetela and Rich, n.d., but after 1944), p. 27.

20. See Springfield Town Records, City Hall vault, VII, 295, for the initial town meeting on the matter, December 25, 1847. For minutes and summary of debate, see *Springfield Daily Republican* December 24, 1847 (hereafter cited as *SR*); *Springfield Weekly Republican*, December 25, 1847; *Chicopee Telegraph*, December 29, 1847; *Springfield Gazette*, December 21, 1847. On the change in character of Cabotville, see Shlakman, *Factory Town*, pp. 65–68.

21. "Citizen" articles are in *SR*, January 4, 5, 15, 24, 1848, with January 5, 24 quoted here. The Dwight quote is from the *Chicopee Telegraph*, February 9, 1848; Barton quote is from the *Springfield Gazette*, December 21, 1847. For reports on other meetings about the matter, see *SR*, December 15, 18, 1847; January 19, 26, 1848.

22. *Hampden Post*, March 22, 1848.

23. The quote is from *Springfield Weekly Republican*, December 25, 1847.

For the general arguments in favor of incorporation and against division, see *SR*, December 18, 20, 1847; January 19, 1848. *Springfield Gazette*, December 21, 1847. "Replies to Citizen," *SR*, January 7, 10, 1848.

24. See *SR*, February 12, 1848 (town meeting rejects division); March 3, 15, 20, 24, 1848 (legislative committee hearings); and April 3, 1848 (town remonstrance). The proposed city charter is *Massachusetts General Court House Documents 1848*, no. 6. For the split itself, see Massachusetts *Acts and Resolves* 1848:189 (hereafter Mass. *AR*). See also Springfield Town Records, VII, 299. There was much wrangling over boundaries and division of property, because each town sought to include valuable lands in its own bounds while letting bridges and roads — and the responsibility for their maintenance — fall to the other. The details and procedure of actually dividing the town are in the "Report of the Selectmen," *Annual Reports of the Town School Committee and Selectmen, &c. during the year 1849*, pp. 17–19, and Springfield Town Records, VII, 322, 338–339.

25. Mason Green, *Springfield*, p. 480. *SR*, March 31; April 2, 3, 4, 16, 17, 29, 1849.

26. The ordeal can be followed in effective outline through the procedural minutes of the town meetings, in Town Records, VII, 503–507. For highlights in the press, with specially valuable issues italicized, see *SR*, April 8, 14, 15, *25, 29*; May 12, 19, 20, *29*, 31, 1851.

27. Mason Green, *Springfield*, p. 461; *SR*, February 11, March 1, April 13, 19, 22, 1852. *Hampden Post*, April 13, 19, 1852. One riddle is why it took Springfield three years to reach 12,000 once again, an increment of only a thousand. There are no references to a recession or slowed population growth elsewhere or in Springfield during this period. It perhaps had more to do with statistical variations in these unofficial and probably unreliable censuses.

28. See Town Records, VII, 508–512. For the new charter, see Mass. *AR*, 1852: 94. Also, "Report of the Board of Five Men for Dividing the City into Wards," *Municipal Register for 1852* [*MR*, 1852], appendix. See also *SR*, April 22, 1852; *Hampden Post*, April 1, 1852.

29. Town Records, VII, last page. For the new government's inaugural ceremonies, see *SR*, May 26, 1852. The city seal is explained in Barrows, *History of Springfield for the Young*, pp. 132–133.

2. The Meaning of Community

1. See especially Michael Zuckerman, *Peaceable Kingdoms: New England Towns in the Eighteenth Century* (New York: Alfred A. Knopf, 1970), which will be important in the argument of this chapter, and also Kenneth A. Lockridge, *A New England Town: The First 100 Years* (New York: W. W. Norton, 1970). Page Smith, *As A City Upon a Hill: The Town in American History* (New York: Alfred A. Knopf, 1966) is also excellent social history, but is much less satisfactory as an interpretation of the town as an institution, concentrating instead on the many aspects of life within towns.

2. H. Paul Douglass, *The Springfield Church Survey* (New York: George H. Doran, 1926), pp. 51–57. Rev. John J. McCoy, *History of the Catholic Church in the Diocese of Springfield* (Boston: Hurd and Everts Co., 1900), pp. 98–100. *History of St. John's Congregational Church* (Springfield: History Committee of St. John's, 1962) is the best survey of the background of the Negro community in Springfield.

3. The development of this aristocracy is well described in Margaret E. Martin, *Merchants and Trade of the Connecticut River Valley, 1750–1820* (Northampton, Mass.: Smith College, 1938) and to some extent in Robert J. Taylor, *Western Massachusetts in the Revolution* (Providence, R.I.: Brown University Press 1954), as well as in the standard local histories mentioned in the notes to the first chapter. For a somewhat contrasting approach, which will be explicitly considered later in this study, see Robert Dahl, *Who Governs?* (New Haven: Yale University Press, 1961), especially the long historical introduction to his analysis of contemporary New Haven, pp. 11–86, and 25–28 in particular. See also E. Digby Baltzell, *The Protestant Establishment: Aristocracy and Caste in America* (New York: Random House, 1964), pp. 7–10, 18–21, which defines the aristocracy as those upper-class families possessing authority and status not only by virtue of birth, but through wealth and other forms of leadership. In fact, asserts this sociologist, the "aristocratic process" itself, by which this group is created, "means that the upper class is open."

4. A. F. Weber, *Growth of Cities* has some excellent statistics on this for a somewhat later period, pp. 265–266, showing that in Massachusetts only 35 percent of the population were born in the census town. This concept is fully explored, but mostly in relation to working classes, in Stephan Thernstrom, *Poverty and Progress: Social Mobility in a Nineteenth Century City* (Cambridge, Mass.: Harvard University Press, 1964), a remarkable study of Newburyport, Massachusetts based solidly on manuscript census returns. See A. F. Weber, *Growth of Cities*, especially pp. 84–90, 198–200.

5. Charles Wells Chapin, *Sketches of Inhabitants and Other Citizens of Old Springfield of the Present Century, and its Historic Mansions of "Ye Olden Tyme"* (Springfield: Springfield Printing Co., 1893).

6. Smith, *City Upon a Hill*, includes a good sketch of the social life of small towns during this period, pp. 157–178. For a more analytic discussion, see Thernstrom, *Poverty and Progress*, which attacks what is seen as a myth of "democratic paradise" by discussing social controls formal and informal in the old town, pp. 33–39. The most sophisticated treatment is Zuckerman's discussion of socialization, in *Peaceable Kingdoms*, pp. 46–84.

7. George S. Merriam, *The Life and Times of Samuel Bowles* (2 vols.; New York: Century Co., 1885), is a really excellent biography including many of Bowles's letters, by one of his Springfield contemporaries. It is also a valuable source on the newspaper, the town, and the issues of the time, much more satisfactory than the useful later study by Richard Hooker, *The Story of an Independent Newspaper* (New York: Macmillan Co., 1924).

8. Smith, *City Upon a Hill,* discusses religion and socialization, pp.75–77.

9. Joseph Gusfield, *Symbolic Crusade: Status Politics and the American Temperance Movement,* (Urbana, Ill.: University of Illinois Press, 1963), pp. 44, 69, and p. 36 quoted. See especially chap. ii "Status Control and Mobility," pp. 36–60, and chap. iii, "Assimilative Reform and Social Dominance," pp. 61–86, as well as Gusfield's theoretical conclusion, chap. vii, "A Dramatistic Theory of Status Politics," pp. 166–188.

10. *SR,* December 11, 1857; "Mayor's Address," *MR,* 1859, p. 18.

11. For background on this phase of the temperance movement, see Smith, *City Upon a Hill,* pp. 145–156, and J. C. Furnas, *The Life and Times of the Late Demon Rum* (New York: G. P. Putnam's Sons, 1965), pp. 165, 174–175. For a view from the inside of the crusade, see George Faber Clark, *History of the Temperance Reform in Massachusetts, 1813–1883* (Boston: Clark and Carruth, 1888), pp. 86–94.

12. *SR,* December 6, 1858.

13. Zuckerman, *Peaceable Kingdoms,* chap. v, "Sense of the Meeting," pp. 154–186, especially 166–167, 176–177.

14. See Lee Benson, *The Concept of Jacksonian Democracy* (Princeton: Princeton University Press, 1961), pp. 64, 82–85, 141, 177–184, 275–281, 292–293; Dahl, *Who Governs?,* p. 28.

15. See Edward C. Banfield and James Q. Wilson, *City Politics* (Cambridge, Mass.: Harvard University Press, 1965), p. 22, and Arthur J. Vidich and Joseph Bensman, *Small Town in Mass Society* (Princeton: Princeton University Press, 1958), pp. 109–110. On the other hand, for a good illustration of the class-dominated rhetoric of the period, see the fiery Locofoco broadside reprinted in Chapin, *Old Inhabitants,* pp. 243–244.

16. See Martin, *Merchants and Trade,* p. 223, and Taylor, *Western Massachusetts,* pp. 11–26, 75–102, 175–177. Taylor makes the additional point that even after the Revolution, hostility toward the East and general loyalty to the region solidified support for the local establishment. See also Thernstrom, *Progress and Poverty,* p. 41. The classic description of deference politics in an early-American setting is Charles S. Sydnor, *American Revolutionaries in the Making,* (New York: Collier Books, 1962; first published as *Gentlemen Freeholders,* Chapel Hill: University of North Carolina Press, 1952), especially pp. 60–73.

17. The following figures, compiled from Springfield city directories, include all of the fifty-two men who held the seventy-two annual seats on the Board of Aldermen between 1852 and 1860. Categories are of necessity somewhat arbitrary, and it was often difficult to assign individuals to one or another, as in the cases of artisan-entrepreneurs, or middle-level factory officials; in addition, directory descriptions were themselves often inconsistent. However, familiarity with the community and the individuals involved hopefully permitted meaningful assignation in most instances. The exact title of the city directory varied from year to year.

1852–1860

1.	Merchants, businessmen	14 men	26.9%	21 terms	29.2%
2.	Manufacturers, rail- roaders, builders, etc.	10 men	19.3%	14 terms	19.4%
3.	Professionals, bankers, insurance	6 men	11.5%	9 terms	12.5%
4.	Artisans, workingmen, foremen	17 men	32.7%	21 terms	29.2%
5.	Farmers	5 men	9.6%	7 terms	9.7%
		52 men	100%	72 terms	100%

18. Zuckerman, *Peaceable Kingdoms*, p. 189. More generally, see his chap. vi, "A Happy Mediocrity," pp. 187–219, esp. pp. 189–206, and also appendices 6–9, pp. 274–282.

19. Oscar Handlin and Mary Flug Handlin, *Commonwealth* (New York: New York University Press, 1947), p. 139, and also pp. 53–85. John F. Sly, *Town Government in Massachusetts, 1620–1930* (Cambridge, Mass.: Harvard University Press, 1930), pp. 38–39. A particularly good discussion of the general questions involved is Carter Goodrich, *Government Promotion of American Canals and Railroads, 1800–1890* (New York: Columbia University Press, 1960), especially chap. i, "The Spirit of Improvement," pp. 3–16, and chap. viii, "Public Promotion and Private Enterprise," pp. 265–297. In addition, see Zuckerman, *Peaceable Kingdoms*, pp. 71–72, 134–135.

20. Zuckerman, *Peaceable Kingdoms,* pp. 166–167. See also pp. 105–107 and chap. v, "Sense of the Meeting," pp. 154–187.

21. "Table Showing the Growth of Expenditures . . . from 1845 to 1876," *MR*, 1877, follows p. 203 (foldout).

22. Max Weber's distinction is relevant here between government involvement in private law, concerning relations between individuals, and public law, concerning the community as a whole. See the *Essays in Sociology*, a collection edited by H. H. Gerth and C. Wright Mills (New York: Oxford University Press, 1946), p. 239.

23. Chilton Williamson, *American Suffrage from Property to Democracy* (Princeton: Princeton University Press, 1960), pp. 270–271.

24. This point is discussed in Arthur J. Vidich and Joseph Bensman, *Small Town in Mass Society* (Princeton: Princeton University Press, 1958), pp. 116–118.

25. "Mayor's Address," *MR*, 1857, p. 24. Resentment of the center continued to breed secession spirit in the outskirts, for which see "Mayor's Address," *MR*, 1854, p. 61, and *SR*, March 17, 1856. Hostility to the idea of a centralized city fire department kept it from being included in the city charter, and only after the charter was amended (Mass. *AR*, 1852:175) could the step be taken. Such opposition easily intimidated the new government. One of the city's first official actions, symbolically enough, was a refusal to grant traditional funds for the Fourth of July celebration. And so unsure were the city fathers in their new powers that when in 1853 they faced a difficult decision about the building of

an expensive new city hall, they called for a public assembly indistinguishable from the old town meeting, and proceeded with the project only after approval by this body. See "Records of the Mayor and the Board of Aldermen," MS (M-Ald) I, June 8, 28, 1852, on the July Fourth discussion (meeting dates are a better reference than the frequently omitted or jumbled ledger page numbers). On the town hall meetings, see M-Ald I, January 24; February 7, 1853.

26. The best study of this development is George H. Martin, *The Evolution of the Massachusetts Public School System* (New York: D. Appleton and Co., 1923; first published 1894), chaps. i–iv. See also William C. Webster, *Recent Centralizing Tendencies in State Educational Administration*, Columbia University Studies, 8 (New York: Columbia University, 1897), pp. 23–26; and Robert Harvey Whitten, *Public Administration in Massachusetts*, Columbia University Studies, 8 (New York: Columbia University, 1898), pp. 40–44.

27. Martin, *Massachusetts School System*, 92; see also pp. 90–96, 114–130, 148–164, and 203–209. Mann is quoted in Webster, *Educational Administration*, p. 23. For general background, see Lawrence Cremin, *The American Common School: An Historic Conception* (New York: Teachers College, Columbia University, 1951), pp. 60–71.

28. For background on this local situation, see Alfred M. Copeland, *Our Country and Its People: A History of Hampden County, Massachusetts* (Boston: Century Publishing Co., 1902), II, 113–115, 122–124. See also *1839 Report of the School Committee*, p. 7; *1842 Report*, p. 11; *1849 Report*, p. 13; *1851 Report*, pp. 12–13, all of these bound in *Town of Springfield Annual Reports*, 1839–1852. On the district battle, see "Report of the School Committee" in *MR*, 1852, pp. 29–30; 1855, pp. 69–71; 1856, pp. 26–30; 1857, pp. 31, 39; and "Mayor's Address," in *MR*, 1856, pp. 19–20; 1857, pp. 20–21; in 1858, p. 18. See also "Ordinance 32," *MR*, 1855, pp. 69–71; "Ordinance 33," *MR*, 1857, p. 104; "Ordinance 42," *MR*, 1859, p. 150. Finally, see MS "Record Book of School District 2," meetings of March 6, 1851; June 10, 1852; May 15, 1854.

29. Michael B. Katz, *The Irony of Early School Reform: Educational Innovation in Mid-Nineteenth Century Massachusetts* (Cambridge, Mass.: Harvard University Press, 1968). See esp. part 1, "Reform by Imposition: Social Origins of Educational Controversy," pp. 19–112. It is interesting to note that the figures Katz bases his argument upon can be read quite differently. His tables suggest, for instance, that geographic and neighborhood groupings correlate with recorded votes at least as significantly, and usually more so, than do the categories of occupation and wealth that he emphasizes, which seems to indicate the need for a more multifaceted interpretation of the dynamics of educational controversy in the Massachusetts town context. See Appendix D, "Beverly: Analysis of the 1860 Vote on the High-School Issue," pp. 274–279.

30. *SR*, April 17, 1849, contains the quoted passage. See *1850 Report of School Committee*, p. 10, and *1851 Report*, p. 11. See also William Orr, *The History of the Classical High School* (Springfield: Classical High School Alumni Association, 1936), pp. 13–18, 38–50, and Gladys A. Midura, "A Critical His-

tory of Public Secondary Education in Springfield, Massachusetts," unpub. diss., University of Connecticut, 1961, pp. 83–108. The high school law was Mass. *AR*, 1848: 293. Katz's computer analysis of the relationship between community structure and high school establishment is a model of methodology and interpretation. See Katz, *Irony of Early School Reform*, Appendix B., "Communities and Education: An Analysis of Variance," pp. 225–269.

31. Hans Paul Bahrdt, "Public Activity and Private Activity as Basic Forms of City Association," in Roland Warren, *Perspectives on the American Community* (Chicago: Rand McNally, 1966), 78–85. Bahrdt's discussion is closely related to Max Weber's analysis of public and private, cited above in Gerth and Mills's collection of his essays, p. 239. See also Oscar and Mary Handlin, *Commonwealth*, passim, but especially pp. 53–72, 147–166, 195–205; and Zuckerman, *Peaceable Kingdoms*, p. 188.

32. There is an important discussion of similar points in Zuckerman, *Peaceable Kingdoms*, pp. 92–102, where it is argued that even the formal institutions that did exist in developed form depended critically upon informal consensus and controls for both their legitimacy and their effectiveness.

3. Springfield and the Civil War

1. Most of the standard local histories are good on the attitudes toward slavery in the prewar years. In addition, see the full discussion in John F. Mitchell, "Springfield in the Civil War," unpub. diss., Boston University, 1960, pp. 10–15, 22–27. On John Brown, see Harry Andrew Wright, "John Brown in Springfield," in *The Story of Western Massachusetts*, II (New York: Lewis Historical Publishing Co., 1949), 406–422. See also Wilbur H. Siebert, *The Underground Railroad in Massachusetts* (Worcester: American Antiquarian Society, 1936), pp. 68–72.

2. The entire process for Springfield is traced in Mitchell, "Springfield in the Civil War," pp. 10–15. The general story in the state is still best followed in some recent biographies, such as David Donald, *Charles Sumner and the Coming of the Civil War* (New York: Alfred A. Knopf, 1960); and Martin Duberman, *Charles Francis Adams* (Boston: Houghton Mifflin, 1960). On Bowles, the *Republican*, and Springfield, see George S. Merriam, *The Life and Times of Samuel Bowles* (New York: Century Co., 1885), I, parts 3 and 4; and Mitchell, "Springfield in the Civil War," pp. 56–81, a detailed account of Bowles's political role, which includes references to many specific editorials. Bowles often subordinated his own political views, explaining to a friend that "an individual can be Wendell Phillips, but a newspaper cannot and have circulation and tolerance" (quoted in Merriam, *Bowles*, I, 393).

3. Mitchell, "Springfield in the Civil War," p. 141, concluded that the *Republican* reflected general public opinion and followed the administration in that it "arrived at its position on most of the important political issues . . . at about the same speed and generally with the same results as Mr. Lincoln." On all these points, see also Roberta Fraser Morris, "The Editorial Policy of the

Springfield *Republican* During the Civil War," unpub. M.A. thesis, Smith College, 1950, esp. chap. ii.

4. Merriam, *Bowles*, I, 354. The emancipation call was issued by a group of Springfield ministers in *SR*, October 2, 1861. Merriam traces the developing attitude toward slavery, pp. 349–355; as does Mitchell, "Springfield and the Civil War," pp. 125–140; and Morris, "Editorial Policy of the *Republican*," chap. iii. The following issues of the *Republican* contain representative illustrations of changing opinions: *SR*³ June 8, July 15, October 2, 7, November 13, and December 5, 1861; *SR*, January 9, 18, May 23, 1862; *SR*³ August 30, September 24, 1862; January 2, 14, 1863.

5. The *Union* soon grew to a circulation of 4,000 with its advertising space fully taken. It covered local news and events vigorously, and would take issue with the *Republican* on almost any pretext. Bowles, in turn, replied with an unbreachable silence, rarely even acknowledging the existence of a rival. For an illustration of the *Union's* radicalism, see *SU*, January 5, 28, 1864, calling for distribution of confiscated plantation land to poor farmers, black and white. On the collapse of the center, see Mitchell, "Springfield and the Civil War," chap. vii. On the Irish in the war's early years, see *SR*³, June 1, 1861; and December 21, 1861. *SR*, January 10 and July 26, 1862 discuss Irish volunteers.

6. For Andrew's victories, see *SR*³, January 7, 1860; November 4, 1861; November 5, 1862; November 4, 1863; November 7–9, 1864. On the political scene and the People's Party convention, held in Springfield, see *SR*³, September 5, October 8, 25, November 3, 5, 7, 1862. See also a letter describing local meetings and organization, William Stowe to Henry L. Dawes, October 26, 1862. Dawes Papers, Library of Congress, box 18. Throughout 1862 Bowles was in Europe on his intermittent but endless search for sound health. During his absence the paper was run by the noted J. G. Holland, whose more conservative views are evident in the *Republican* during this period. See Merriam, *Bowles*, I, 357–359.

7. Mitchell, "Springfield and the Civil War," pp. 159–164 lists nineteen basic criticisms of the president found in the *Union*, from his being soft on Copperheads to being swayed by Mrs. Lincoln's "secesh relations." The Bowles quote is in Mitchell, p. 137, but for his eventual endorsement of Lincoln, see Merriam, *Bowles*, I, 413. See also *SR*, April 9, September 16, 1864, and *SU*, June 9, July 8, 1864. On the election, see *SR*, October 3, 21, November 7, 8, 1864. There is a statistical comparison of the 1860 and 1864 votes, by wards, in *SR*, November 9, 1864. See also Joanna Coleman, "A Social, Economic, and Political History of Springfield, Massachusetts from 1860 to 1865," unpub. M.A. thesis, Smith College, 1928, pp. 110–115.

8. Mitchell, "Springfield and the Civil War," chap. vi, drawn totally from regimental histories, is reliable on the formation and adventures of the local units. See also the standard local histories for references to regimental sources.

9. *SR*, June 17, 21, July 17, 1861. Mitchell, "Springfield and the Civil War," pp. 102–106.

10. See for instance *SR*, June 17, 1862 when the Tenth was hit hard and its commander seriously wounded. There are interesting statistics in the regimental

histories, suggesting that the famous battles were not the only ones to penetrate to the local level. The Tenth Regiment, in major actions, suffered a total of 15 percent dead; the Thirty-seventh fought in the war's major campaigns and lost 17 percent; but the Twenty-seventh, which spent years in peripheral and undramatic skirmishing in North Carolina, lost a shocking 24 percent. See Mitchell, "Springfield in the Civil War," pp. 105–109 for figures and citations.

11. SR^3, May 3, July 19, 24, September 6, 27, December 13, 1861. SR January 20, February 7, 12, March 18, and June 17, 1862. Justice Willard to Henry L. Dawes, May 5, 1862, Dawes Papers, LC, box 18.

12. SR^3, Sept. 5–20, 1862 esp. The quotation is from John Wells Alexander to Henry L. Dawes, March 4, 1863, Dawes Papers, LC, box 18.

13. "Mayor's Address," *MR*, 1863, p. 11.

14. "Mayor's Address," *MR*, 1864, p. 17. Also, E. A. Newell, *"Rest," A Memorial* (Springfield: Soldiers' Rest Fund, 1881), pp. 8–9.

15. *SR*, Dec. 10–27, 1864, esp. Dec. 10 and 24. Newell, *"Rest,"* pp. 12–16; Coleman, "Springfield 1860–1865," pp. 24–25.

16. For "culture," see *SR*, January 28, February 18, 1862; February 10, 1865. On the more garish amusements, see *SR*, May 17, 1861; November 25, 1863, for illustrations. See also Coleman, "Springfield 1860–1865," pp. 41–43 for a summary, including Booth's appearance in 1863.

17. Coleman takes the frivolity at face value, "Springfield, 1860–1865," pp. 43–44, as does Mitchell, "Springfield and the Civil War," pp. 105, 230–231, while most of Springfield's local historians of an earlier day ignored it entirely as an embarrassment, or as irrelevant. J. G. Randall and David Donald, *Civil War and Reconstruction* (Boston: Heath Co., 1961), hint at a similar view, p. 486. On Washington, see Constance Green, *Washington, I, Village and Capital* (Princeton: Princeton University Press, 1962), p. 267.

18. This gap has now been partially filled by a serviceable general study by Eugene C. Murdock, *Patriotism Limited, 1862–1865: The Civil War Draft and Bounty System* (Kent, Ohio: Kent State University Press, 1967).

19. James L. Bowen, *Massachusetts in the War* (Springfield: Clark W. Bryan, 1888), pp. 27–31; *Report of the Adjutant General, Public Documents of Massachusetts for 1861*, pp. 30, 69–70.

20. SR^3, April 9, 24, 29, 1861. "Records of the Mayor and Aldermen," (M-Ald.), April 18, 24; July 13, 1861.

21. William Schouler, *A History of Massachusetts in the Civil War* (Boston: E. P. Dutton, 1868), II, 14, 18. Bowen, *Massachusetts in the War*, pp. 44, 48, *Report of the Adjutant General, Public Documents 1862*, no. 7, pp. 45–46 and 468. Schouler was adjutant general throughout the war, and wrote the voluminous and scholarly reports for these years, as well as the long compendium published shortly afterward cited here.

22. *SR*, August 13, 15, 1862. "Report of the Springfield City Clerk" in Schouler, *Massachusetts in the Civil War*, II, 319.

23. M-Ald., August 26, 27, 1862; July 16, 1863; Schouler, *Massachusetts in the Civil War*, II, 319, 15; *Report of the Adjutant General, Public Documents*, 1862, no. 7, p. 37. For general comments, see Murdock, *Patriotism Limited*, chap. ii, "The Bounty System," pp. 16–41.

24. See *SR*[3], August 27, 1862; February 13, 1863 for illustrations. *Report of the Adjutant General, Public Documents 1862*, no. 7, also discusses this. Fred Shannon, *Organization and Administration of the Union Army* (Cleveland: H. Clark Co., 1928), II, 57, corroborates the impression that this opprobrium did not in the least attach to the hiring of substitutes or the paying of commutation, both of which were done with honor. See Mayor Briggs's address in *MR*, 1865, p. 10, lauding Springfield's accomplishment, including the 318 commutees in the praise. On the meaning of the draft, and fear of it, see Murdock, *Patriotism Limited*, chap. iii, "The Draft," pp. 42–62.

25. *SR*[3], July 15, 1863; M-Ald., July 14, 1863; *Report of the Adjutant General 1863, Public Documents*, no. 8, pp. 15–19 on the drafting. Figures on p. 26 do not include data for Springfield, but the Tenth Congressional District, dominated by the city, showed figures in keeping with statewide proportions. Throughout the state, 32,000 were called, 22,000 exempted, 3,000, in the idiom of the day, skedaddled, 6,700 were "held to service," over half of whom paid the $300 commutation fee. In the Tenth District, 3,395 names produced 89 conscripts, 53 substitutes, and 689 commutees, a total of 831 held to service. According to statistics in Murdock, *Patriotism Limited*, p. 13, the figures from Springfield and Massachusetts parallel national averages. In all cases, only about 25–30 percent of the names called were "held to service," and only about 10 percent of these were drafted. Among those escaping, however, there were significant differences between local and national figures in the ratio of those obtaining substitutes to those paying commutation. On draft insurance societies, see Murdock, pp. 60–62, and *SR*[3], July 10, 1863; *SU*, July 20, 1864.

26. *SR*[3], November 2, 19, 1863; *SR*[2], January 23, February 6, 17, 1864. On further drafting, and the near panic at the abolition of commutation, see *SR*[2], June 15, July 27, 1864; *SU*, June 6, 7, 1864. See also Randall and Donald, *Civil War*, for a discussion of these issues, pp. 314, 315.

27. *SU*, July 9, 1864.

28. *Acts and Resolves Passed by the General Court of Massachusetts in the Year 1863* (*AR*), 1863: 91, 218, 254, Law of November 18, 1863. *Report of the Adjutant General, 1863, Public Documents*, nos. 8, 9. Springfield apparently was less strained than other areas, for its $44,000 in 1862 bounties was $5,000 less than the "balanced" share it was asked to contribute in taxes for the reimbursement, and the city lost money in the transaction. "Report of the Finance Committee," *MR*, 1866, p. 142. See also Murdock, *Patriotism Limited*, pp. 16–41, 107–131.

29. "Report of the Special Committee of the City Council, June 12, 1865", reprinted in *SR*, June 13, 1865. See also Shannon, *Union Army*, II, 92, on bounty-piling in general.

30. *Report of the Adjutant General, 1865, Public Documents*, no. 7, p. 10. Schouler, *Mass. in the Civil War*, I, 667; II, 18. "Report of the Finance Committee," *MR*, 1866, p. 142. Figures in "Civil War Records," MS ledger, City Hall Vault, show $116, 924 in direct bounty payments. Excerpts from this are reprinted in *SR*, March 16, 1867. Schouler's figures, II, 319–320, corroborate Springfield statistics.

31. Mass. *AR* 1864:103. "Report of the Finance Committee," *MR*, 1866, p. 142.

32. Mass. *AR* 1865:162. The city council had reversed an earlier decision and borrowed, rather than taxed, for the money in 1864, one reason why it received little attention at the time. M-Ald., May 2, August 1, 1864. On the 1865 actions, see *SR*, November 16, 27, 30, 1865.

33. *SR*, November 22, 24, 1865. These are letters to the paper. The *Republican* more or less opposed refunding, but uncharacteristically refrained from taking a clear position. Murdock, *Patriotism Limited*, points out that the trend in most communities throughout the war was toward financing through property and other general taxes, rather than through volunteerism or more particularized contributions or assessments. This would tend to support, at least historically, the arguments of the refunders.

34. *SR*, November 18, 20, 25, 1865.

35. Oscar Handlin and Mary Flug Handlin, *Commonwealth* (New York: New York University Press, 1947), p. 242. *SR*, December 4, 1865.

4. The War Boom

1. The best study, although somewhat inaccessible, is Constance Green, "History of the Springfield Armory," unpub. and incomplete typescript, microfilm in Springfield City Library. The Armory sources used by Mrs. Green and Derwent Whittlesy, "The Springfield Armory: A Study in Institutional Development," unpub. diss., University of Chicago, 1918, comprise an excellent and thorough record, including complete correspondence files, payrolls, and other documents. These sources are now in the National Archives in Washington. Other secondary sources cited on Armory matters here also rely heavily on these records. See, in addition, Whittlesy, "Extracts from Original Sources Made for the Purpose of Writing a Thesis on 'A History of the Springfield Armory,'" typescript, 7 vols., 1918–1920, which covers the period just up to the beginning of the Civil War.

2. Constance Green, "Armory," pp. 113, 124–125, 129–131; John F. Mitchell, "Springfield, Massachusetts in the Civil War," unpub. diss., Boston University, 1961, pp. 203–205, 209–211. See also Father Peter G. Loughran, "Western Massachusetts and the Arms Supply in the Civil War," M.A. thesis, Catholic University, 1958, pp. 32, 35–38, 43, 46; and Felicia Deyrup, *Arms and Armsmakers of the Connecticut Valley*, Smith College Studies, 33 (Northampton, Mass.: Smith College, 1948), pp. 189–191, 196. Beyond expanding plant and equipment, the Armory shifted many operations from the Watershops to the newly steam-powered Hill facilities, while leaving heavy procedures, like barrel rolling and drawing, at the Mill River. See SR^3, April 15, 22, July 12, August 12, 30, 1861, for contemporary discussion of expansion problems; for discussion of labor matters, see *SR*, April 4, 8, 1862; SR^3, February 2, 1863; April 2, 1864. Wages rose during the war by about 20 percent, averaging $3 per day at its close, and ranging from $1.25 to $4.50. See Deyrup, *Armsmakers*, appendix D, table 2, p. 240, for figures on conditions, hours, and wages.

3. Deyrup, *Armsmakers*, p. 201 (quoted). On specialization, see chart from official records, appendix D, table 1, p. 240. On costs, see appendix B, table 1, pp. 228–229. Most contemporary sources mentioned $9, while Deyrup cites Ordnance Department estimates of $14; her own "real cost" estimates are higher. Constance Green, "Armory," p. 117, arrives at a figure of $11.70.

4. See charts in Deyrup, *Armsmakers*, appendix B, table 2, p. 233 for employment figures.

5. Official figures cited in ibid., appendix B, table 2, p. 233; also Mitchell, "Springfield," p. 205.

6. G. B. Prescott, "The U.S. Armory at Springfield," *Atlantic Monthly*, 12 (October, 1863), 436.

7. The standard local histories discuss this background in great detail, especially the conflict between Ripley and the colorful Charles Stearns, a builder and businessman who was one of the town's most controversial figures, a stubborn man who always preferred a lawsuit to a compromise, and who cultivated a passionate hatred for Ripley. On the superintendency question, see the review of the 1852 investigations, *The National Armories, a Review of the System of Superintendency, Civil and Military, Particularly with Reference to the Economy and General Management at the Springfield Armory* (Springfield: G. W. Wilson, 1852).

8. *SR*[3], June 29, 1860; February 20, April 22, August 21, 26, 1861. The firing of Dwight did not escape becoming a political issue by very much, apparently, for the important George Ashmun had written to Henry L. Dawes that the action "takes all of us by surprize and me more than anyone else." Arguing that officers were most needed in the field, Ashmun urged Dawes to bring his political influence to bear and secure a reversal. See George Ashmun to Henry L. Dawes, August 17, 1861, Dawes Papers, LC, box 18.

9. *SR*[3], April 22, October 30, November 27, 1861; July 4, 5, 1862.

10. Whittlesy, "Armory," pp. 216, 225.

11. While figures and percentages from the decennial industrial censuses are of highly questionable accuracy, and structural differences between the 1855 and 1865 compilations make any calculation of growth rates suspect, general observations can still be drawn from comparison of city statistics within this framework, for basic functional discrepancies can be assumed to be more or less evenly distributed. The figures are further qualified by other limitations. The forms were filled out by individual businesses, often less than candid because they found it "next to impossible to divest themselves of the impression of an intimate connection between [their] answers and the assessment of [their] taxes." For this and other comments on procedure in the industrial census, see *Statistical Information Relating to Certain Branches of Industry in Massachusetts for the Year Ending June 1, 1855* (Boston: William White, 1856), pp. xiv, xi–xiii. The figures cited here are calculated from the Springfield items and state total in this 1855 industrial census, pp. 233–237 and the 1865 compilation (same title, Boston, 1866), pp. 266–271. The quote in the text is from the general introduction to the 1865 statistics, p. xxi.

12. "Mayor's Address," *Municipal Register* (*MR*), 1861, p. 24. *SR*[3], August 5,

1861 (quoted). On economic conditions see SR^3, February 8, May 31, September 16, 18, 1861; and especially a long survey on May 10, 1861. Consumer industries were severely depressed at first, and rail traffic was reported off by a third. The Indian Orchard Mills had stockpiled much cotton against the emergency of a supply cut-off.

13. Deyrup, *Armsmakers*, pp. 184–185; 1865 Mass. *Industrial Census*, Springfield section, pp. 266–271; Loughran, "Arms Supply," p. 66.

14. Ames had been close to the Government for years, and in 1869 had represented it on a trip to England in search of dependable supplies of iron. Loughran, "Arms Supply," pp. 53–63, discusses the role of the Ames Company, and see also SR^3, June 19, 1861. The dividend records from the Ames Papers are quoted in Mitchell, "Springfield," pp. 2, 3. The Ames Company was actually located in Chicopee, but because of the scale of its operations was an integral part of Springfield's economic life.

15. Harris letter of May 7, 1861 quoted in Mitchell, "Springfield," p. 244. See also SR^3, September 9, 1861; SR, August 8, 1862.

16. SR^3, September 4, October 10, November 6, 1861; 1865 Mass. *Industrial Census*, Springfield section, pp. 266–271.

17. SU, March 17, 18, 19, 1864; SR^3, March 19, 1864. Due mainly to Ripley's conservatism, the breech-loading step was delayed for years, at what some have seen as a great price in lives and money through the prolongation of the war. The muzzle-loaders fired only a single shot and took almost two minutes to load again. The long debate is one of the main focuses of Robert Bruce, *Lincoln and the Tools of War* (Indianapolis: Bobbs-Merrill, 1956).

18. SR^2, January 28, 1861; July 4, 1864; SU, February 1, 1864. Loughran, "Arms Supply," pp. 68–69.

19. SR^3, July 10, August 21, 1863 summarizes these developments. See 1865 Mass. *Industrial Census*, pp. 697, 718, for Springfield's domination of the production of the collars and photo albums. See also Joanna Coleman, "A Social, Economic, and Political History of Springfield, Massachusetts, from 1860 to 1865," M.A. thesis, Smith College, 1928, pp. 58–60.

20. Calculated from the Springfield section in the 1865 *Industrial Census*, pp. 266–271.

21. Coleman, "Springfield," p. 59. SR^3, February 18, August 31, October 7, 1863 on income taxes and property valuation of various businesses and individuals. On the paper industry, see major survey in SR, September 27, 1865, also October 14, 1863; April 12, 1865. On the important Power's Paper Company, see sketch in Moses King, *King's Handbook of Springfield* (Springfield: James Gill, 1884), pp. 324–328.

22. Henry-Russell Hitchcock, *The Architecture of H. H. Richardson and his Times* (rev. ed., Hampden, Conn.: Archon Books, 1961), pp. 14–15, 71, and also Hitchcock, "Catalogue of an Exhibit of Photographs of Springfield Architecture, 1800–1900," typescript, 1934, Springfield City Library, p. 8.

23. SR^3, September 23, May 6, June 19, 1863; SR^2, January 22, 1864; SR, December 3, 1864; July 22, November 25, 1865.

24. *SR*, December 2, 3, 1864; November 26, 1865, special year-end surveys of building.

25. *Abstract of the Census of Massachusetts 1865* (Boston: Wright and Potter, 1867). Remarks, pp. 207, 265; table 7, pp. 180–205; table 13, p. 261. Percentages calculated by author from these official figures, here and below.

26. *1865 Mass. Census Abstract*, table 8, p. 240; table 9, p. 208.

27. *1865 Mass. Census Abstract*, table 13, pp. 248–249, 261; table 16 A, p. 268.

28. *1865 Mass. Census Abstract*, p. 299, compared with *Mass. Abstract of U.S. Census, 1860*, table 6, p. 128, and *1855 Mass. Census Abstract*, table 4, pp. 145, 239. Throughout the 1850's, the number of census "families" — anything from a full family to a bachelor living alone — was proportional to the general population. But in the war, the number of families rose by 75 percent, far more than the total population, indicating the presence of a great many more single or two-person households. Seen another way, the figures show average family size decreasing from 4.8 persons in 1860 to 3.96 in 1865, also indicating a sudden increase in unattached and childless newcomers.

29. *1865 Mass. Census Abstract*, table 21, p. 281; table 1, pp. 24–47, compared with *Abstract of the Census of Massachusetts from the Eighth U.S. Census, 1860* (Boston: Wright and Potter, 1863), table 1, pp. 26–29.

30. *1865 Mass. Census Abstract*, table 31, p. 297, and table 32, p. 298, compared with *1855 Mass. Census Abstract*, table 3, p. 132. It should be noted that after 1861, though foreign born were only a fifth of the population, total births to immigrant parents began to outnumber births to natives. See *1865 Mass. Census Abstract*, table 30, p. 294.

31. *SR*[3], January 17, 1860; August 2, 1861; *SR*, March 18, 31, 1862; October 28, 1863.

32. *SR*[3], August 2, 1861; October 28, 1863. See also special business summaries, *SR*[3], March 18, 1862 and *SR*[2], January 24, 1864.

33. See the business summary of *SR*[2], January 2, 1864, and *SR*, November 25, 1865. Also *SR*[2], March 30, May 17, 1864; March 25, 1867; and Coleman, "Springfield," p. 67. The figures on dwellings and construction are drawn from *1855 Mass. Census Abstract*, table 4, p. 145; *Mass. Abstract of U.S. Census 1860*, table 6, p. 128; and *1865 Mass. Census Abstract*, p. 299.

34. William Orr, *The History of the Classical High School* (Springfield: Classical High School Alumni Association, 1936), pp. 71–72.

35. *SR*[3], June 16, 1863; *SR*[2], January 2, 1864; *SR*, May 2, 1859; October 22, 1864; August 29, 1859; February 10, 1862.

36. *SR*[3], March 13, September 30, 1863.

37. *SR*, September 20, 1859.

38. H. Paul Douglass, *The Springfield Church Survey*, (New York: George H. Doran, 1926), pp. 54–60, noted that the movement of churches toward the center of town had begun in the 1840's. Denominations that had started on the Hill soon had branches downtown, and these eventually became the main churches of the denomination, as with the Baptists and Methodists.

39. *SR*, November 14, 1865 has these figures. It should be remembered that wards one through five, often called the "city wards" had three Common Councilmen apiece, while the "suburban" wards had only one each. On the tax breakdown, see *SR*, February 25, 1865; on voters see *MR*, 1866, p. 141; on nationality and ward, see *1865 Mass. Census Abstract*, table 2, pp. 68–69.

5. Institutional Responses to City Growth

1. See *SR*^{3}, June 28, 1861 editorial on "The Americanizing effect of the War." On temperance, see *SR*^{3}, December 2, 7, 1860; *SR*^{2}, November 7, 1867.

2. Joanna Coleman, "A Social, Economic, and Political History of Springfield, Massachusetts from 1860 to 1865," M.A. thesis, Smith College, 1928, pp. 12–13, on crime. Statistics show no increase of serious crime, but a larger number of the petty offenses disturbing to the community – drunkenness, prostitution, gambling, brawling. On attitudes, see *SR*, March 4, 1862; *SU*, February 11, 1864, and "Mayor's Address," *MR*, 1862, pp. 22–23.

3. See the historical sketch in the *Report of the City Library Association for 1879* (Springfield: Published by the Association, 1879), pp. 8–11. *SR*^{2}, June 1, 1864 is quoted, from a sophisticated discussion of "institutions," as is the "Mayor's Address," *MR*, 1863, pp. 11–13. See also "Mayor's Address," *MR*, 1865, pp. 17–18, and Mass. *AR*, 1864: 142. On the local role, see "Mayor's Address," *MR*, 1862, p. 12; and *SR*^{3}, February 6, December 9, 1863; *SR*, January 27, 30, October 3, 1864.

4. *SR*, December 13, 1859; *SR*^{3}, November 29, December 24, 1860. The election was a close one, ending in a tie and requiring a revote. See also Henry M. Burt, ed., *Memorial Tributes to Daniel L. Harris with a Biography and Extracts from His Journal and Letters* (Springfield: Privately printed, 1880), pp. 193–195.

5. "Mayor's Address," *MR* 1861, p. 10; *SR*, December 25, 1865.

6. *SR*^{3}, December 1, 3, 1862; December 5, 1863.

7. *SR*^{2}, November 28, December 5, 1864 (quoted).

8. "Table, showing the Growth of Expenditure, etc. . . . from 1845 to 1876," *MR*, 1877, follows p. 203. Valuation and tax figures listed in every *MR*, also tabulated in *Springfield, 1852–1952* (Springfield, 1952), p. 6.

9. "Mayor's Address," *MR*, 1863, p. 9; *MR*, 1867, p. 26. *SR*, October 3, 1864.

10. "Report of the School Committee," *MR*, 1861, pp. 30, 71.

11. "Report of the School Committee," *MR*, 1863, p. 23. Following this report in the annual *MR*, there was usually a chart giving schools, teachers, number of students, attendance, etc.

12. "Report of the School Committee," *MR*, 1863, p. 23; *MR*, 1864, p. 29. "Mayor's Address," *MR*, 1864, pp. 9–10.

13. Hooker served the committee for twenty-two years, twenty as chairman. He had at this time been on the board without interruption since 1852, and had served in earlier years as well. He wrote the reports while chairman, and they

were unusually extensive and reflective, truly fine essays about the state of the schools, and education in general, often discussing questions of curriculum and teaching. On Hooker, see Charles Wells Chapin, *Sketches of the Old Inhabitants* (Springfield: Springfield Publishing Co., 1893), p. 223.

14. "Report of the School Committee," *MR*, 1863, p. 29 (quoted); *MR*, 1864, pp. 29–30; *MR*, 1865, pp. 25–28. "Mayor's Address," *MR*, 1865, p. 13; *SR*, April 10, 1863.

15. George H. Martin, *The Evolution of the Massachusetts Public School System* (New York: D. Appleton and Co., 1923, first published 1894), pp. 192–195. See also *19th Annual Report of the Board of Education (1856), Public Documents of Massachusetts*, on this general trend. See especially the recent study by Michael B. Katz, *The Irony of Early School Reform: Educational Innovation in Mid-Nineteenth Century Massachusetts* (Cambridge, Mass.: Harvard University Press, 1968), an important reinterpretation confirmed in some ways by the developments in Springfield and, as will become clear, seriously qualified in others.

16. "Report of the School Committee," *MR*, 1866, p. 33. Also *MR*, 1863, pp. 25–28; *MR*, 1864, pp. 30–31.

17. *SR*[3], March 11, September 19, 1863; *SR*, January 30, 1864. See Hooker's special appeal, *SR*[3], April 10, 1863; also "Mayor's Address," *MR*, 1864, pp. 9–12. On the general situation, see *27th Annual Report of the Board of Education (1863), Public Documents*, pp. 36–38.

18. These are drawn from the statistical tables in the Board of Education reports for 1860–1865, *Public Documents*. See also "Report of the School Committee," *MR*, 1864, p. 30.

19. "Mayor's Address," *MR*, 1862, p. 14; *SU*, May 18, 1864.

20. Follow this procedure in the "Records of the Mayor and the Board of Aldermen," (M-Ald), II and III, September 7, 21, 28, October 12, 1863; February 29, May 10, October 17, November 21, 1864; February 27, March 13, 1865. See also *SU*, November 2, 1864; *SR*, February 18, March 4, 1865.

21. For a discussion of such problems in the statewide context, see Martin, *Massachusetts Public School System*, p. 94.

22. "Mayor's Address," *MR*, 1865, pp. 12–13; "Report of the School Committee," *MR*, 1865, pp. 68–69. The development of the office elsewhere is discussed in Robert H. Whitten, *Public Administration in Massachusetts* (New York: Columbia University Studies, 1898), pp. 28–31.

23. Katz, *Irony of School Reform*, p. 131. Martin, *Massachusetts Public School*, p. 266. "Report of the School Committee," *MR*, 1865, pp. 65–66.

24. The Stearns Aqueduct controversy is discussed thoroughly in most of the standard local histories. For contemporary sources on this battle over corporate powers and meaning, see [Charles Stearns], *A Statement of Facts in Connection with the Petition of Charles Stearns and others for an Act of Incorporation as an Aqueduct Company* (Springfield: John M. Wood, 1848), and Joseph Pynchon, *A Reply to Charles Stearns' "Statement of Facts, etc."* (Springfield: Horace S. Taylor, 1849). On the general development of the water supply prob-

lem in America, see Nelson Blake, *Water for the Cities* (Syracuse: Syracuse University Press, 1956), which provides a valuable context for the emerging debate in Springfield at mid-century.

25. "Report of the Chief Engineer," *MR*, 1862, p. 78; *MR*, 1863, p. 71. Thomas F. Loorem, *A Souvenir History of the Fire Department of Springfield, Massachusetts* (Springfield: Veteran Volunteer Fireman's Association, 1913), p. 149.

26. *Report of the Board of Water Commissioners of the City of Springfield for the year 1874* (Springfield: Clark W. Bryan, 1875), pp. 6–7. (An historical sketch of the city's water supply development is included in this report.)

27. M-Ald., II, June 25, 1860. See also *SR*[3], June 20, 1860, for text of this report.

28. The election, which produced a tie and a subsequent revote, saw ward five vote against Harris by 165–71 in the first count, 243–85 in the second. For debate on this controversy, see *SR*[3], December 12, 24, 1860. On the broader issues, and the aftermath, see "Mayor's Address," *MR*, 1861, pp. 20–22; and "Report of the Special Committee," M-Ald., II, June 6, 1861.

29. See the original Harris Plan report, M-Ald., II, June 25, 1860. On the Worthen Report, see M-Ald., II, April 28, July 28, 1862; and *SR*, May 13, 19, 1862. The text of the report is an appendix to *MR*, 1864, pp. 157–168.

30. "Report of the Chief Engineer," *MR*, 1865, p. 101; *SR*[2], July 27, October 15, 1864. Haynes threatened to sue for criminal neglect, finally settling for a tax abatement from the city. See M-Ald., III, December 12, 1864.

31. *Report of the Board of Directors of the Springfield Aqueduct Company, July 1, 1867* (Springfield: Union Printing Co., 1867), pp. 3–6; *Fifth Annual Report of the Springfield Aqueduct Company, July 1, 1870* (Springfield: Union Printing Co., 1870), p. 9. For the reorganization act, see Mass. *AR* 1864: 165.

32. *SR*[2], February 27, 1864. See also *SU*, July 17, 25, 1864.

33. *SR*, May 29, 1865; M-Ald., II, March 27, 1865. The contract is reprinted in the *1874 Water Commissioner's Report*, pp. 117–119.

34. See the company's charter, Mass. *AR* 1863: 121, also *SR*[2], February 3, July 30, 1864.

35. See representative letters and comment, *SR*[3], December 2, 1863; *SU*, February 2, 1864.

36. M-Ald., II, June 29, December 2, 28, 1864; M-Ald., III, February 1, 29, March 14, 1864; *SU*, March 21, 1864; *SR*[2], July 30, 1864. Whitten, *Public Administration*, p. 112. See also the first general law for incorporation of such companies, Mass. *AR*, 1864: 229 which specified a strip narrower than the one Springfield demanded — this law called for eighteen inches on each side of the tracks, which would come to about six feet in all.

37. See *City Charter and Amendments, City Ordinances, Rules, and Orders . . . of the City of Springfield* (Springfield: Samuel Bowles, 1860), pp. 49, 55, 57 for these processes.

38. "Mayor's Address," *MR*, 1865, pp. 7, 15–16; "Report of the City Engi-

neer," *MR*, 1866, p. 69. For the fire district ordinances see, "Ordinances 119, 120 passed 9/16/61," appendix to *MR*, 1862, and "Ordinance 174, passed 9/19/64," appendix to *MR*, 1865.

39. On these legal problems, including necessary revisions of some of the procedures, see M-Ald., II, May 20, 1861; *SR*, March 7, 1862. Mass. *AR* 1863:204 clarified the city's powers.

40. "Mayor's Address," *MR*, 1864, p. 7; *MR*, 1865, p. 14; *MR*, 1866, p. 16. "Report of the City Engineer," *MR*, 1866, pp. 69–70.

41. Mass. *AR*, 1863:107. The city may have had power to proceed with these extensive improvements under its charter, but wished to remove all possibility of doubt.

42. *SR*, Aug. 22, 1865. See M-Ald., III, March 13, Aug. 22, 1865. The cases all involved technical objections to the assessments. For representative illustrations of the problems encountered, see *Springfield v. Gay*, 94 Mass. 612 (1866), and *Brewer v. Springfield*, 97 Mass. 152 (1867), both Massachusetts Supreme Court cases.

43. "Report of the City Engineer," *MR*, 1862, pp. 70–71.

6. Prosperity and Growth

1. *SR*, May 24, October 6, 1865; *SU*, May 1, 1866; March 21, 1867.

2. *SR*, May 24, 1865 (quoted); October 6, 1865; *SR*², May 11, June 3, 1866; August 7, 1867; April 1, 1868. Armory figures, drawn from official government records, are in Felicia Deyrup, *Arms and Armsmakers of the Connecticut Valley*, Smith College Studies 33 (Northampton, Mass.: Smith College, 1948), appendix B, table 2, p. 233, and appendix D, table 4, p. 245. On the Armory, see also Derwent Whittlesy, "The Springfield Armory", unpub. diss., University of Chicago, 1920, p. 260.

3. *SR*, October 17, 1865; *SR*², January 16, 30, March 20, 1867; February 5, 1865.

4. Census figures on industry for 1865 and 1875 almost defy comparison, because of differences in categories and standards of evaluation. Comparison is misleading also because the 1875 tally depicted a society in the second year of depression and is thus a poor guide to the dimensions of the boom period. Nevertheless, as with earlier censuses, there is still validity in comparing the relative performances of various towns and cities within the statistical framework, whatever its general weaknesses. See *The Census of Massachusetts:1875* (3 vols.; Boston: A. J. Wright, 1876–1877), II, xv–xvi, on changes in methodology of the industrial census. Also, pp. xx for summary of growth.

5. *Mass. Census:1875*, II, table 1, pp. 1–186 (Springfield figures 67–70) and table 12, pp. 339–360.

6. *Ninth Census of the United States, 1870* (3 vols.; Washington: G.P.O., 1872) III, table 2, p. 37; *Mass. Census:1875*, II, table 1, pp. 67–70; *Springfield City Directory for 1873*, pp. 374–389.

7. Among the important additions were several firms that were to win a

lasting place in Springfield's life: the Gilbert and Barker Company, a gas-equipment manufacturer that remained in the area until 1966; and a dry goods store at Main and Vernon called Forbes and Smith that, soon becoming Forbes and Wallace, is today the city's leading department store and still occupies the same central corner. There are good summaries of business development in the annual city directories for 1870–1873, and also in *SR²*, December 22, 1869, and *SU*, December 13, 1872. On the specific firms mentioned here, see also Moses King, ed., *King's Handbook of Springfield* (Springfield: James Gill, 1884), pp. 328, 335, 346; and Alfred M. Copeland, *Our County and Its People: Hampden County, Massachusetts* (Boston: Century Publishing Co., 1902), II, 227. See also, on new companies formed, *SR²*, February 10, 24, 1866.

8. *City Directory for 1870*, pp. 22–23 (quoted); *SR²*, February 26, August 8, 1868; *SR*, November 28, 1872.

9. *SR*, May 24, 1872, and *SU*, March 16, 1872 are quoted. See also *SR²*, January 13, 1866; *SR*, November 20, 1872; January 28, 1873 on banking developments.

10. *SR²*, June 3, 1868 (quoted); see also *SU*, May 1, 1866; March 21, 1867; *SR²*, February 16, 1867; *City Directory for 1868*, pp. 233–234; *for 1872*, pp. 375–379.

11. The special report on wholesaling takes up five columns in *SR²*, Dec. 22, 1869. Also *SR²*, March 23, 1867; and *City Directory for 1870*, p. 23 (quoted).

12. Springfield, by this time, completely dominated the new paper collar industry, a position recognized when a quite inclusive manufacturers association, for the protection of patent rights, was located there in 1866. On all this specialization, see *Ninth U.S. Census, 1870*, III, table 11; *Mass. Census: 1875*, II, table 1, pp. 1–186; table 3, pp. 231–250. Also, *SU*, January 3, 26, February 7, May 9, 19, 1866 on the paper businesses as well as a series on them in *SR*, February 13, March 18, June 24, 1873.

13. *Mass. Census: 1875*, II, table 1, pp. 1–186; table 12, pp. 339–360.

14. The most remarkable increases were in the Boston area, with Cambridge jumping 60 percent in the decade, and Somerville twice that. Factory towns also grew furiously, such as Fall River by 175 percent and Holyoke by 300 percent. See *Mass. Census: 1875*, I, xxix–xxxii on the urban trend, and also Horace G. Wadlin, "The Growth of Cities in Massachusetts," *Publications of the American Statistical Association*, n.s. 13 (vol. 2, March 1891), 159–162. For specific town figures, the basis of percentages calculated by the author, see *Mass. Census: 1875*, I, table 25, pp. 733–751; table 1, pp. 3–8.

15. *Mass. Census: 1875*, I, table 24, pp. 725–731; table 25, pp. 733–751.

16. Ibid., I, table 25, pp. 733–751; table 1, pp. 3–8.

17. The 1875 Springfield figure represents a slight retreat from the peak of just over 25 percent recorded in 1870. *Ninth U.S. Census, 1870*, I, table 3, pp. 165–168; *Mass. Census: 1875*, I, xxxviii; table 8, pp. 273–284; table 10, pp. 311–378. It should be noted that there were many foreigners farming in rural country through this period, particularly Irishmen. See interesting items in *SU*, November 19, 1868 or *SR*, August 8, 1876 where the middle-class "exodus"

from large cities is seen as having the advantage of reclaiming the backcountry from Irish control.

18. In 1875, on the question of age distribution, 51 percent of the native-born males in Springfield were over twenty, while 85 percent of the foreign born were above that age. For these and other figures, see *Mass. Census: 1875*, I, Table 1, pp. 3–8; table 7, pp. 71–270; table 8, pp. 273–284; table 10, pp. 311–378; table 30, II, p. 294. See also explanatory notes on I, xliii. For the figures on children with native-born parents, see in addition *Ninth U.S. Census, 1870*, I, table 5, p. 312. The statistics estimate that 60 percent of the native born had one or both parents foreign born. With 75 percent of the population native, this means that only 40 percent of this 75 percent – 30 percent of the total population – were native born of two native parents.

19. *Mass. Census: 1875*, I, table 7, pp. 273–284; table 9, pp. 285–339; table 5, pp. 45–56. See also *Abstract of the Census of Massachusetts:1865* (Boston: Wright and Potter, 1867), table 12, pp. 222–234. On the Negroes, see *History of St. John's Congregational Church* (Springfield: History Committee of St. John's, 1962), pp. 25–35 and 131–132. The Negroes were somewhat organized in politics as well, as witness the club formed to work for Grant in 1872 (*SR*, August 12, 1872) or the earlier organized celebration of the fifteenth Amendment (*SR²*, April 29, 1870).

20. *SU*, March 12, 1866; *SR²*, October 3, 1866; September 2, 23, 27, 1870. See also John J. McCoy, *History of the Catholic Church in the Diocese of Springfield* (Boston: Hurd and Everts Co., 1900), pp. 11–12, 102–103.

21. *SU*, March 21, 1871; May 7, 1872 discuss role of Catholics in temperance matters. See also *City Directory for 1872*, pp. 63–64, and *King's Handbook*, p. 278.

22. *SU*, November 28, 1868.

23. *Mass. Census Abstract:1865*, table 1, pp. 24–27; table 2, p. 68; table 3, p. 102. Also, special abstract from returns, in *MR*, 1866, p. 141. The 1875 figures are not cited now; the situation changed so drastically between 1872 and 1875 that those figures are best reserved for later discussion.

24. *SR²*, September 26, 1868, and *SU*, August 16, 1869 are quoted. Any number of others could be cited: *SR²*, February 9, 1867; *SU*, April 21, 1866: January 8, July 16, 1867; June 25, 1871. The *Union's* stand is particularly revealing in that the paper, through several changes of owners, tried to present itself as the friend of the "people," labeling its rival as too aristocratic.

25. *SR²*, March 19, 21, 1868; September 1, 1871; *SR*, May 3, July 20, September 25, 1872. See also *History of the Central Labor Union of Springfield, Massachusetts* (Springfield: n.p., n.d. but after 1912), pp. 7–8, 50, 74–76.

26. *SR²*, December 23, 28, 1868; March 17, April 21, July 28, September 12, 1869; *SU*, April 26, May 20, August 12, 1869.

27. *Mass. Census:1875*, II, table 13, pp. 361–370, *Fifth Annual Report of the Bureau of Statistics of Labor* (1874), *Public Documents of Massachusetts*, table 1, p. 55, also p. 132; *Seventh Annual Report* (1876), pp. 79–81. This last is

part of an important report on the statistics of eight selected cities and three large towns, pp. 78–113.

28. *SR*², March 19, 1868; February 10, 1871; *SR*, September 21, 1872 on Catholic events; *SR*, June 5, 1867; January 8, 1868; March 13, October 23, 1869; January 6, 1871 on other events and groups.

29. *SR*², April 27, 1867; September 26, 1871; and *King's Handbook*, p. 268, on the Springfield Club; Solomon Bulkley Griffin, *People and Politics Observed by a Massachusetts Editor* (Boston: Little, Brown and Co., 1923), p. 81, and George S. Merriam, *The Life and Times of Samuel Bowles* (New York: Century Co., 1885), II, 76 give details on "The Club," See also *City Directory for 1872*, pp. 69–70.

30. *SR*², August 28–31, 1867 on the revived Horse Show; on other events, see *SR*², October 21, 24, 1868; *SR*, July 7 (quoted), July 13, 25, 1872.

31. *SU*, December 15, 1869; *SR*², January 1, 1870; *SR*, January 22, February 2, 1872 on the Agricultural Society. The quote is from *SR*², December 28, 1867. On the Mechanics Fair, see *SR*², February 5, 15, 20, 1868.

7. Physical Change and the Community

1. Kevin Lynch, *The Image of the City* (Cambridge, Mass.: M.I.T. Press, 1960), passim, but especially chap. i. Although Lynch deals with the urban metropolis of the present era, the image area he studies is only the central section of these cities, about 2½ by 1½ miles. This is not very much bigger than the settled area of Springfield in 1865.

2. *Census of Massachusetts:1875* (Boston: A. J. Wright, 1876–1877), I, table 1, pp. 3–8, table 8, pp. 273–284.

3. *SR*, November 24, 1869; *Mass. Census:1875*, I, table 3, pp. 19–24, and *City Directory for 1872*, p. 18.

4. Comparison of 1865 and 1869 city maps, frontispieces to the municipal registers for these years. Also *SR*², October 20, 1866; June 26, 1867; January 29, 1869, (long surveys of building growth).

5. Comparison of 1869 and 1873 city maps, frontispieces to the municipal registers for these years. Also *SR*², January 16, 1870; *SR*, March 16, November 22, 1872 (long surveys of building growth); *SU*, April 9, 1873; "Records of the Mayor and Board of Aldermen" (M-Ald.), V, March 10, 1873, on the city and the Jefferson Avenue project.

6. *SR*², April 25, 1871; *SR*, January 23, August 4, 1873 (long survey); *SU*, April 9, 1873; also *City Directory for 1871*, pp. 19, 27; *for 1873*, p. 19.

7. *Highland Community* (Springfield: Highland Cooperative Bank, 1921), pp. 3–7. A good deal of the land, in fact, was the property of a wealthy Negro farmer named Primus Mason, who became even wealthier as he sold parcel after parcel to real estate men.

8. Comparison of 1869 and 1873 city maps; *SR*², April 12, May 24, December 16, 1870. Also, *City Directory for 1871*, pp. 19–20; *for 1872*, pp. 18–19; *for 1873*, p. 26.

9. *SR*[2], January 20, 1869; *SR*, August 10, 1872 (quoted). See also *SU*, November 21, 1868; May 4, 1872; April 9, 1873; *City Directory for 1867*, pp. 38–40; *for 1873*, p. 25.

10. Comparison of 1869, 1873 city maps; *SR*[2], September 26, 1871; *SU*, July 7, 15, 1869; April 9, 1873.

11. *Acts & Resolves* (Mass:*AR*), 1864:229 (the general street car act); 1868: 63 (the Springfield company's charter); M-Ald., III, July 20, 1868. There was a last-minute threat to the project, when the Boston & Albany secured an injunction preventing the horsecars from crossing its tracks at the depot. But the differences were settled and the railroad relented. For this and related matters, and the inception of service, see *SR*[2], November 24, 27, December 27, 1869; March 11, 29, 1870; *SU*, January 8, 1869; August 3, 1872.

12. Even the expansions were on an unusual basis: The Mill River extension was granted only after residents gave the company a $5,000 bonus, while the Winchester Park extension cost that neighborhood $500 plus the cost of a turntable there: *SR*[2], July 3, 1869; January 15, 1870; April 7, 1871; *SR*, July 31, August 3, 1872; January 2, 10, February 1, 8, 1873. Both extensions were in operation by June 30, 1873.

13. *SR*, February 8, 1873. The company's charter permitted it to operate such intertown lines. On the industry's general development and impact at this time, see Sam B. Warner, Jr., *Streetcar Suburbs* (Cambridge, Mass.: Harvard University Press, 1962), pp. 26, 49–62.

14. *City Directory for 1866*, pp. 17–18; *for 1872*, pp. 14–16; *for 1873*, p. 18.

15. *SU*, August 4, 1866; also *SR*, October 9, 1867 for similar proposals. See a solid discussion of the need and the Market Street issue in "Petition of G. R. Townsley, August 13, 1866," MS petition in 1866 bundle, City Hall Vault.

16. *SU*, May 23, July 20, 1868; *SR*[2], June 30, 1868 summarizes City Council meetings on the subject.

17. *SR*[2], January 1, 1870, summary article. On the specific improvements mentioned, see *SR*[2], May 28, July 20, 1868; *SU*, January 13, 1869 for Dwight and Harrison Streets; *SR*[2], April 21, 1871; *SR*, May 30, 1872; *SU*, September 14, 1871 on Matoon Street. The townhouses still stand on Matoon Street as of this writing, although they are long vacant and have been condemned by the city.

18. City maps, 1869 and 1873. Also, *SR*[2], and *SU*, June 9, 1871. For general discussion of the larger context of park discussion, and references to the literature, see Blake McKelvey, *The Urbanization of America* (New Brunswick, N.J.: Rutgers University Press, 1963), pp. 116–117; and Charles Glaab and A. Theodore Brown, *A History of Urban America* (New York: Macmillan Company, 1967), pp. 254–256.

19. St. Michael's was followed immediately after the war by the new Unitarian Church just across State Street, and the Memorial Church in the North End. These set the tone, and other congregations followed. By 1870, the State Street Baptist, Trinity Methodist, and St. Paul's Universalist had been completed, and Springfield stood third in Massachusetts in the value of church

property. The North Congregational, State Street Methodist, and South Congregational were substantially done by 1873, and, despite depression difficulties, the building wave was rounded out by the Christ Church (Episcopal), Grace Methodist, and St. Joseph French Catholic Churches finished somewhat later: *SR*[2], December 21, 1861; April 12, 1865. *City Directory for 1870*, pp. 18–19; *for 1873*, p. 28. See the section on churches in Moses King, *King's Handbook of Springfield* (Springfield: James Gill, 1884), pp. 178–204.

20. *City Directory for 1873*, p. 28. *King's Handbook*, pp. 198, 200; [Rev. Charles A. Humphreys], *A Sketch of the History of the First Half Century of the Third Congregational Society of Springfield* (the Church of the Unity) (Springfield: Samuel Bowles, 1869), pp. 25, 47; *History of South Congregational Church* (Springfield: Centennial Committee, 1942), pp. 35–39.

21. Henry-Russell Hitchcock, "Catalogue of an Exhibit of Photographs of Springfield Architecture, 1800–1900" (Springfield, 1934, typescript, City Library), pp. 7–10. See also for descriptions, *City Directory for 1867*, p. 30; *for 1873*, p. 34. *SR*[2], November 25, 1865 discusses the Memorial Church. South Church is also treated in Henry-Russell Hitchcock's, *The Architecture of H. H. Richardson and His Times* (Hampden, Conn: Archon Books, 1961; first published 1936), p. 152.

22. Hitchcock, "Catalogue" p. 1, *Richardson*, pp. 61–62. See Lewis Mumford, *The Brown Decades* (New York: Dover Publications, 1955; first published 1931), chap. iii, for an excellent discussion of Richardson, and his place in American architecture.

23. Hitchcock, *Richardson*, p. 62 (first quote); see also "Catalogue" pp. 7–8. Also *SR*[2], January 20, 1869 (second quote) and *City Directory for 1867*, p. 29.

24. *SR*, April 19, 1872; *City Directory for 1872*, p. 26. Although planning began in 1868, the church was not built until 1871, the year work started on Richardson's great – and quite different – Trinity Church in Boston.

25. *King's Handbook*, pp. 178–204 gives locations in the individual church sketches. See also *SR*, October 20, 24, November 17, 1871.

26. In this context, it is significant that the first new church in the area was Catholic, and the Irish can hardly be considered as courting wealthy parishoners in the fancy neighborhoods. Rather, they chose the site partly because it was attractive, partly because they had been unable, some say prevented, from obtaining a plot in the more populous downtown sections. See *SR*[3], December 21, 1861, for this background, and also Rev. John J. McCoy, *History of the Catholic Church in the Diocese of Springfield* (Boston: Hurd and Everts Co., 1900), pp. 99–103.

27. "Mayor's Address," *MR*, 1873, p. 19; *Report of the City Library Association for 1879* (Springfield: Published by the Association, 1879), (an historical sketch), pp. 10–12, 41–42. See also *City Directory for 1871*, p. 58, and *King's Handbook*, pp. 151–154.

28. Hitchcock, *Richardson*, pp. 125–129. The building was drastically remodeled in 1906, with the high roof and the double stairs removed. This, Hitchcock feels, destroyed much of the structure's proportion and grace.

29. The decision to build had been made in 1869, but there followed a long and bitter dispute between the city and the county commissioners over the site choice. The commissioners had first decided on a State Street lot which they already owned adjoining the new Unitarian Church, but pressure from the legal and business community convinced them that Court Square would be better. The only available land here, however, was owned by the city – the soon to be abandoned West State Street schoolhouse. The dispute came over a proposed trade, whereby the city would give this land to the county, in exchange for the county's lot on State Street, where a new High School would be built. Much of the delay, apparently, was due to stalling by the city government, since agreement would commit it to the controversial high school project, some said prematurely. See *SR*[2], January 9, 23, 1869; January 13, February 21, March 14, 21, April 14, August 18, September 29, October 27, and December 12, 1871. Also, *SU*, January 25, June 22, 26, 1871.

30. Hitchcock, *Richardson*, pp. 70–75 (first quote from 71). See also *SR*[2], Jan. 20, Nov. 24, 1869 on Agawam Bank. On SIS block, see *Richardson*, p. 75, and *City Directory for 1867*, p. 31 (second quote). Also, *SR*[2], January 24, 1866; June 5, 1867. See McKelvey, *Urbanization of America*, pp. 76–80, for a good discussion of general styles in business building during this period.

31. *City Directory for 1867*, pp. 38–40; *for 1871*, pp. 28–31.

32. *SR*, June 23, 1860. A somewhat similar point is developed in Edward Kirkland's interesting essay, "The Big House" in *Dream and Thought in the Business Community, 1860-1900* (Ithaca, N.Y.: Cornell University Press, 1956), pp. 29–49. Speaking more of the fabulously rich, Kirkland notes that "some commentators held that the failure of the capitalist to build a big house was an indictment of selfishness and greed. It was an obligation of the rich to live lavishly" (p. 38). He also notes that muckraker Ida Tarbell criticized John D. Rockefeller for his unpretentious home and miserly style.

8. Community Change and the Public Interest

1. "Report of the School Committee," *MR*, 1867, p. 32; 1868, p. 37; 1872, p. 42. "Report of the Superintendent of Schools," *MR*, 1869, pp. 54–55. "Mayor's Address," *MR*, 1867, pp. 13–14; 1870, p. 16. Also *SR*, January 3, 1866; July 6, 1867.

2. "Report of the Superintendent of Schools," *MR*, 1872, pp. 36–37. Other figures appear in Alfred M. Copeland, *Our County and Its People, a History of Hampden County, Massachusetts* (Boston: Century Publishing Co., 1902), II, 136. Also, *SR*[2], May 22, 25, June 12, 1867; *SU*, May 21, 1867.

3. *Fifth Annual Report of the Springfield Aqueduct Company, 1870* (Springfield: Union Printing Co., 1870), pp. 5–9; also *SR*, September 22, 1866 (quoted) and February 27, 1867.

4. "Report of the Chief Engineer," *MR*, 1868, pp. 65–69; 1869, pp. 69–71; "Mayor's Address," *MR*, 1869, p. 32. "Ordinance of 3/19/66" reorganized the Fire Department, *MR*, 1867, pp. 154–156. See also Thomas F. Loorem, *A*

Souvenir History of the Fire Department of Springfield, Massachusetts (Springfield: Veteran Fireman's Association, 1913), pp. 65–66. The firemen were still far from professionals, however, and the companies still served a social role. Thus the George Dwight Engine Company was composed of twenty-five young men, shoemakers, teamsters, blacksmiths, florists, and the like. The Hanson Company was in 1867 all Irish, most probably by choice. See Loorem, pp. 101-103.

5. These ordinances are in the respective annual *MR*, or can be seen in the 1868 revised ordinances: *City Charter and Amendments, City Ordinances, Rules and Orders, etc.*, (Springfield: Clark W. Bryan, 1868).

6. *SR²*, December 29, 1866; *SU*, May 29, 1866.

7. *SU*, May 19, 1866 (quoted). Progress can be followed in "Report of the City Engineer," *MR*, 1867, pp. 81–83; 1868, p. 88; "Mayor's Address," *MR*, 1867, p. 15; 1868, pp. 29–30. "Report of the City Treasurer," *MR* 1869, pp. 142–147 itemizes recent work. See also *SR²*, May 23, August 11, November 3, 1866; May 8, 1867.

8. The city engineer's reports cited above also discuss street work. See in addition "Mayor's Address," *MR* 1869, pp. 24–28; 1871, p. 15; and *SR*, January 1, 1870, Mayor Winchester's farewell address.

9. Mass. *AR* 1866:172 is the Boston Betterment Act, applied to Springfield by 1867:94. See *SR²*, June 19, 1867 for its local acceptance; on sewer costs and assessments, see "Mayor's Address," *MR* 1867, pp. 15–16 and *SR²*, September 18, 1867. For illustrations of betterment procedures and districts, see M-Ald., III, October 28, 1867, and IV, December 27, 1869.

10. *SU*, May 29, 1866; June 8, 1868 (first quotes) and June 8, 1868 (second quote). See also "Mayor's Address," *MR*, 1869, p. 21; *MR*, 1871, on this general problem. For typical remonstrances, see "Notice from Tilly Haynes," in MS Miscellaneous Papers for 1867, City Hall Vault.

11. "Table, Showing the Growth of Expenditures, . . . from 1845 to 1876," *MR*, 1877, follows p. 203. This includes expenditures, debt, and tax information. See also the annual City Treasurer reports: the annual *MR* gives valuation and tax rates, but a handy table is in *Springfield, 1852–1952* (Springfield: n.p., 1952), p. 6.

12. The best general background, although quite sketchy, is still Edith Ware, *Political Opinion in Massachusetts During Civil War and Reconstruction* (New York: Columbia University Studies, 1917).

13. Each *MR* would list all officials for the year. For biographical information, see Moses King, *King's Handbook of Springfield* (Springfield: James Gill, 1884), pp. 39–42.

14. George Faber Clark, *History of the Temperance Reform in Massachusetts, 1813–1883* (Boston: Clark and Carruth, 1888), pp. 76–77, 135–140. The statewide effort to enforce prohibition, and the relation of police forces, state and local, to this drive, is discussed at length in Roger Lane, *Policing the City: Boston, 1822–1885* (Cambridge, Mass.: Harvard University Press, 1967), pp. 39–45, 63–64, 87–90, 133–141, 222.

15. For general issues, see *SR²* and *SU*, passim during the spring legislative session or the fall elections for 1866–1869. Important editorials are in *SR²*, April

28, 1866; March 20, 1869; *SU*, May 15, 1866; February 26, 1870. On the PLL, see *SR*², September 4, 7, 10, 16, November 6, 26, 30, December 18, 1867; *SU*, August 19, September 2, 20, 28, October 26, 31, November 5, 16, 1867.

16. See illustrative editorials, especially concerning events in New York City, *SR*², February 13, 1867; February 3, 1868; February 4, 1869; *SU*, December 2, 1869. There is an important chapter on "The War against Corruption" by one who lived through it in George S. Merriam, *The Life and Times of Samuel Bowles* (New York: Century Co., 1885), II, 86–109. Merriam, in addition to describing Bowles's new crusade, including his famous run-in with Jim Fisk, discusses in sophisticated terms the nationwide fixation, suggesting that in part it was a guilt reaction to the country's new materialistic involvement, after the higher concerns supposedly dominant during the war.

17. *SR*², January 6, April 21, 1869; *SU*, April 20, 1869. Also, see "Report of the City Treasurer," *MR*, 1869, 1870.

18. *SR*², November 6, 1869 (quoted); *SU*, November 4, 26, 30, 1869.

19. *SU*, December 8, 1869; *SR*², January 5, 1870.

20. "Mayor's Address," *MR*, 1870, pp. 10–13 (quoted); 1871, pp. 10–11; 1872, p. 12; 1873 p. 11. "Report of the City Treasurer," *MR*, 1871, pp. 99–105; 1872, pp. 127–133; 1873, pp. 139–145; *SR*², December 2, 6, 1870; November 14, December 5, 1871; *SR*, January 2, 1872; *SU*, November 19, 1870; January 1, 1872.

21. See the city treasurer's reports, *MR*, 1871–1875, or the "Table showing the growth of expenditure," *MR* 1877, follows p. 203.

22. William Orr, *The History of the Classical High School, Springfield, Massachusetts* (Springfield: Classical High School Alumni Association, 1936), pp. 76–77.

23. "Report of the School Committee," *MR*, 1867, p. 69. Also *MR*, 1868, p. 38; *MR*, 1869, pp. 48–49; *33rd Annual Report of the Board of Education 1869, Public Documents of Massachusetts*, p. 115. See also Gladys Midura, "A Critical History of Public Secondary School Education in Springfield, Massachusetts," unpub. diss., University of Connecticut, 1961, pp. 115–116. For a stimulating new interpretation of this larger reform movement, especially concerning the establishment of secondary education, see Michael B. Katz, *The Irony of Early School Reform: Educational Innovation in Mid-Nineteenth Century Massachusetts* (Cambridge, Mass.: Harvard University Press, 1968), particularly P. 1, "Reform by Imposition," and Appendix B, "Communities and Education." See also Chapter 5, above, where some of Katz's arguments are considered in both the text and the notes.

24. "Report of the Superintendent of Schools," *MR*, 1869, p. 56; *MR*, 1870, p. 38. See also the MS "Report of the Special Committee on the High School," in Misc. Papers for 1871, City Hall Vault. The majority report, dated May 29, 1871, is a long and eloquent study written by C. R. Ladd; the minority report is briefer, but valuable. Partial texts of both are in *SR*², May 30, 1871; see also *SR*², June 6, 1871; *SR*, April 9, 1872. The building was designed by S. J. Thayer of Boston, and is described well in the *City Directory for 1872*, p. 26.

25. "Report of the School Committee," *MR*, 1873, p. 42; Midura, "Second-

ary Education," pp. 127–131; and Appendix E, pp. 409–411, which lists the curriculum. As an illustration, here are the courses in the winter term of the third year: *Classical Course:* Virgil, Cicero, Greek Reader, Latin, French, German; *English Course:* Rhetoric and English Literature, Natural History, Bookkeeping, Trigonometry, French, German; *General Course:* Virgil, Rhetoric and English Literature, Natural History, Trigonometry, French, German.

26. On this last point, see *SR*, March 1, 1872. For developments elsewhere at this time, see Nelson Blake, *Water For the Cities* (Syracuse, N.Y.: Syracuse University Press, 1956); Blake McKelvey, *The Urbanization of America* (New Brunswick, N.J.: Rutgers University Press, 1963), pp. 90–91, 105–106; and Charles Glaab and A. Theodore Brown, *A History of Urban America* (New York: Macmillan Co., 1967), p. 97.

27. The report is in *SR*, January 1, 1872. See also *1874 Report of the Board of Water Commissioners* (Springfield, 1875), pp. 9–10, 78–83, 91–96, for most of the text of the report.

28. *Report of the Committee of the City Council of the year 1872 on the Subject of Supplying the City with Water* (Springfield: Clark W. Bryan, 1872), pp. 12–15, 19–20; *SR*, March 16, June 19, 1872. See also McKelvey, *Urbanization of America*, pp. 105–106.

29. The new commissioners, including Daniel Harris and Albert Briggs, were also chosen in this May 1872 election. Mass. *AR* 1872:345 established the board. A clarifying act, 1873:75, increased some powers, but reserved final authority over bond issue to the City Council. On the board and the referendum, see *SR*, February 14, March 23, April 8, 30, May 21, 29, 1872.

30. On government resentment of the board, see "Mayor's Address," *MR*, 1873, pp. 33–34.

31. On the water crisis, see the company's statements in the *1874 Report of the Board of Water Commissioners*, p. 12, and the government's emergency responses, M-Ald., V, June 24, 1872. Also, *SR*, June 25, 26, September 26, 1872 (quoted).

32. *1874 Report of the Board of Water Commissioners*, pp. 14–16 (quoted), 18–19. Many earlier committee and expert reports are included here, pp. 35–52. See also "Mayor's Address," *MR*, 1874, p. 23; "Report of the City Treasurer," *MR*, 1874, pp. 214–219.

33. The case was *Day v. City of Springfield*, 102 Mass. 310 (1870). See also *SR*[2], May 6, 1870 (quoted); *SU*, February 8, 1870. Also "Mayor's Address," *MR*, 1872, pp. 24–25.

34. A similar plan had been offered in 1869 by Tilly Haynes, but he was more successful when he brought the idea up as an alderman in 1872. On the earlier proposals, see *SU*, May 14, December 10, 1869, and "Report of Special Committee, November 22, 1869," in MS Reports for 1869, City Hall Vault. The new act was Mass. *AR* 1872:334. See also "Report of the Special Committee, January 22, 1872" in MS Reports for 1872, and the embodying "Ordinance #59, June 24, 1872", *MR* 1873, 186–191. The Charter Revision was Mass. *AR*, 1873:126.

35. *The Report of the State Board of Health for 1872*, pp. 19–133, and for 1873, pp. 63–115, illustrate the attention being devoted to the question of water supply, sewage, and cities. See also Glaab and Brown, *Urban America*, pp. 164–165.

36. "Mayor's Address," *MR*, 1879, p. 22 (first quote); *MR*, 1868, p. 30 (second quotes). See also *SR*², March 13, 1867; *SU*, May 29, 1866.

37. "Report of the Board of Public Works, including Engineer Ball's Report, June 9, 1873", *MS* Reports for 1873, City Hall Vault, also reprinted in *SR*, June 17, 1873. The debate is summed up well in *SU*, July 30, 1873. See also special address by the mayor in favor of the plan, *SU*, September 23, 1873.

38. BPW, "Report of June 9, 1873," MS Reports, City Hall Vault.

39. *SR*, October 14, 1873.

9. Suspicion, Confusion, and Crisis

1. Edward C. Kirkland, *Men, Cities and Transportation, A Study in New England History* (Cambridge, Mass.: Harvard University Press, 1948), II, 306–309 (quoted). See also Kirkland, *Charles Francis Adams, Jr.* (Cambridge, Mass.: Harvard University Press, 1965), p. 36. On the general question see an excellent discussion in Harry H. Pierce, *Railroads of New York: A Study of Government Aid* (Cambridge, Mass.: Harvard University Press, 1953), chap. iii, "The Period of Promotion," pp. 41–59. Also see, for a more general overview and discussion, Carter Goodrich, *Government Promotion of American Canals and Railroads, 1800–1890* (New York: Columbia University Press, 1960).

2. Kirkland, *Men, Cities, and Transportation*, I, chap. xi, "The Boston and Albany," especially pp. 366–372. The company remained almost a family operation until the twentieth century, for Chapin was succeeded by his sons-in-law, William Bliss and James Rumrill. On the New Haven road, see Kirkland's chap. xviii, "The Consolidated," especially pp. 72–80. The road at this time was still under Connecticut, not New York control, and the major route to Boston from New York was still up through Hartford and Springfield and then east.

3. Ibid. II, 311.

4. *Third Annual Report of the Board of Railroad Commissioners* (1872), *Massachusetts Public Documents*, p. cxlv. Also, Mass. *AR* 1849:232; 1856:156 1864:81, for earlier charters for similar efforts. Neither of these projects, incidentally, envisioned a future as an operating railroad; both planned to build the tracks and stations, and then conclude a profitable leasing arrangement with the larger connecting systems.

5. *SR*², May 15, 1869 (quoted); June 9, 1869; *SU*, February 2, 3, 24, May 15, 1869; Mass. *AR* 1869:69, 70 for the relevant charters. See Goodrich, *Government Promotion*, pp. 290–292, and also all of chap. viii, "Public Promotion and Private Enterprise."

6. *Third Report of the RR Commissioners* (1872), p. cxlv; *Fourth Report of the RR Commissioners* (1873), p. 136. On the difficulties encountered, see also

SR [2], July 24, 1869; November 29, 1870; *SR*, January 23, February 6, 9, March 26, May 6, 7, August 14, 1872; *SU*, May 27, November 18, 23, 1872. See also "Mayor's Address," *MR*, 1870, p. 25.

7. See the classic discussion of the meaning of corporation in developing New England, Oscar and Mary Handlin, *Commonwealth* (New York: New York University Press, 1947), passim but especially pp. 230–233. Goodrich has a good discussion of the decline of the public assistance concept, *Government Promotion*, pp. 250–262.

8. Kirkland, *Men, Cities, and Transportation*, I, 269.

9. The finest discussion of the imbroglio is in ibid., I, chap. xii, "The Great Bore."

10. See the thorough discussion in ibid., II, chap. xvii, "This Infant Hercules." The veto message is quoted from *SR* [2], June 21, 1870; follow the issue as seen in Springfield in *SR* [2], February 4, March 11, May 13, 27, June 10, 1870. These incessant efforts to tap the trade of the west then going to New York, and thus make Boston the great metropolis of the east, were part of an old dream, based on what Charles F. Adams later termed the stubborn fallacy that "steam could run uphill cheaper than water could run down" (ibid., I, 156).

11. *Third Report of the RR Commissioners* (1872), p. clxxxiii; *SR*, April 15, June 6, 1872; March 13, 1873.

12. Moses King, *King's Handbook of Springfield* (Springfield: James Gill, 1884), p. 94; Charles Wells Chapin, *Sketches of the Old Inhabitants, etc.* (Springfield: Springfield Printing Co., 1893), pp. 303–304.

13. *Third Report of the RR Commissioners* (1872), p. clxxii–iv. The road was defended by Phelps's son in a letter, *SR*, May 28, 1872. See *SU*, April 8, 1872 and *SR*, March 25, April 8, 23, 1872 for further discussion. The road's charter is Mass. *AR* 1872:154.

14. See *SR*, February 16, May 29, 1872; also, "Mayor's Address," *MR*, 1873, pp. 31–32; *Fifth Report of the RR Commissioners* (1874), pp. 74–75; Mass. *AR*, 1873: 16.

15. *SR*, February 17, 24, March 6, 1873.

16. See "Report of the Finance Committee," MS Reports for 1873, City Hall Vault; also, *SR*, March 11, April 19, 23, 28, May 6, August 2, 17, 1873; *SU*, April 18, 26, May 10, 1873.

17. *SR*, November 12, 26, 27, 1873, on the Thompson question; for the famous Tweedism editorials, see *SR*, November 29, December 1, 1873. Also, George S. Merriam, *The Life and Times of Samuel Bowles* (New York: Century Co., 1885), II, 310–312.

18. The general finance act was Mass. *AR*, 1874: 251; the Longmeadow Act, 1874: 372. See "Report of the Finance Committee," M-Ald., V, June 29, 1874. And, on the debate and the election, see *SR*, January 3, 18, February 24, March 13, June 9, 22, 30, July 4, 22, 26, 1874; *SU*, July 16, 18, 20, 21, 1874. The dispute preceding the road's opening involved many interesting questions of public-private relationships in the management of the corporation. See *SR*,

January 25, 28, March 16, August 12, November 17, 1875; *SU*, January 28, August 17, 1875.

19. The case, tried before a single justice, rather than a jury, at Bowles's request, is not listed in the official Mass. Reports. The details were fully given in both papers, including transcripts of briefs, summary of testimony, and the like. The accounts, however, are much fuller and detailed in the *Republican*, and so it is cited here, notwithstanding the irony of its greater reliability in the reporting of a suit that challenged its integrity. See both *SR* and *SU*, April 27 to May 6, 1875; and *SR*, April 29, 30, 31, for testimony, May 5, 1875 for briefs. It was apparently Bowles's choice that the matter was tried before a judge, and not a jury. See F. W. Bird to Samuel Bowles, May 8, 1875, Bowles Papers, Yale University Library, Box II.

20. Richard D. Hubbard to Samuel Bowles, May 6, 1875, Bowles Papers, Box II. See the decision, *SR*, May 6, 1875; also *SU*, May 6, 1875 (quoted) and *SR*, May 6, 8, 1875.

21. *Tenth Report of the RR Commissioners* (1879), pp. 95–98; *Twelfth Report of the RR Commissioners* (1881), pp. 191–193 on these later developments. See also Merriam, *Bowles*, II, p. 318; *King's Handbook*, pp. 91–92; and *SR*, January 4, 1878; February 27, June 8, 1877; February 5, August 4, 1880; *SU*, February 16, 1880. On the Chapin affair, see Kirkland, *Men, Cities and Transportation*, I, 376–377, and *SR*, April 25, 29, 1876. There was another embarrassment when former mayor A. D. Briggs, one of Adams's Railroad Commissioners and a close friend, was discovered to have a conflict of interest between his post and some private business. The issue was shown to be a misunderstanding in which Briggs was fully blameless but not until a minor tempest had erupted. See *SU*, March 28, 1876 for a report on this.

22. William D. Mallam, "Butlerism in Massachusetts," *New England Quarterly*, 33 (June 1960), 186–206, has the best discussion of the phenomenon. Recent biographies of Butler, of which there are several, none very good, all concentrate on his controversial military career, with sketchy attention to the significance of his later political life. For a sample of contemporary attacks on Butler, see the writings of the noted columnist "Warrington," who appeared for many years in the *Republican*, as collected by his wife, Mrs. W. S. Robinson, in *"Warrington" Pen Portraits* (Boston: Lee and Shepard, 1877), chap. viii, "Butlerism," pp. 130–148, and also pp. 439–453.

23. Samuel Shapiro, "'Aristocracy, Mud, and Vituperation,' The Butler-Dana Campaign in Essex County in 1868," *New England Quarterly*, 31 (September 1958), 340–360.

24. Mallam, "Butlerism," pp. 193–196, 205–206. On the 1871 campaign, see Merriam, *Bowles*, II, 106–108; *SR*[2], August 25, September 26, October 6, 24, 1871; *SU*, September 12, 23, 1871. The *Union's* support for Butler at this time was based on his alliance of convenience with the prohibitionism the paper then espoused, as well as the fact that he had been opposed so staunchly by the rival *Republican*.

25. Bowles Papers, Box I, show Samuel Bowles's painful journey to independence. See his famous correspondence feud with James G. Blaine in 1868, for example, anticipating his later position. The letters for 1872 repeatedly warn close friends that he will bolt the party if necessary, even at the cost of old friendships and loyalties. See Bowles to Charles Sumner, March 30, 1872; Bowles to Judge J. C. Collins, March 22, 1872; Bowles to B. Gratz Brown, April 5, 1872; and especially a long letter, Bowles to Frederic Law Olmsted, May 21, 1873, for good illustrations. Also, for Bowles's reluctant acceptance of Greely as a reform standard-bearer, see Bowles to Henry L. Dawes, May 21 and May 28, 1872.

26. The best study is still Earl D. Ross, *The Liberal Republican Movement* (New York: Holt and Co., 1919). Merriam, *Bowles*, II, 175-200 is quite perceptive. Eric Goldman, *Rendezvous with Destiny* (New York: Alfred A. Knopf, 1952), chap. ii, "Thrust from the Top," is excellent. Schurz is quoted here, p. 20. On the crucial Cincinnati convention, see Ross, pp. 86-105, Merriam, II 175-200, and Martin Duberman, *Charles Francis Adams* (Boston: Houghton Mifflin, 1960), chap. xxv, "Adams and the Liberal Republicans." A recent reinterpretation challenging Ross' view of the convention as "Reformers vs. Politicians" is Matthew T. Downey, "Horace Greely and the Politicians: The Liberal Republican Convention in 1872," *Journal of American History*, 53 (March 1967), 727-750. In addition to the manuscript letters cited in n. 25, the Bowles Papers, Box I, contain many valuable letters to and from Bowles concerning the developing campaign. Also see the Henry L. Dawes Papers, Box 21, folders d,e,f,g,h, and i, LC, which contain a number of very important letters, focusing on the split between Bowles and Dawes, who finally decided to endorse Grant publicly.

27. Merriam, *Bowles*, II, chap. xl, "Dissolution of Partnership," 201-209. Solomon B. Griffin, *People and Politics Observed by a Massachusetts Editor* (Boston: Little Brown and Co., 1923), p. 132. On the campaign, see Ross, *Liberal Republicans*, pp. 106-128. The *Republican*, despite disappointment, stuck with Greely through the campaign, stressing sectional reconciliation as its theme. See daily editorials through the election. See also Edith Ware, *Political Opinion in Massachusetts During Civil War and Reconstruction* (New York: Columbia University Studies 1917), pp. 171-172, and Appendix 1, follows p. 199. See Bowles's letters on the campaign in Merriam, *Bowles*, II, 210-221.

28. The *Union*, an earlier supporter, now denounced Butler as a "blackguard" and a threat to the survival of the Republican Party and decent politics: *SU*, August 25, 27, September 1, 1873; *SR*, September 3, 10, 1873.

29. Ware, *Mass. Political Opinion*, pp. 193-195; *SR*, June 24, October 8, November 4, 5, 1874; *SU*, August 9, November 4, 5, 1874. See also Merriam, *Bowles*, II, pp. 264-272.

30. *SR*, August 31, 1876; Merriam, *Bowles*, II, pp. 278-306; Duberman, *Adams*, pp. 390-394; Ware, *Mass. Political Opinion*, pp. 182-193; also Hans L. Trefousse, *Ben Butler — The South Called Him BEAST!* (New York: Twayne Publishers, 1957), pp. 234-243. On the 1876 election, see *SR*, August 31, September 6, November 8, 1876.

31. Samuel Bowles to Henry Alexander, October 19, 1874, Bowles Papers, Box II; *SR*, October 17, 30, 31 (quoted), November 9, 1874; *SU*, October 6, 10, 22, 1874; Merriam, *Bowles*, II, pp. 269-271.

32. On the Jackson Club, see *SU*, November 6, 1873; January 29, 30, February 3, May 28, 1874; July 21, 1875; *SR*, October 13, 14, 1875; September 29, 1876. The statistics on voters are from *Census of Massachusetts: 1875* (Boston: A.J. Wright, 1876-1877), I, table 2, pp. 11-16; table 8, pp. 273-284; table 10, pp. 341-378.

33. Biographical notes on these men found in *SU*, December 5, 1871; December 18, 1873; January 29, 1874; *SR*, January 28, 1874.

34. *SR*, December 21, 1873; *SU*, March 5, 1874. On the cleavage in the party see *SR*, July 21, 1875; November 11, 1876; *SU*, October 15, 1874; December 6, 1875. On the control of the City Committee, see *SR*, October 13, 1875; June 10, 1876; *SU*, September 9, 1878. Also, see Griffin, *People and Politics*, pp. 188-190.

35. *SR* and *SU*, September 20, 22, 24, 1873; *SR*, September 26, 29, October 1, 2, 8, 1873; March 19, August 26, 1874.

36. *SR*, March 19, July 14, 1874. Both local papers published occasional reviews of the effects of the depression. See the detailed and thorough articles in *SR*, September 22, 1874, and *SU*, September 19, 22, 24, 1874, the first anniversary of the Panic. E. Ray McCartney, *Crisis of 1873* (Minneapolis: Burgess Publishing Co., 1935), is still a somewhat serviceable monograph. For more sophisticated recent treatment, see Walter T. K. Nugent, *Money and American Society, 1865-1880* (New York: Free Press of Glencoe, 1968) which focuses on the depression and its effects; and Irwin Unger, *The Greenback Era* (Princeton: Princeton University Press, 1964), especially chap. vii, "Panic and Inflation."

37. See subsequent reviews of conditions, *SR*, January 13, November 13, 1877; January 1, 1878; also, see April 28, 1875; June 4, 1877 on the Armory. For bankruptcy figures, see *SR*, January 29, 1876; March 5, 1878; *SU*, August 11, 1877; May 1, 1878. Also, McCartney, *Crisis of 1873*, p. 100 on this general trend.

38. *SR*, November 15, 1875; May 9, August 7, 9, 1876 on real estate dealings. Valuation figures listed each year in table at end of *MR*, and compiled in *Springfield, 1852-1952* (Springfield: n.p., 1952), p. 6.

39. *Ninth Annual Report of the Bureau of Statistics of Labor* (1879), pp. 3-4, 7-9; *SR*, August 10, 11, 12, 22, 1876; *SU*, August 10, 22, 1876; M-Ald., VI, August 21, November 16, 1876.

40. Robert Wiebe, *The Search for Order* (New York: Hill and Wang, 1967), 1. Also, Nugent, *Money and Society*, pp. 175-178, makes a similar point.

41. *Census of Massachusetts: 1880 . . . from the Tenth Census of the United States* (Boston: A. J. Wright, 1883), pp. xii, 17-23, 31, 59-60, 96.

42. "Mayor's Address," *MR*, 1874, p. 17; 1875, pp. 10-12. "Report of the City Treasurer," *MR*, 1874-1879, especially 1877. Relevant here is Nugent's conclusion, pp. 177-178, that "The depression following the Panic of 1873 was mainly noticeable where it was most unsettling politically and socially . . . Its

harshest effects were its most visible ones. It functioned less as an economic disaster than as an event which provoked divisions among the country's ideological, social, and political groups, and helped shatter the rhetoric that had helped bind them."

10. A Disturbing Self-Examination

1. For a good discussion of this national mood, see Robert Wiebe, *The Search for Order* (New York: Hill and Wang, 1967), pp. 1–10, 44–75.

2. *SR*, October 29, November 17, 21, 24, 29, 1873; *SU*, November 10, 24, December 1, 1873. On the offer to Bowles, see *SU*, September 16, November 15, 1873; also, George S. Merriam, *The Life and Times of Samuel Bowles* (New York: Century Co., 1885), II, 309–311, and Bowles's letter declining, 332. The actual petition, with signatures, is in the Samuel Bowles Papers, Box II, Yale University Library, and includes the names of almost every prominent leader, including those of the Irish community. See also a letter there from the editor of the *Union*, Clark W. Bryan, to Samuel Bowles, November 15, 1875, concerning Bowles's decision not to accept. In addition, in Box V there are many clippings from papers all over the country commenting on the offer and Bowles's response, most of them congratulating him for deciding he served Springfield best by maintaining his independence as a journalist.

3. "Mayor's Address," *MR*, 1874, p. 15; *SR*, April 25, November 16, 19, 24, 30, December 1, 5, 8, 9, 1874; *SU*, December 7, 8, 9, 1874.

4. On Wight, see Moses King, *King's Handbook of Springfield* (Springfield: James Gill, 1884), p. 13, 297; *SU*, January 25, 1875; *SR*, December 15, 1874. See also "Mayor's Address," *MR*, 1875, pp. 9–11; p. 25 is quoted.

5. *SU*, December 29, 1874; January 4, 1875; *SR*, January 4, 25, 1875.

6. Henry M. Burt, *Memorial Tributes to Daniel L. Harris, with Biography and Extracts from His Journal and Letters*, (Springfield: Privately Printed, 1880), p. 29; Solomon B. Griffin, *People and Politics Observed by a Massachusetts Editor* (Boston: Little, Brown, and Co., 1923), p. 58; Daniel L. Harris, *Municipal Extravagance* (Philadelphia: n.p., 1876), pp. 4–5. Also, *SU*, March 9, 1875; March 11, 1876 (quoted), September 9, 1876.

7. Irwin Unger, *The Greenback Era* (Princeton, N. J.: Princeton University Press, 1964), p. 138. See also pp. 136–139, 237 on the A.S.S.A. Wiebe, *Search For Order*, p. 121, points out that the group was a direct precursor of the major academic professional associations, such as the American Historical Association, the American Sociological Association, the American Political Science Association, the American Economic Association, and so forth. At this time, however, it was as much composed of gentlemen and businessmen as academics. See also Edward C. Kirkland, *Dream and Thought in the Business Community* (Ithaca, N.Y.: Cornell University Press, 1956), pp. 15–17 on business involvement in the Association.

8. Harris, *Municipal Extravagance*, text and tables, pp. 9–10, 16–17, 19. See his other tables and research, *SR*, June 27, July 27, August 3, 1876; and his

"Table showing the Growth of Expenditures, etc. from 1845 to 1876," *MR*, 1877, follows p. 203. The final quote is from *SU*, March 11, 1876.

9. Mass. *AR*, 1875: 209; *SU*, May 8, 1875. See also Royal S. Van de Woestyne, *State Control of Local Finance in Massachusetts* (Cambridge, Mass.: Harvard University Press, 1935), pp. 26–28.

10. "Mayor's Address", *MR*, 1874, p. 15; *SU*, February 3, 1876. On salary fights, see *SR*, January 27, February 10, March 17, 1874; March 9, 30, April 6, 25, 1875; January 18, March 23, 1876; January 18, March 20, 23, 1877. The last quote is from *SR*, April 13, 1875. The City Council itself was unsalaried.

11. *SU*, February 17, November 27, 1876.

12. "Mayor's Address," *MR*, 1876, pp. 13–15; 1877, pp. 23–25; *SR*, January 4, 5, March 9, April 11, 1876; February 10, 1877; *SU*, January 3, 1876; March 21, 1877.

13. "Report of the School Committee," *MR*, 1876, pp. 40–44; 1877, pp. 40–42 (quoted); 1878, pp. 30–41; 1880, p. 54; "Report of the Superintendent of Schools," *MR*, 1876, pp. 37–41; "Mayor's Address," *MR*, 1878, pp. 21–22; 1879, p. 35; "Report of the City Treasurer," *MR*, 1879, pp. 238–244.

14. "Mayor's Address," *MR*, 1878, pp. 9–12 (the address was a summary of Wight's progress entitled "Three Years of Economy."); *MR*, 1879, pp. 14–15; "Report of the City Treasurer," *MR*, 1876–1879; Valuation and tax rates listed at the back of each *MR* are also available in a handy table, in *Springfield, 1852–1952* (Springfield: n.p., 1952), p. 6.

15. Calculated from Harris' 1845–1876 chart cited earlier, *MR*, 1877, follows p. 203.

16. Carter Goodrich, *Government Promotion of American Canals and Railroads, 1800–1890* (New York: Columbia University Press, 1960), p. 283. See also Wiebe, *Search For Order*, pp. 44–75 on a similar theme in the context of community responses. As he notes (pp. 45–46), "community boosters who had courted a factory for years would suddenly find it a tyrant and turn violently against it." It is questionable, however, whether Wiebe's generalization that "the most significant characteristic shared by these many anxieties was the desire for community self-determination" (p. 52) is demonstrated in his work, or adequately explains the complex responses he describes.

17. "Mayor's Address," *MR*, 1878, p. 16; "Report of the Special Committee on Improvements, 11/30/75," MS Reports for 1875, City Hall Vault; *SU*, April 10, 1877. On the details of specific improvement problems, see *SR*, December 19, 1874; December 14, 1876; *SU*, November 30, 1875; December 3, 1876.

18. *SR*[2], December 18, 1869 discusses the background and details of this issue. See also, on 1870 hearings about it, *SR*[2], April 8, June 15, 21, 1870; *SU*, April 4, 5, 8, 1870.

19. For the various hearings, investigations, and proceedings, see the heavily detailed accounts in *SR*, September 10, 26, October 21, November 7, 1872; January 13, 18, 20, 1873; *SU*, November 19, 20, 1873. This last describes an elaborate plan for a grand tower-terminal-overpass complex, with preliminary sketches by H.H. Richardson printed. On the County Commission hearings and

the court deliberations in 1874, see *SR*, February 2, 11, May 4, 7, 8, 15, 28-30, August 28, September 4, 11, 28, and especially October 24, November 10, 1874; *SU*, May 2, 7, 11, and especially November 20, 1874.

20. See *SR*, January 23, February 7, March 4, 15, 1865 for one of many unsuccessful earlier efforts. The new bridge acts by the legislature were Mass. *AR* 1872: 130, 131; 1873: 20. See also *SR*, February 3, 7, 9, 26, 1872; *SU*, February 2, April 27, 1872.

21. "Mayor's Address," *MR*, 1877, p. 13; 1879, pp. 14-15. *SR*, May 8, 22, June 10, 19, July 4, 1876; July 11, August 25, December 15, 1877; November 3, 1879. Also, *King's Handbook*, p. 76.

22. *SR*, November 16, 1874 is quoted. See also *SR*[2], September 26, 1871; *SR*, March 18, 1872; *SU*, November 30, 1875.

23. Wiebe, *Search for Order*, pp. 44-75. See also Walter T. K. Nugent, *Money and American Society, 1865-1880* (New York: Free Press of Glencoe, 1968), p. 241.

24. *SR*[2], April 18, 1871; see also February 29, 1868; November 22, 1870. The best interpretive study is Seymour Mandelbaum, *Boss Tweed's New York* (New York: John Wiley and Sons, 1965). Valuable also, perhaps more so, is the dissertation from which this book grew, "Community and Politics: New York City in the 1870's," (unpublished Ph.D. Thesis, Princeton University, 1961), which is tied less rigidly to the communications theory Mandelbaum's book develops. Perhaps even more relevant to Springfield's problems were developments in Washington, D.C., where Alexander Shepherd's fantastic building and improvement program, though not touched by major scandal, brought the capital to bankruptcy in 1873 and 1874, a lesson not lost elsewhere. See the best account, Constance Green, *Washington, Village and Capital* (Princeton: Princeton University Press, 1962), pp. 335-351.

25. *SR*, January 7, December 21, 1875; January 25, 1877. See also *SU*, June 1, 1877.

26. On the charter movement, see *SR*, January 6, March 10, 13, 15, 1877; *SU*, January 6, March 3, 9, 1877; for the text, see Mass. *AR*, 1877: 146.

27. For discussion of the charter, see *SR*, June 13, 16, 17, 1877; *SU*, June 5, 9, 13, 1877. *SR*, January 25, 1875 is quoted.

28. *SR*, June 11, 1877. See *SR*, June 19, 1877 for the election results.

29. These objections are discussed in *SR*, March 7, 1877; *SU*, June 2, 5-9, 16, 1877.

30. *SR*, June 19, 22, 1877; Wiebe, *Search for Order*, p. 162.

11. Community as Interdependence

1. See summary of the movement, *SU*, December 27, 1878. Its development can be seen in *SR*, January 3, 1874; June 11, 1875; *SU*, October 19, 1875.

2. Both *SR* and *SU*, July 21-24, 1877; *SU*, August 20, 1877, quoted. Local detachment undoubtedly owed something to the fact that New England was the only section of the country not touched by rioting during the 1877 labor disturbances.

3. The license law was Mass. *AR* 1875:99. On the implementation and enforcement in Springfield, see the valuable MS ledger, "Liquor License Data Book," City Hall Vault, which includes fee receipts, list of licensed locations, denied petitions, and the like. See licensing statistics in *SR*, March 26, April 20, 1880, and newspaper accounts of license debates, *SU*, July 27, 1875; November 15, 17, 18, 19, 1879; *SR*, April 28, 1877; April 17, 20, 30, 1878.

4. *SU*, January 15, 17, 30, 1878; *SR*, January 12, 15–23, 1878 on Murphy's appearance. See J. C. Furnas, *The Life and Times of the Late Demon Rum* (New York: G. P. Putnam's Sons, 1965), for background on this colorful crusader, pp. 176–178. For Dwight Moody in Springfield, see *SR*, January 19, February 2, 9, 13, 16, 23, 1878.

5. For background on Gladden and the movement, see Charles H. Hopkins, *The Rise of the Social Gospel in America* (New Haven: Yale University Press, 1940); Henry F. May, *Protestant Churches and Industrial America* (New York: Harper Bros., 1949); Aaron Abell, *The Urban Impact on American Protestantism* (Cambridge, Mass.: Harvard University Press, 1943). See also Gladden's autobiographical memoir, *Recollections* (Boston: Houghton Mifflin 1909), with discussion of his Springfield experience on pp. 159–161, 239–241, 248–263. See also a recent biography, helpful in both narrative and analytic detail: Jacob H. Dorn, *Washington Gladden: Prophet of the Social Gospel* (Columbus, Ohio: Ohio State University Press, 1966).

6. *Sunday Afternoon*, I, (January 1878), 85. See a discussion of this magazine in Dorn, *Washington Gladden*, pp. 67–70.

7. See *Working People and Their Employers* (Boston: Houghton Mifflin, 1876), and Gladden's comments, *Recollections*, pp. 255–257. The other quoted evaluation is Hopkins, *Social Gospel*, p. 27.

8. Arthur E. Morgan, *Edward Bellamy* (New York: Columbia University Press, 1944), pp. 57–63, 82–89, 178, 193–198, 101–105. Morgan cites and quotes many of Bellamy's articles, including illustrative examples from *SU*, August 30, 1872; June 15, 1873; and Bellamy's Lyceum speech, pp. 98–100. See notice of his departure, *SU*, December 1, 1877.

9. For the background of this system, see Robert Harvey Whitten, *Public Administration in Massachusetts* (New York: Columbia University Studies, 1898); F. B. Sanborn, *The Public Charities of Massachusetts* (Boston: Wright and Potter, 1876); John Cummings, *Poor Laws of Massachusetts and New York* (New York: American Economics Association, 1895); Robert W. Kelso, *History of Public Poor Relief in Massachusetts* (Boston: Houghton Mifflin, 1922).

10. Mass. *AR* 1874:274 reduced residence requirements from ten to five years. See *Eleventh Annual Report of the Board of State Charities* (1875), *Public Documents of Massachusetts*, pp. 88–93. Also, see Cummings, *Poor Laws*, pp. 60–62 and Kelso, *Public Poor Relief*, p. 65, on settlement law.

11. See "Report of the Overseers of the Poor," *MR*, 1874, pp. 132–143; *MR*, 1877, pp. 141–144; "Mayor's Address," *MR*, 1872, p. 24.

12. "Report of the Overseers of the Poor," *MR*, 1876, pp. 137–138; *MR*, 1877, p. 151. See *Sunday Afternoon*, I, 3 (March 1878), 277, Gladden's lead editorial on these "social parasites." Also, see *Twelfth Report of the Board of*

State Charities (1876), pp. 165-167. That the city was being imposed upon seemed demonstrated by the sudden drop in the number appearing each evening after a new law permitted the city to ask tramps to work on the woodpile in exchange for their blanket and supper.

13. "Mayor's Address," *MR*, 1867, p. 21; *MR*, 1876, pp. 23-24; "Report of the Overseers of the Poor," *MR*, 1879, p. 172. "Report of the Overseers and A. B. Harris on the Pauper Department, April 25, 1877", MS Reports for 1877, City Hall Vault, table 3.

14. "Mayor's Address," *MR*, 1877, pp. 32-33. On the Bartlett issue, see *SR*, December 20, 1876; May 8, 22, 27, 29, 1877; February 4, 1879; *SU*, January 5, 1879. "Report of the Overseers and A. B. Harris on the Pauper Department, April 25, 1877," *MS* Reports for 1877, City Hall Vault; also see *SR*, March 19, 1877.

15. George S. Merriam, *The Life and Times of Samuel Bowles* (New York: Century Co., 1885), II, 325; Gladden, *Recollections*, p. 248; *Clara Temple Leonard: A Memoir of Her Life by her Daughter* (Springfield: Loring-Axtell Co., 1908), pp. 106-131, 161-215. This was a fascinating but frail and complex woman, well fitting the age's understanding of the euphemism neurasthenic. While on the Board of Health, she became a politically important figure by resisting Governor Ben Butler's efforts to remove her for political reasons. Curiously, for such an aggressive woman, she staunchly opposed woman suffrage, and actively campaigned against it. Her statement of this position became a circulated tract and is reprinted in this memoir, pp. 217-223.

16. *First Annual Report of the Union Relief Association* (Springfield: Atwood and Noyes, 1877) complete text also in *SR*, September 28, 1877. On the Children's Aid Society, see *SR*, December 13, 1878; September 25, 1879. *Fifteenth Report of the Board of State Charities* (1879), pp. 109-112. Championed by Mrs. Leonard and later institutionalized in the Hampden County Children's Aid Society, established in 1878, this was a new idea in Massachusetts, and Springfield's success with it was widely hailed.

17. "Mayor's Address," *MR*, 1878, p. 22; "Report of the Overseers of the Poor," *MR*, 1880, pp. 188-190; Mass. *AR* 1878:97 affected the reorganization of the Pauper Department.

18. *Report of the Union Relief, 1879* (also in *SR*, September 25, 1879); Washington Gladden, "Report of the Committee on Organization," in *Report of the Union Relief, 1877*. "Committee on the Pauper Department, Report of the Minority, December 20, 1877", MS Reports for 1877, City Hall Vault. (The majority and minority reports differed only on the Bartlett question, and were in substantial agreement on the points discussed here.) "Mayor's Address,' *MR*, 1877, pp. 32-33.

19. *Report of the Union Relief, 1879*, also in *SR*, September 25, 1879. See also *Sunday Afternoon*, I, 1 (January 1878), 85, and Gladden's speech on "True Charity," *SR*, November 25, 1878. See, in addition, a good discussion of the Union Relief in Dorn, *Washington Gladden*, pp. 268-275.

20. *Report of the Union Relief, 1879*, also in *SR*, September 25, 1879. Roy

Lubove, *The Professional Altruist: The Emergence of Social Work as a Career* (Cambridge, Mass.: Harvard University Press, 1965), p. 14.

21. Lubove, *Professional Altruist*, p. 15.

22. *SR*, January 23, 1880; see also Merriam, *Bowles*, II, 325 and *Memoir of Clara Leonard*, pp. 161-162 on the "new charity."For a thorough discussion of very similar developments in a pace-setting city at the same time, see Constance Green, *Washington*, II, (Princeton, N.J.: Princeton University Press, 1963), 61-70. By 1881 sixteen major American cities had adopted the "Associated Charities" approach, most since the late 1870's. See Lubove, *Professional Altruist*, chap. i.; also Blake McKelvey, *The Urbanization of America* (New Brunswick, N.J.: Rutgers University Press, 1963), pp. 141-146.

23. *Report of the Union Relief, 1879*, also in *SR*, September 25, 1879; see also *Report of the Union Relief, 1880*, in *SR*, December 2, 1880.

24. "Ordinance no. 92," *MR* 1877, pp. 255-261; *SR*, May 16, 1876. See also the "Report of the City Physician," *MR*, 1877, p. 160. Dr. Clark started out by making a determined effort to devise an efficient system for licensing and supervising private garbage collectors, setting up zones, rates, inspection, etc. The city depended on these contracted collectors, having no services of its own. See "Report of the City Physician," *MR*, 1877, pp. 161-167; *MR* 1880, pp. 222-223.

25. Mass. *AR* 1867:107 was the charter. "Report of Special Committee," MS Reports for 1868, City Hall Vault (quoted); see also "Mayor's Address," *MR*, 1870, p. 24; 1871, p. 21; "Report of the City Physician," *MR*, 1870, pp. 96-98. The City Charter revision of 1873 explicitly recognized the city's right to tax for support of the hospital.

26. "Mayor's Address," *MR*, 1872, p. 26; 1874, p. 18; 1875, p. 28. "Report of the Board of Managers of the City Hospital," *MR*, 1872, p. 111; 1874, p. 155 (quoted); 1875, pp. 149-150.

27. *Report of the Union Relief, 1877*, also *SR*, September 28, 1877. Also, *Report of the Union Relief, 1878*, in *SR*, November 18, 1878.

28. "Mayor's Address," *MR*, 1880, p. 28. See also "Report of the Committee on the Management of the City Hospital," *MR*, 1879, pp. 161-167; "Report of the Board of Trustees of the City Hospital, including the Report of the Medical Staff," *MR*, 1880, pp. 172-175. On public debate of the reorganization, see *SR*, December 17, 18, 1878; January 3, 24, 1879.

29. *SR*, October 14, 1874 reviews the construction. See also "Mayor's Address," *MR* 1875, p. 11; 1877, pp. 26-28; 1880, p. 17; and *Report of the Board of Water Commissioners for 1874* (Springfield: Clark W. Bryan, 1874), pp. 18-20; *for 1875*, pp. 36-39.

30. *Water Commissioners' Report, 1874*, pp. 17-18; *1875*, pp. 48-49; *1876*, pp. 41-43. See also *SR*, July 14, 17, 23, 1875.

31. *Water Commissioners' Report, 1877*, 23-25. "Mayor's Address," *MR*, 1878, pp. 26-28; "Report of the City Physician," *MR*, 1877, pp. 165-166. For the use of statistics, see the retrospective "Table of Consumers" in the *Water Commissioners' Report, 1881*, p. 16. The water rates charged by the city were

not considered extravagant — $8 per year for a faucet in a single family house, $4 per family in multiple dwellings, with tubs and waterclosets extra.

32. See the above-mentioned "Table of Consumers," and also *Water Commissioners' Report, 1876*, p. 7; *1879*, pp. 8–9; *1880*, pp. 4–7.

33. *Water Commissioners' Report, 1874*, p. 21. "Mayor's Address," *MR*, 1879, p. 32.

34. "Report of the City Physician," *MR*, 1874, pp. 149–152; also 1877, pp. 163–164. "Mayor's Address," *MR*, 1876, pp. 22–26; 1877, pp. 20–22. "Report of the Superintendent of Sewers," *MR*, 1881, pp. 245–249; 1876, pp. 142–145. See the map of the entire system, appended to "Report of the Special Committee on Sewer Entrances, 12/30/80," *MR*, 1881, pp. 250–254.

35. "Mayor's Address," *MR*, 1877, p. 20; 1880, p. 20.

36. See the series on the new system, *SR*, November 24, December 18, 27, 1879; and "Report of the City Physician," *MR*, 1880, pp. 229–230. The relationship of household drains to sewer gas and public health in general was well discussed in the *Seventh and Eighth Annual Reports of the State Board of Health* (1876 and 1877), which helped bring the problem to Springfield's attention.

37. "Mayor's Address," *MR*, 1877, pp. 20–21.

38. "Report of the City Physician," *MR*, 1877, pp. 163–164; *MR*, 1880, pp. 222–227.

39. "Mayor's Address," *MR*, 1880, pp. 36–37. See also *SR*, February 3; March 2, 8, 16, 23, 26, 1880.

40. "Report of the Special Committee on Sewer Entrances, 12/30/80," *MR*, 1881, p. 252. On rates, see M-Ald., VII, December 30, 1880. The number of entrances at the lower rate was 224, whereas the previous annual average had been only 90 at the higher rate.

41. "Report of the City Physician," *MR*, 1880, p. 222.

12. An Urban Community: 1880 and Beyond

1. "Mayor's Address," *MR*, 1878, pp. 11–12.

2. *SR*, December 3, 1878. On the election, see *SR*, November 27, 28, 30, December 2, 4, 1878; *SU*, November 27, December 2, 4, 1878. See also reminiscences in Solomon Bulkley Griffin, *People and Politics Observed by a Massachusetts Editor* (Boston: Little, Brown and Co., 1923), pp. 58–59.

3. Griffin, *People and Politics*, pp. 59–60. See also "Mayor's Address," *MR*, 1879, pp. 12–13, and, on Powers, Moses King, *King's Handbook of Springfield* (Springfield: James Gill, 1884), pp. 324–328.

4. For obituaries of Alexander and Harris, see *SR*, July 25, 1878 and July 12, 1879; for comments on and tributes to the latter, see Henry Burt, *Memorial Tributes to Daniel L. Harris with Biography and Extracts from his Journal and Letters* (Springfield: Privately printed, 1880), pp. 21–33, 235–240. On Bowles's death, see the *Republican* from his first stroke on December 1, 1877 until his death on January 17, 1878, and also *SR*, January 24, 1878 for funeral and

memorial tributes from all over the country. See also George S. Merriam, *The Life and Times of Samuel Bowles*, (New York: Century Co., 1885), II, 427–461 which includes the text of many of these tributes. There is, in addition, a full collection of memorabilia, clippings, letters, official resolutions, and other documents relating to Bowles's death and the public reaction to it locally and elsewhere, in the Samuel Bowles Papers, Box V, Yale University Library.

5. *SR*, May 28, 29, June 13, 17, 30, July 5, 8, 1879 describe the Independence Day gala; see *SR*, December 27, 1880 for Sarah Bernhardt's visit; April 12, 1880 for the D'Oyly Carte. On new clubs and associations, see *SR*, December 18, 1878; January 22, April 16, 21, 1879. On the new art galleries, see *SR*, July 4, 1879, April 21, 1880; *King's Handbook*, pp. 344–345.

6. On this recovery, see *SR*, April 15, October 3, 17, 1879; *SU*, October 8, December 31, 1879; *SR*, April 21, 1880. For a general overview of Springfield's economic and social life in 1880, see the helpful *Report of the Social Statistics of Cities*, pt. 1 (vol. 18 of the *Tenth Census of the United States, 1880*) (Washington: G.P.O., 1886), pp. 307–314.

7. *SR*, January 11, 14, 21, February 26, 28, March 8, 31, April 8, May 16, October 27, 1879. The invention was not a total success at first. The cost to subscribers was a flat $40 annually, and in 1880, calling this excessive, a number of local doctors and druggists decided phone service was not worth the price, and dropped their lines.

8. See Chapter 2, Note 17 for the sources and methodology involved in these calculations. The data suggest considerable qualification of the schematization, discussed earlier, offered by Robert Dahl in *Who Governs?* (New Haven: Yale University Press, 1961), a study of political power in New Haven, Connecticut. See particularly pp. 11–86, where Dahl sees an historical progression from ruling dynasties of patricians to entrepreneurs to ex-plebes.

9. *Springfield Daily News*, November 24, 1880.

10. On the new business group, see "Mayor's Address", *MR*, 1879, p. 39; also, *SR*, March 19, April 2, 9, 1879; *SU*, June 6, 24, July 15, 1880.

11. *SR*, March 3, 5, 1880 on new labor activity. See also *History of the Central Labor Union of Springfield, Massachusetts* (Springfield: n.p., n.d. but after 1912), pp. 62–64, 127–131. The only extant file of Bellamy's paper, and this fragmentary, is in the offices of the *Springfield Daily News*. The first few years of the journal are disappointing. The *News* was obviously struggling with the business of producing a daily paper and winning a large audience; there were many small items of popular interest, but few extended stories and almost no reflective editorials. It is easy to see why Edward Bellamy found this less than satisfying and soon left the venture. See *Springfield Penny News*, February 24, March 11, 13, 1880 and *Daily News* September 24, November 23, December 8, 1880. See also Arthur E. Morgan, *Edward Bellamy* (New York: Columbia University Press, 1944), pp. 62–64, 127–131.

12. Robert Wiebe, *The Search For Order* (New York: Hill and Wang, 1967), esp. pp. 44–75, but also passim. For horizontal/vertical typologies, see Roland L. Warren, *Community in America* (Chicago: Rand McNally, 1963). For an

excellent discussion of American urban theory, particularly in relation to classic European sociology, see Don Martindale, "The Theory of the City," introduction to Max Weber, *The City* (Glencoe, Ill: Free Press, 1958).

13. Samuel P. Hayes, "The Politics of Reform in Municipal Government in the Progressive Era," *Pacific Northwest Quarterly*, 55 (October 1964), 157–169.

Index

Haynes, Tilly, 83, 162
Hays, Samuel, 248
Herschell, Clement, 168
Hitchcock, Henry-Russell, 151
Holyoke, Mass., 84, 119, 123f
Hooker, Josiah, 97, 98, 101, 102, 158
Housing: construction, 136: shortage, in wartime, 85–87

Immigrants: French Canadians, 33, 125; Irish, 33, 89, 125–126, 194–196; local settlement of, 89; new force in government, 246; and skilled labor (*see* Labor force); statistics for, 85, 124–125, 195
Incorporation, municipal, debate over, 22–28
Industry. *See* Manufacture
Irish. *See* Immigrants: Irish

Jackson Naturalization Club, 195

Kansas-Nebraska Act, 54
Kibbee, Horace, 154
King Philip's wars, Springfield's destruction in, 12
Kirkland, Edward C., 180

Labor force, 41, 74, 125; elimination in government of, 244. *See also* Labor movement
Labor movement: failure of unionism, 127–129, 219–220; first successful union organizing, 245
Lampard, Eric, 3
Lee, Horace C., 56
Leet, C. D., 118
Leet, C. D., manufacturing co., 80
Leonard, Mrs. Clara. 225, 230
Liquor licensing. *See* Temperance movement
Lincoln, President Abraham, 54, 56
Longmeadow, Mass., 13
Looking Backward, 222
Lowell, Mass., 84
Lubove, Roy, 227, 228
Ludlow, Mass., 84, 169
Lynch, Kevin, 133–134
Lynn, Mass., 118

McClellan, Gen. George, 56
Mcknight brothers (retailers and developers), 121, 138
Main Street, 20–21, 83, 139, **152, 153**; and railroad construction, 209

Mann, Horace, 45, 46
Manufacture, 17; diversification in, 118–120, 122; in wartime, 77–82. *See also* United States Armory
Massachusetts: and "Butlerism," 191f; and control of local finance, 205, economic lag in, in wartime, 77–78; educational reform in, 98, 101; growth in population of, 13–15, 83, 85, 123–124; military mobilization in (*see* Civil War); and public assistance to private corporations, 183–184; welfare policy, 223
Massachusetts Agricultural College, 93n
Matoon, William, 143
Mill River. *See* Planning
Morgan Envelope Company, 119–20
Morris and Clement Company, 80
Murdock, Eugene, 69n

Negro community, 33, 138
New York City, 63, 214
Northampton, Mass., 13
North End, development of. *See* Population: shifting movements of

O'Keefe, James, 195
O'Reilly, Bishop P. T., 154, 196n
Osgood, Rev. Samuel, 36

Park, Robert E., 2
Party organization: Democrats, 38, 162, 195–96; People's Party, 55; Republicans, 54, 162, 191f
Penny News, (*Springfield Daily News*), 245–246
Personal Liberty League (PLL), 163
Phelps, Ansel Jr. (mayor), 44
Phelps, Henry, 188
Phelps, John, 188n
Phelps, Willis, 185–186, 188–190
Pittsfield, Mass., 13
Planning: decentralization of city attempted, 141–142; first rational attempts at, 137–138, 145; and formation of Board of Public Works, 170–171; and development of Mill River, 139; and proposed park system, 143. *See also* Roads; Sanitation; Streetcar system
Politics, local: as agent of public interest, 48; before Civil War, 38–42; postwar, 162; changes in role of, 1840–1880, 242; and immigration (*see* Immigrants: new force in government)